Rebecca Riots!

True Tales of the
Transvestite Terrorists
who Vexed Victoria

by Henry Tobit Evans,
Gwladys Tobit Evans,
George Rice Trevor,
and George Thomas

Evans, Henry Tobit (1844–1908)
  Rebecca Riots!: True Tales of the Transvestite Terrorists who Vexed Victoria / by Henry Tobit Evans;
  ISBN   1-4515-9086-5
  EAN-13 978-1-4514-9086-9

order additional copies at:
http://www.createspace.com/3444853

Copyright © 2010 by David M. Gross
All rights reserved.

For more information about tax resistance,
see *The Picket Line*:
http://sniggle.net/Experiment/

10 9 8 7 6 5 4 3 2 1

Cover incorporates art by Kenny Cole
http://www.flickr.com/photos/kennycole/
License: http://creativecommons.org/licenses/by/2.0/deed.en
(Creative Commons Attribution 2.0 Generic)

Foreword

This book contains the complete text of Henry Tobit Evans's and Gwladys Tobit Evans's *Rebecca and Her Daughters: Being a History of the Agrarian Disturbances in Wales Known as "The Rebecca Riots"* and two additional appendices with supplemental information about the Rebecca Riots.

Note from G.T. Evans

The editing of this *History of the Rebecca Riots*, written by my late father, has been to me a very pleasing and at the same time a very sorrowful task; pleasing, inasmuch as I was able to gather together his copious notes, the result of years of research, sorrowful, insomuch that he was not spared to complete the work, for doubtless then the book would have assumed a more polished style.

The arrangement of the notes into chapters has proved difficult. It is with diffidence that I let the MS. go out of my hands, for I am fully conscious of its shortcomings, yet I trust that the book will meet with the approval of those best qualified to judge of its merit and worth.

My subscribers I heartily thank. Many a cheery message have I received from them which has helped me over black days when "Rebecca" was unusually hard to deal with. A kind word goes far—may the critics remember that when they judge.

Gwladys Tobit Evans
Trewylan, Sarnau Henllan, Cardiganshire, May 9th, 1910

Foreword

In editing this *History of the Rebecca Riots* the following books, periodicals, newspapers (among others) for the period 1842–43–44 have been consulted:

1. *The Report of the Commissioners of Inquiry for South Wales.*
2. *The Rebecca Rioter*, a novel, by Miss E. A. Dillwyn.
3. *Y Diwygiwr.*
4. *Y Gwladgarwr.*
5. *Y Bedyddiwr.*
6. *Seren Comer.*
7. *Yr Haul.*
8. *The Welshman.*
9. *Gweithiau, "S. R."*
10. *The Red Dragon.* Vol. XI.
11. The files of the following newspapers:
    - *The Times.*
    - *The Standard.*
    - *The Cambrian.*
    - *The Carmarthen Journal.*
    - *The Bristol Mercury.*

Contents

Foreword	**iii**
Introduction	**1**
Events leading up to 1843	**25**
Mob Law Commences	**29**
The Evil Spreads	**35**
The Rioters Grow Bolder	**41**
Rebecca and Her Legions at Carmarthen	**51**
Rebeccaite Correspondence	**61**
Cardigan, Newcastle Emlyn, and Carmarthen	**67**
Rebecca's Tactics Continued	**75**
A Rebeccaite Conference	**85**
Rebecca at Swansea—Capture of some Rebeccaites	**93**
Another Important Conference	**101**
Further Riotous Proceedings	**111**
An Address to the Inhabitants of Conwil Caio	**119**
A Farmers' Meeting	**125**
Attacks on Private Houses	**133**
"Some Exciting Incidents"	**141**
Destruction of Pontardulais Gate	**149**
A Petition to the Queen	**153**
The Law in Motion	**159**
Rebecca on the Stage	**165**
Some Threatening Letters	**171**
Rebeccaites at Rhayader	**177**
A Table of Grievances	**183**
Becca Before the Bar	**193**
Appendix A	**201**

Appendix B - - - - - - - - - - - - - - - - - - - **207**
Appendix C - - - - - - - - - - - - - - - - - - - **209**
Appendix D - - - - - - - - - - - - - - - - - - - **213**
Appendix E - - - - - - - - - - - - - - - - - - - **215**
Chronological Index - - - - - - - - - - - - - - - **223**
General Index - - - - - - - - - - - - - - - - - - **227**
Index of Persons - - - - - - - - - - - - - - - - **235**

Introduction

Many interesting and romantic stories are frequently related about "Rebecca" and her "daughters," but the actual exploits of this renowned band have not, so far as is known, been collected and set down in book-form.

Nothing has been published except the *Report of the Commissioners for 1843*, a novel called *The Rebecca Rioter*, a few scattered articles in various publications, and the reports of the riots in the newspapers of the period, to give any idea of the wave of indignation which spread through Wales almost a century ago a wave which rose higher and higher, till it broke at last in open rebellion against the oppression of the Government and the tyranny of those in authority.

What were the "Riots"? What were the causes? And who were "Rebecca" and her "daughters"? are some of the questions which naturally arise in the minds of those who are strangers to the history of this rebellion against the despotism of those times, and whose forebears were not participators in the revolt.

Wales is generally regarded as a very peaceful country, and its people as a peace-loving nation, who prefer to suffer wrong and indignity with meekness and resignation, rather than to boldly retaliate and proclaim their rights in unmistakable manner, and when reading the accounts of these wonderful riots, one is easily persuaded that it is an account of passionate Ireland in the throes of the Land League agitation, rather than of quiet, peaceful Wales.

"Rebecca" and her "daughters," realising that they had no power to bring about reform by moral suasion and legitimate agitation, resorted to open revolt against their oppressors, and took the law into their own hands. This cannot be glossed over; their action may not be approved of, nevertheless they succeeded in drawing attention to the grievances

Introduction

from which they sought to be rid, and undoubtedly from their point of view and the welfare of their children, the means justified the end.

The riots were but a part of the agrarian disturbances which took place in various parts of the country. In some districts they took the form of the Chartist Riots, while the revolt of the peasants in Wales has become known as the Rebecca Riots. All the disturbances had a common root; they sprang from the same great grievance, but each district had its own particular form of rebellion, just as each district had its own distinctions and characteristics.

It has been well said[1] that the Chartists might be roughly divided into three classes—the *political* Chartists, the *social* Chartists, and the Chartists of *vague discontent*, who joined the movement because they were wretched and felt angry. Truly this might be taken as a description of the Rebeccaites. We come across the exploits of the *political* Rebeccaites, who rebelled against the operation of the Poor Law Amendment Act, the weak administration of Justice by local magistrates, and agitated unceasingly for Free Food. The *social* Rebeccaites sought to better the lot of the agricultural labourer by sustaining a revolt against the unequal distribution of rent charges, the increase in the amount payable for tithes, and the increasing cost of all necessaries of life; for the excessive tolls exacted from the farmers naturally had their counterpart in the higher cost of all commodities. The grievances of the Rebeccaites of *vague discontent* were legion, and these malcontents of vague ideas and loose principles tended eventually to lessen the effectiveness of the greater movement, and weakened the case of those leaders who, at great personal sacrifice of life and freedom, willingly placed themselves at the head of a movement which their principles and their convictions forced them to start, and which they honestly believed to be their only method of redressing their grievances. Some people have a hazy idea, due to the gathering mist of passing time, that the Rebecca Riots were merely a nightly gambol of reckless spirits let loose on the countryside, whose sole object was to enjoy themselves in uproarious fashion a boisterous gang going about destroying toll-gates

---

1 Justin McCarthy's *Short History of Our Own Times*, p. 18.

for a pastime, and firing toll-houses for a recreation. This is not so; the Rebeccaites were instigated to their revolt by strong convictions of their grievances, and they were firmly determined to do away with the monster of tyranny, which they regarded as sucking their life blood. The attacks on the toll-gates were undertaken simply because it was a glaring fact forced into their minds every day of their lives that the heavy tolls demanded from them on all goods were the direct cause of the high cost of living in their districts; therefore, though nominally a revolt against the toll-gates, really it was a great movement among the peasantry of South and West Wales for untaxed food and cheaper living. It was thus part of the great epidemic of revolt which swept the country, finding its counterparts in the Chartist Riots in Monmouthshire, the Anti-Corn Law Agitation in England, and the cry of Ireland after the failure of the potato crop. It was the spirit of democracy wearied of its chains and bonds of slavery, crying aloud for freedom and redress.

Of all the counties affected, Glamorganshire alone at that time possessed any paid constabulary, or any force that could be of service. The other counties relied upon the services of pensioners, or special constables sworn in on any particular occasion, therefore when the riots were at their height, they were obliged to have recourse to the military for help to protect property and lives.

Finding that restoring gates, rebuilding houses, and offering large rewards for the apprehension of the rioters failed to produce any satisfactory results, the trustees lost heart, and roads were left free of toll. This was the popular triumph.

Undoubtedly the origin of all this turbulence was the resistance to the payment of turnpike tolls. The farmers complained of the expense of paying these tolls, and when it is recollected that in Carmarthenshire alone there were eleven toll-bars on nineteen miles of road, besides additional bars on the by-roads, it is apparent to everyone that they had good reason for complaint. They also suspected that the proceeds from the tolls were not fairly expended on the roads.

Among the subjects of complaints in the meetings on hillsides, by mountain streams, and at many out-of-the-way places, held for the discussion of grievances, were the following:

1. Tolls had to be paid every third time of passing.

Introduction

2. Mismanagement of funds applicable to turnpike gates.
3. Amount of payment of tolls.
4. Illegal demands of certain toll-collectors.
5. Increase in the amount payable for tithes.
6. Unequal distribution of rent charges.
7. Operation of the Poor Law Amendment Act.
8. Weak administration of justice by local magistrates.
9. Excessive cost of recovery of small debts.
10. Multiplication of side-bars by private individuals.
11. Monoglot Englishmen holding office in Wales.
12. Increased County Rates.

About this time (1838) and before the introduction of railways, the magistrates in these districts had set themselves to make new roads as well as to widen and improve the gradients of the old ones; to pay the cost of these improvements, they had increased the number of the turnpike gates in such a manner that there was scarcely a town or village that was not approached by a gate.

The turnpike roads were held under separate trusts, and the trustees found it necessary, in order to protect the interest of the tallyholders, to place their gates near the confines of their respective districts, so as to prevent persons from other districts travelling over their roads free of charge.

It therefore frequently happened that persons living and travelling within any given district, were only charged one toll for the use of a considerable length of the road, while those living on the borders, and having occasion to travel out of the district, had frequently to pay at two gates within a comparatively short distance.

There were five different trusts leading into the town of Carmarthen, and any person passing through the town in a particular direction had to pay at three turnpike gates in a distance of three miles.

About the year 1834 a turnpike road was made between Pembroke and Carmarthen, with the intention of gaining pedestrians along it between London and Ireland. The promoters of the scheme were, however, disappointed with the result, inasmuch as they left only thirty-two miles of road between Carmarthen and Milford as a road to the mail-coach, which often carried but three or four travellers in the day.

Owing to this, not enough money was raised to pay the interest on the capital expended, much less to keep the road in repair.

The trustees had a right to set up toll-gates on lanes, and to throw the costs of the main roads on the parishes, and they exercised that right to the full. The toll on the road amounted to 12s. 6d. for every market cart for thirteen miles. Besides this the people had to repair the roads.

At the instigation of some Englishmen, four additional gates were demanded on parish roads near Whitland, in order to create an increased source of revenue. These toll-gates were accordingly erected, and completed by the month of March, 1839. They stood at Cefnbralam crossroads, Llanfallteg, Cwmfelinboeth, and Pantycaws near Efailwen.

After they were opened, farmers were compelled to pay heavy taxes on the haulage of lime and culm (the ordinary fuel in Wales), over roads maintained by themselves, and hitherto free. To redress their grievances, the farmers upon finding that their petitions were not receiving desirable consideration, formed a League, and after holding conferences at different places, it was agreed that such tyranny could no longer be tolerated and they decided to remove the oppression.

About six o'clock one evening in the summer of 1839, a large number of farmers, chiefly from the neighbourhood of Efailwen and Llandyssilio, assembled at Whitland, and after exchanging their views on the matter and expressing some threatening epithets in reference to the trustees, they decided to demolish the four toll-gates. A movement was made towards Cwmfelinboeth, accompanied by discordant music and disturbances, and the four gates were that night destroyed without the slightest opposition or interference being made. The rioters were disguised, and had their faces blackened; but they had not then adopted the name "Rebecca." It was feared that these gates would be re-erected; but through the instrumentality of Mr. Powell of Maesgwynne, better counsel prevailed. It was hoped that the high feeling which prevailed among the farmers against the payment of tolls would gradually cool down, but unfortunately this outbreak was only a forerunner of further agitation and tumults. For a time peace and goodwill appeared to reign, but owing to the number of toll-gates and the amount of toll paid

Introduction

by some farmers, disturbances and agitations again took the field, and for a long time predominated. Eventually the League was revived, and secret meetings were called in West Carmarthenshire and East Pembrokeshire, the most enlightened members of the Society being selected to go about expounding their policy, and to deal with the imposition and injustice of the trustees.

To the neighbourhood of Efailwen must be given the first and foremost place in connection with the formation of the Rebecca Movement, and to the people of that district must be given the credit of providing the movement with a leader. It was decided at Efailwen and Whitland, that the rioters should be clothed in women's dresses with blackened faces, and fern in their white caps. Their arms were to consist of sticks, pikes, spades, hatchets, old swords, guns, in fact any weapon they could get hold of. The leader, to be called "Rebecca," was invariably to be mounted and accompanied by a bodyguard. All their doings were to be conducted under the superintendence of "Mother Rebecca," and all arrangements and commands were to be made and given by her. Many guesses were hazarded on the subject of "Rebecca"; "Rebecca" was elusive, "Rebecca" was unknown. Some[2] suggested "she was a disappointed provincial barrister," others asserted that "she was a political agitator bent on making the abolition of tolls the seventh point in the Chartist programme." A writer of the period, dealing with this subject very pointedly, remarks: "The supposed sole chief and director of the campaign must have been gifted with ubiquity, for Rebecca was in three of four counties at the same moment."

"Methinks there be *two* Richmonds in the field."

The truth is, that each district had its own Rebecca, who planned the various enterprises, and who was recognised as chief by the rest of the band. Whether the districts worked independently or had a common centre of action is uncertain.

It is intensely interesting to read the letters and the proclamations issued by "Rebecca." They are written either in colloquial Welsh, with complete unconcern as to grammar and spelling; or in English, which would be a literal rendering of a similar expression in the Welsh language.

---

2 James Mason in *Leisure Hour*, August, 1891.

Some of these letters are genuine enough in their mistakes of grammar, and orthography; but one is convinced when reading other manifestoes and circulars, that they are the work of a person who seeks to hide his identity under a cloak of ignorance. Some of the leaders were unquestionably men of position and learning, for their political knowledge and their legal learning as expressed in the garb of bad Welsh and worse English, proclaim them as men above the ordinary peasant. Their thoughts, though expressed in uncouth terms, betray the political thinker and the social reformer.

In this connection it is interesting to note that Mr. Hugh Williams, a solicitor, residing and practising at St. Clears, and a native of Machynlleth, took a very active part in the Rebecca movement, and did all the legal work for the rioters, also drafting various petitions for them. He was a prominent member of the Chartist movement, acting as their solicitor, and he defended the prisoners at Welshpool Assizes in July, 1839, for taking part in the Chartist Riots. He rendered similar services to the Rebecca prisoners gratuitously; but was eventually reported to the Lord Chancellor and struck off the Rolls.

He, however, continued to do a considerable amount of legal work, and whenever it became necessary for him to appear in court, he invariably employed Mr. Thomas Davies, solicitor, Carmarthen (who had been articled to him), to appear for him. He was looked upon as one of the ablest and keenest solicitors in the Principality. For many years he lived at St. Clears, but at last removed to Ferryside, where he died.

The first leader, who was present at Efailwen and Whitland, was one of the most important persons in the whole movement, and no apology is needed for a detailed reference to him.

Thomas Rees, *alias* "Twm Carnabwth," residing at a place called "Carnabwth," in the parish of Mynachlogddu, in the county of Pembroke, was, in the year 1842, made a leader of the Rebecca rioters. He was then about thirty-six years of age, and considerably above middle stature, possessing great muscular power, and was a noted pugilist. He frequently gave ample proof of his powers at fairs or local festivities, where fights and other disturbances so often took place; his services at those places were frequently in requisition to separate the combatants. When Twm was chosen leader, and it was decided that the rioters should wear women's garments, considerable trouble was experienced in procuring a gown large enough to fit him; several gowns were borrowed, but to no purpose, and it was feared that a new one would have to be made. At last, however, the rioters came across a tall and stout old maid named "Rebecca," and after undergoing some alterations, her dress was made to fit Thomas Rees tolerably well. From this circumstance the name *Rebecca* was adopted, and not, as some say, from having taken Genesis xxiv. 60[3] as a motto.

It was a curious coincidence that at Efailwen Gate, the toll-keeper's wife should be known as "Becca," her full name being Rebecca Davies. Thomas Davies, her husband, was unable to attend to the gate, owing to his vocation (that of a coachman) compelling his frequent absence from home; consequently, that duty fell on his wife's shoulders. Some people assert that the rioters assumed their "nom de guerre" in derision of her valiant efforts to defend Efailwen Gate from their attack.

Thomas Rees distinguished himself greatly as a leader, and succeeded beyond measure in destroying the toll-gates which were so numerous. He soon established a name for himself in the agitation. Most of the followers wore bet-gowns (the peasant dress of Welsh women), and were frequently called Mary, Jane, or Nelly, after the names of the women whose gowns they wore. "Rebecca" pretended to be the "Mother," and the others her "daughters"; and they addressed each other as such when attacking the toll-gates.

When more than one attacking party was organised for the same evening, another leader had to be chosen; and he, of course, was styled "Rebecca" for that occasion.

After the Riots were at last put down, Thomas Rees continued his hold over the district in which he lived, and whenever a pugilist visited the place, he was always put up as champion, invariably giving a good account of himself in all the combats in which he took part.

In November, 1847, a hawker, named Gabriel Davies, twenty-two years of age, who lived at Carmarthen, came to

---

[3] "And they blessed Rebekah, and said unto her, Thou art our sister, be thou the mother of thousands of millions, and let thy seed possess the gates of those which hate them."

the district. He took up his abode at Pentregalar public-house, which was on the main road between Crymych and Narberth. He was very strong, and his reputation as a pugilist had reached the district long before him. After having been at Pentregalar for several nights, a quarrel arose between him and his landlord, in consequence of which he removed to a public-house called "The Scamber Inn," situated about a mile nearer Llandyssilio. The landlord of Pentregalar was much annoyed at this, and declared he would have his revenge on him. There also existed considerable feeling in the district as to the superiority of Gabriel and Twm Carnabwth in the pugilistic world. In order to decide which was really entitled to the coveted honour of being champion, it was arranged to bring about a rupture between the two men if possible.

The landlord of Pentregalar Inn was deputed to wait on Twm; the following day he went in search of him, and brought him to his own house, where, after giving him some alcoholic drink, he offered Twm a gallon of beer if he would give Gabriel Davies a sound thrashing. Being thirsty, and believing himself to be the better man, Twm at once accepted the offer, and proceeded to the Scamber Inn. Gabriel was kept in total darkness as to what was going on; though an occasional fight was more delicious to his palate than a good breakfast, yet, as the fighting capabilities of Twm were well known, it was more than probable had the hawker been informed of Twm's object, he would have beaten a hasty retreat to some secluded spot, so as to obviate the necessity of coming in contact with the Welsh "lion." Such intimation, however, was not given, and early in the afternoon of that day, Twm Carnabwth entered the Scamber Inn and called for a pint of beer. Gabriel, who happened to be sitting down near the fireplace, wished him "Good afternoon," and endeavoured to carry on a conversation with him, but Twm's repulsive demeanour soon made it clear that he was not of the same sociable turn of mind. The latter next tried to pick a quarrel; but Gabriel was too old a bird to be drawn into his net, and instead of retaliating, sang his praises as a leader and a fighter, and wound up with an appeal to drink beer and be happy. Quart after quart was called for by Gabriel, but instead of indulging in it too freely himself, he quietly disposed of his share by pouring it into a corner close by.

Introduction

Twm on the other hand continued to drink, and instead of exercising the necessary precaution against over-indulgence, imbibed too freely of the beverage, and eventually got intoxicated. When St. Peter's boy observed the state of his antagonist, he thought that the time had come when he could take a more active part, and at once threw down the gauntlet. A fierce fight ensued, and owing to Twm's drunken condition, he was soon thrown to the ground, one of his eyes having been gouged out by Gabriel. The combatants were then separated, and the fallen warrior was taken home. He suffered great pain for some time afterwards, and as inflammation set in his life for a time was despaired of. Gradually he recovered, after which he joined the Baptist Church at Bethel Mynachlogddu, where he remained a zealous member till his death. It will therefore be seen that Gabriel Davies, though unwittingly, was the means of converting one sinner from being a terror and a drunkard, to be a decent member of society. After his conversion he became a very genial and benevolent person, highly respected by all his acquaintances.

On 17th November, 1876, Thomas Rees, at the age of seventy years, was found dead in the garden adjoining his own house. This house was situated on the bank of a tributary to the Cleddau river, at the foot of Prescelly Top, Pembrokeshire. It is supposed that his death was caused by a fit of apoplexy or a stroke while gathering vegetables for dinner. His remains were interred at Bethel burial ground on Sunday the 22nd.

A tombstone was subsequently erected over his grave, and on it is the following inscription:

>Er cof am
>Thomas Rees, Trial[4]
>Mynachlogddu;
>Bu farw Tachwedd 17^{cg} 1876
>Yn 70 mlwydd oed.
>
>Nid oes neb ond Duw yn gwybod
>Beth a ddigwydd mewn diwarnod;
>Wrth gyrchu bresych at fy nghinio
>Daeth angeu i fy ngardd i'm taro.

Many strange and weird stories are related about the person of Rebecca. People drew largely on the imagination when

---

[4] Trial was the name of the house in which he lived.

describing the night attacks of the dreaded lady. Yet the manner of attack and the dress of Rebecca and her Daughters were in the main alike on all occasions.

As to the "form and mode" of attack, the following vivid pen-picture[5] is a good description:

> The secret was well kept, no sign of the time and place of the meditated descent was allowed to transpire. All was still and undisturbed in the vicinity of the doomed toll-gate, until a wild concert of horns and guns in the dead of night and the clatter of horses' hoofs, announced to the startled toll-keeper his "occupation gone." With soldier-like promptitude and decision, the work was commenced; no idle parleying, no irrelevant desire of plunder or revenge divided their attention or embroiled their proceedings. They came to destroy the turnpike and they did it as fast as saws, and pickaxes, and strong arms could accomplish the task.
>
> No elfish troop at their pranks of mischief ever worked so deftly beneath the moonlight; stroke after stroke was plied unceasingly, until in a space which might be reckoned by minutes from the time when the first wild notes of their rebel music had heralded the attack, the stalwart oak posts were sawn asunder at their base, the strong gate was in billets, and the substantial little dwelling, in which not half an hour before the collector and his family were quietly slumbering, had become a shapeless pile of stones or brick-bats at the wayside.
>
> Meantime all the movements of the assailants had been directed by a leader mounted and disguised like his bodyguard in female attire, and having like them his face blackened, and shaded by a bonnet or by flowing curls, or other headgear. ... Day comes and the face of the country wears its accustomed aspect.

Rebecca and her daughters becoming accustomed to notoriety, and reckless in the face of danger, undertook to redress all wrongs, and put themselves in the role of judges, determining the course of action in connection with many grievances. In the pages following will be found many such instances, some of the most interesting being the care that 'Becca took of bastard children. The following rather gruesome story is a peculiar instance of Rebecca's interference in

---

5 *The Red Dragon*, Vol. xi.

Introduction

order to right a seeming wrong, and to settle a point which for years had given occasion to doubt and misgiving.

In the month of August, 1838, a parishioner of Trelech, of the name of William Jones, who lived on his own farm, Croes Ifan, of the value of about £80 a year, died and was buried in the parish churchyard. He left a lonely widow behind him. Apparently there was a marriage settlement between them.

William Jones's brother, thinking that he was the rightful heir, took possession immediately on William's death, having understood that he was to pay a yearly sum to the widow. Some little time after the burial he asked the widow for all the deeds of the place, when she informed him that she knew nothing about them, and that the last she had seen of them was in a red handkerchief 'neath her husband's arm shortly before he died. They failed to proceed any further, and things quieted down somewhat. In a short time a rumour passed through the neighbourhood that the deeds were in the coffin, and the hubbub occasioned was great. The brother talked of opening the grave or vault, and demanded from the widow the key of the iron railings which surrounded it; but she refused to give it up. This naturally strengthened the opinion that the deeds were in the coffin; but the brother, having no substantial evidence, gave up the idea of opening the grave.

Not very long after, another rumour arose about the deeds, and in order to settle the uncertainty about their location in the coffin, on Sunday evening the 5th of April, 'Becca and her children resorted to the graveyard of the church of Trelech and Bettws. Rushing towards the grave or vault, they wrenched off the iron railings which surrounded it, opened it, as well as the coffin, and made a thorough search for the deeds; the body was mixed up and the whole place left in the greatest disorder. They disappeared secretly, leaving the grave and coffin open. Having spent some hours in a search for the missing deeds which were not discovered,[6] and having done much damage to the body, they evidently made a hurried retreat. It is impossible to find words strong enough to condemn their inhuman actions in disturbing the repose of the dead, and inflicting so grievous a wound on the feelings of the living.

---

6 See *Yr Haul*, May, 1843. *The Welshman* for the same date states the deeds were found.

Rebecca after her first successes at Efailwen and Whitland, made the necessary arrangements for attacking Trefechan or Trevaughan near Whitland, on 16th January, 1843, and without much ceremony demolished the gate. "Nothing succeeds like success," and 'Becca's daughters increased in number and power daily. Toll-gates disappeared nightly, but, strange to say, not a single capture was made until the end of May in that year. Persons more unscrupulous than the original malcontents were soon associated with the disturbances, which speedily assumed a serious aspect, culminating in threatening letters, theft, arson, and even murder!

Many of the country gentlemen appealed to the better feelings of the people, but unfortunately without the desired effect.

The story of the attack on Efailwen Gate is typical of other attacks. The gate, which was a wooden one, was cut down with hatchets, saws, and bars, and an attempt was made to burn down the house, but unsuccessfully. The gate-posts were cut down, carried away, and thrown into the river Cleddau. Shortly after, another gate was erected, which was made of wood, plated with iron, so as to prevent its being cut down with hatchets and saws, whilst the posts were made of cast-iron.

An account is given in the history of the demolition of gate after gate, with the doings of Rebecca on each occasion. One of the most serious of the disturbances occurred at Carmarthen on 19th June, 1843, which culminated in the attack on the Workhouse, where, on the arrival of the soldiery, several of the Rebeccaites were taken prisoners within the Workhouse walls.

We follow them to Cardigan, where they attacked the Rhos Gate on the road leading to Aberayron, on 23rd June, 1843. There were present many of the town people and inhabitants of the vicinity, who were anxious to see Rebecca, because it was believed she was supernatural, and totally unlike others in appearance.

She was accompanied by about two hundred of her daughters, and when approaching the Rhos Gate called out, "Gate! Gate!" There was no one within, for the woman previously in charge had removed her furniture, and had also gone herself to a public-house called the "Victoria Arms." Being the keeper of both toll-house and public-house, the latter proved to be of valuable service on that occasion.

Rebecca and some of her children had their faces blackened, whilst others had yellow coloured faces. They were dressed in female attire, and among them were both Welsh and English representatives.

The gate and walls were totally demolished in about fifteen minutes; but the house, which was new and very strong, took them an hour to destroy. At the end of that time it looked very much like an old monastery—a little up and a great deal down.

From here, the rioters marched through the main street of the town, shouting, "Powder! Powder!" They proceeded to Rhydyfuwch Gate, which was about three-quarters of a mile from the town on the Newcastle road. They pulled down the gate on the Llangoedmore road, but left the gate on the coach-road unmolested.

They then departed, appearing to be satisfied with the work they had accomplished.

The following day (Saturday) was market day in Cardigan, and every one who drove in was exempted from paying the usual toll, except those who came over the coach-road. The people, looking at things from that point of view, were filled with Rebeccaite enthusiasm. On that day nothing was heard at public-houses but proposals of good health and long life to Rebecca.[7]

New Inn Gate, situated about half-way between Cardigan and Aberayron, was demolished on 26th June. It was put up the following day, and destroyed again the night of the 28th, as also were Abexceri and Henhafod, two bars near Newcastle Emlyn. Rebecca had about 250 followers, and expected a contingent of 700 men from Carmarthenshire to join her, but Mr. Hall (afterwards Mr. FitzWilliams) succeeded in dissuading them from coming. On that night, Rebecca again visited Efailwen, and finding the task of demolishing the gate a difficult one, without having the necessary implements at her disposal, sent two of the company to the blacksmith's shop to demand sledges from the smith, Morris Davies. He at first refused, but upon their threatening to pull down the smithy,

---

[7] *Seven Gomer*, August, 1843.

he threw the key of his shop out of his window to them. The sledges were then brought out, and the posts and gate smashed to atoms. The rioters then dug under the walls, and the toll-house was completely destroyed.

Subsequently the authorities were informed that sledges from Efailwen smithy had been used, and that a farmer named John Davies, residing at Plas Llangledwen had said something relative to the demand made at the smithy. Enquiries were made with a view to procuring sufficient evidence to justify proceedings being taken against someone for the damage, but the blacksmith and John Davies denied all knowledge of the fact. They were in consequence taken into custody, and lodged in Carmarthen Gaol. There they were kept for three months awaiting their trial, but eventually they were discharged.

On the same date a chain was placed across the road, where the Rhos Toll-gate had formerly stood at Cardigan; but almost before it was completed Rebecca and her daughters with picks, shovels, etc., pulled the posts from the ground, and then disappeared. Other attempts were made to put up the chain, but on each occasion were frustrated.[8]

On the 10th, some soldiers arrived at Cardigan, and of these sixty were despatched to Newcastle Emlyn Workhouse. The remaining sixty were quartered at the Free School, Cardigan; some fifty constables were also brought to Cardigan in addition to the twenty already stationed there. By this time it was dangerous to say anything concerning the riots, and people had to be on their guard. One man in a joke said to a toll-keeper's wife that Rebecca was again on the road; though he meant nothing, he had to go before the magistrates, and he had considerable difficulty in keeping out of the county gaol.

Talog, near Carmarthen, was the scene of a riot on 15th July, while on 1st August Pontarllechan Toll-house was destroyed. The house of David Harries, Pantyfenwas, was invaded by 'Becca and her children on August 22nd.

In spite of the many disturbances and the serious riots that occurred, Rebecca always managed to carry on her work so very quietly that even the neighbours were kept in total ignorance of her movements until her arrival on the scene of

---

[8] The chain is now in the possession of Mr. O. Beynon Evans, Cardigan.

Introduction

action. The attack, on 30th June, on Pumpsaint Toll-gate, which stood between Lampeter and Llandovery, showed that Rebecca could be recklessly daring; for it was carried out while the cavalry were fast approaching the place. Yet, it is worthy of note, that during all this period of turmoil and rioting, Rebecca and her daughters were strict Sabbatarians. With one exception, we have no accounts of attacks being made on any form of property, or rebellion against any grievance, taking place on the Lord's Day.

About 11 p.m., on 8th July, a toll-gate some five miles from Llandovery on the Builth road, was demolished. The toll-keeper stood his ground firmly for some time against the intruders; but at last finding that the better part of valour would be to run, he did so without further ceremony. Eight persons were afterwards taken up on suspicion, and were detained for one night, but were subsequently discharged. During the time these persons were in custody, Bronfelin Toll-gate and house were destroyed and afterwards set on fire.

It was this difficulty in laying hands upon the real perpetrators, that nonplussed the authorities. We read continually of persons being arrested on suspicion, and eventually being set free, because of the great difficulty in bringing home the accusation. On 29th September, we find posters being circulated, offering a reward of £500 (!) for the discovery of the ringleader in the riot which had occurred at Pontyberem on the 25th of the same month. This offer shows that the authorities placed a very high value on the ringleaders; but at the same time it clearly illustrates either the inadequacy or the incompetence of the forces whose particular work was to quell the disturbances, and consequently they announced the bribe of £500, hoping that some treacherous companion might sell the leader to them for a bag of gold.

After a series of serious riots had taken place, among which were a riot on 23rd September at Coalbrook Llanon; at Llandebie, where the house of Mr. Rees was demolished on the 28th; and the destroying of Pentrebach Gate on 4th October, we notice that Rebecca, becoming increasingly bold and daring, committed arson at Pantycerrig, attacked Dolauhirion Gate on the 7th, Nantgwyn on the 9th, and on the 10th a place called Pound.

So serious had these constant riots become (for Rebecca was not content now with destroying the toll-gate, but had an increasing love of incendiarism) that detachments of soldiers and London police were drafted into different parts of the country, and during 1843 and 1844 police forces were established for the counties of Carmarthen and Cardigan.

Among the many grievances dealt with by the rioters was the question of free rivers, and on 12th October Rebecca and her daughters proceeded towards Castell Maelgwyn, Llechryd, in full force. After removing a salmon weir, they made for the house, Fortunately Mr. Gower, the owner, happened to be in London, attending to his duties as a Director of the Bank of England. When this became known, 'Becca at once ordered her daughters to retire. They left without committing any damage, neither did they hurt anyone at the house.

During this period, all the gates and bars in the Whitland, Tivyside, and Brechfa Trusts were destroyed. Two gates only out of the twenty-one survived in the Three Commotts Trust, whilst between seventy and eighty gates out of about one hundred and twenty were destroyed in Carmarthenshire. Only nine were left standing out of twenty-two in Cardiganshire.

On Tuesday morning, 19th December, 1843, the dead body of Thomas Thomas, Pantycerrig, in the parish of Llanfihangel-rhos-y-corn, was found in a river near Brechfa! This man had been very much opposed to the Rebecca movement, and on 6th October he had been to Carmarthen to make a complaint to the authorities against some Rebeccaites; on his return home that night he found his house, etc., on fire. Bearing this in mind, together with other circumstantial evidence, it is plain that he had some bitter enemies in the neighbourhood, and it was generally believed that he had been waylaid and murdered. The stream of water where the body was found, was so shallow that his head and right arm could be easily seen. When examined, a deep wound was found on the left temple, and there were other marks on different parts of the body. The deceased had taken out warrants for the arrest of two young men sons of a blacksmith residing at Brechfa for stealing sheep; but as far as it could be ascertained, they had absconded and could not be arrested. Their father, on account of illness, could not leave

Introduction

the house, and being anxious to settle the case, he sent for deceased, who at once obeyed the summons, and proceeded to the blacksmith's house. He left there early in the evening for his home, but was not seen again till his body was found in the river as already described. Close to the place was a piece of timber placed across the river which might have been intended for a footbridge; but as it was round, it would be almost impossible for anyone to walk over it. In the absence of any conclusive evidence, the Coroner's Jury returned an open verdict of "Found dead." The mystery has never been cleared up.

On Friday, 22nd December, 1843, the Carmarthenshire Assizes were opened; but as Christmas Day intervened, business was not proceeded with till the following Tuesday. On this day Justice Cresswell Cresswell arrived. The Solicitor-General, Sir Frederick Pollock, appeared for the Crown, and as he was sent down specially to conduct the prosecution, the rioters were much afraid that heavy sentences would be meted out to them. Sir Frederick, however, instead of being severe, as was anticipated, appeared to be most kind and anxious to establish a reconciliation with the country. Owing to the number of prisoners for trial, Special Sessions to try the Rebecca Rioters were appointed for 1st January, 1844; but as some of the cases were of considerable importance, they were not all disposed of until 21st March before Justice Maule.

"Shoni' Scubor Fawr" and "Dai y Cantwr" (two notorious leaders of the rioters) were tried and found guilty at these assizes.

Dai y Cantwr was a man of considerable ability, and owing to educational advantages was a good bard. He composed many ballads, and while in gaol under sentence, wrote "A Lament" of which the following is a copy of the first verse:[9]

> Drych i fyd wyf i fod,
> Collais glod allaswn gael,
> Tost yw'r nod dyrnod wael
> I'w gafael ddaeth a mi.
> Yn fy ie'nctyd drygfyd ddaeth;
> Yn lle rhyddid, caethfyd maith,

---

[9] See "Lament of DAVID DAVIES (Dai'r Cantwr) when in Carmarthen Gaol for the Becca Riot." on page 220.

'Chwanegwyd er fy ngofid.
Alltud wyf ar ddechreu'm taith,
Ca'm danfon o fy ngwlad;
Ty fy Nhad er codiad tirion,
I blith y duon gor
Dros y mor o'm goror gron;
O! 'r fath ddryghin i mi ddaeth,
Alltud hir gyr hyn fi'n gaeth
Dros ugain o flynyddoedd;
Tost yw'r modd cystudd maith.

When Dai's imprisonment came to an end, he came over to this country, but he only stayed one night at his birthplace, returning to Australia, where he died.

When the Rebecca disturbances started they were confined to a narrow circle, and the newspaper accounts were very meagre in quantity, and very contemptible in tone. It is interesting to notice the development in the attitude of the newspapers as Rebeccaism gained ground. The riots were of such a nature as could not be ignored; they were serious in their results, and they were based on the deep convictions of the perpetrators who thoroughly believed in their cause.

The flame of revolt soon spread abroad, and the circle of action became larger. We find accounts of several disturbances in North Wales which are recorded in the history, and the following account, taken from the *Bristol Mercury*, shows that Rebeccaism was not confined to Wales alone.

> In consequence of an alteration in the line of road leading from Wells through Wedmore to the railway station at Highbridge, several toll-gates have been erected, which appear to have given umbrage to the inhabitants of the localities. In the course of the week ending 31st March, 1843, nightly parties have assembled in great numbers with faces blackened, etc.; and whilst some watched the approaches, others proceeded to demolish the gates with the toll-houses attached: in this manner one in the parish of Mark, and another at Wedmore, have been destroyed.
>
> On Friday night, 24th March, a toll-gate erected a few years since on a new piece of road, between Cheddar and Wedmore, was in a like manner entirely destroyed; and on the following Sunday night another in the same neighbourhood shared a similar fate.

Seven individuals implicated in these outrages were committed to prison. It does not appear that any other description of property was at all injured.

With a little training Rebecca would have had a valuable ally in an elephant, which, with his keeper, left Aylesbury on foot for Amersham. When they arrived at the toll-gate of Missenden, the toll-collector closed the gate against Jumbo, as his keeper refused to pay more for him than he would for a horse. The keeper went forward alone, but he had not gone far, when, to the toll-collector's surprise, the animal quietly took the gate off its hinges, laid it flat on the road, and followed his keeper!

The Welsh grievances had by midsummer of 1843 become famous, and aroused the curiosity, the interest, and the sympathy of many people in England. We find one Dr. Bowring in his address to the electors of Bolton, issued in September, 1843, promising to take up the subject of the Welsh Grievances in Parliament.

At the Royal Amphitheatre, Liverpool, a play called *Rebecca and her Daughters* was enacted on 4th October, 1843.

Turning our attention to the riots themselves, we notice that towards the end of the year 1843, they had become most serious, conflicts with the soldiery being of nightly occurrence, and many being taken prisoners. Several were tried before the Special Commission and found guilty, and some of the leaders were sent to penal servitude across the seas.

The question forces itself upon us "Did any material good come out of all this upheaval?" Much misery and tribulation were caused to a large section of the community. Not only were the toll-collectors going in fear of their lives, anxiously waiting their turn, their visitation from the dread Rebecca, but many of the peace-loving inhabitants of the scattered villages went in fear of the rioters, for one and all were commanded to follow the leader, and heavy was the hand that dealt the punishment to those who neglected or refused to answer the call to follow the "Queen" of the rebels.

Yet looking back upon that distant time, now nearly a century gone, we see that most of their grievances have been righted. The Government very wisely appointed a Commission on 7th October, 1843, to inquire into the condition of things in the Principality, and after a very careful inquiry, and the examination of many witnesses, their report was completed, in which they pointed out the many grievances, making suggestions as to their removal or amelioration.

These were subsequently embodied in the Act of Parliament[10] 7th and 8th Vict. cap: xcl, an Act to consolidate and amend the laws relating to Turnpike Trusts in South Wales, which became law on 9th August, 1844.

Certain it is that the riots hastened the removal of these grievances. Perhaps they would have disappeared with the progress of the people in education and social advancement, but the riots undoubtedly helped to focus the opinion of the country, and to arrest the attention of the Government to the wrongs and the sufferings of the peasantry of Wales.

> "Rebecca" and her children disappeared from the scene as if for ever; but a few old men survived, and a new grievance having sprung up very much after their own hearts, young recruits were not wanting when the enforcement of the law for the protection of salmon by the Board of Conservators made their autumn and winter sport of salmon-spearing a grave offence.[11]

This gives us an insight into the later Rebeccaism, which made its appearance on the banks of the Wye in the autumn and winter of the year 1881.

The common sport of the people had been stopped, and they resented it. They looked upon the rivers and pools as their own peculiar property, and great was their indignation at what they regarded as an interference with their ancient rights and customs.

The people came out nightly to see "Rebecca lighting the water." Tall, well-set men dressed to the waist in white, with bonnets or handkerchiefs over their heads and their faces disguised, would enter the river. Some carried torches and others spears, all spreading out across the river. The salmon, poor and emaciated, were disturbed by the noise and the light, and, scared, they were helpless while the spearman transfixed them with his weapon. The first one speared would be tossed up on high, and a great shout of triumph, taken up by the watchers on shore, rent the air.

---

10 See *Appendix A*, page 201.

11 "Rebeccaism," by R. D. Green Price, an article in *Nineteenth Century*, April, 1881.

Introduction

These disturbances took place regularly for many years, getting more serious as the time passed by. The Duke of Beauport had become Chairman of the Board, and set himself the task of putting down this wanton destruction of fish. During the winter of 1881 twelve riots took place in Radnorshire alone, and the authorities increased the police force by twenty men. This secret organisation of the "later Rebecca" extended over about 150,000 acres, Radnorshire embracing two-thirds and Breconshire the remaining third.

The authorities in this disturbance committed the same grave mistake as they did in the Rebecca Riots, in not realising that the people, rightly or wrongly, believed they had a genuine grievance. The "later Rebeccaite," as Mr. Green Price puts it, said to himself, "I used to be able to get a fish (salmon) when I liked, could catch him with rod and line, or spear, from the common adjoining the river for miles. Now I am not allowed to look at a salmon, to use a spear is unlawful. My old fishing-ground the commons—has been taken away from me by the Inclosure Acts and has gone to the large landowners."

We have set forth some of his grievances. Time has shown him that there was cruelty in his action towards the fish, and time also has made him resigned to the action of the great landowner confiscating his land the common—which the peasant rightly regarded as his heritage.

Earlier in the Introduction the question was asked, "Who was Rebecca?" We can now ask, "What was Rebeccaism?"

Rebeccaism was the spirit of revolt, which filled the whole nature of the peasant against the tyranny of the Government, the oppression of the masses by the classes, the fostering of the individual rights at the expense of the community at large. Rebeccaism was the embodiment of the peasants' anger and righteous indignation at the trampling under foot of his rights and his feelings. Rebeccaism was the spirit of a nation asserting itself against the wrongdoings and evil actions of the few.

Is Rebeccaism dead? Nay, the name may be a forgotten one, but the spirit ever liveth. It is the spirit of democracy crying out against tyranny. To-day it can be heard demanding social reform quite as vehemently, quite as strongly, as did the Rebecca of old demand from the Government of that day, a recognition of its rights and a just treatment of its grievances.

>Gwladys Tobit Evans
>Trewylan,
>9.5.1910

Introduction

Events leading up to 1843

One night about the middle of June, 1839, a mob set fire to, and destroyed, nearly the whole of the toll-house at a place called Efailwen, near Llandyssilio, in the county of Pembroke. A short time after, handbills appeared on many public doors, stating that a meeting would be held at a certain place (fixing the day), near Llandyssilio aforesaid, to take into consideration the propriety of a toll-gate, etc., at Efailwen.

Information of the meeting having been given to the magistrates of the neighbourhood, with a statement that it was expected that the riotous mob would proceed from the same meeting to Efailwen, to destroy the toll-gate and toll-house there, several special constables were sworn in and sent to Efailwen. About 10.30 p.m. of the day mentioned, a mob of about four hundred men, some dressed in women's clothes, and others with faces blackened, marched to the toll-gate, huzzaing for Free Laws and toll-gates free to coal pits and lime kilns; and after driving the constables from their stations, and pursuing them to the fields adjoining, they returned to the gate, and demolished it and the house. In the course of three hours the house was taken down to within three feet of the ground, the gate shattered to pieces with large sledge hammers, and the posts of the gate sawn off and carried away.

On the 15th of the same month, a third riotous mob armed with guns, etc., marched to a toll-gate near St. Clears, Carmarthenshire, and, after firing off several guns, destroyed the gate; and in a short time there was scarcely a vestige of either gate or toll-house to be seen.

In consequence of these acts of violence, a detachment of Her Majesty's 14th Regiment arrived on 5th July at Carmarthen, and thence proceeded to Narberth.

Events leading up to 1843

The Summer Assizes opened on 13th July, before the Hon. Sir John Gurney, Knight, one of the Barons of Exchequer, but there was not a single prisoner for trial either in the Borough or County.

After the destruction of the Efailwen toll-house and gate, a chain was put up, guarded by a body of constables. On Wednesday, 17th July, a mob collected in open day, pursuant to public notice on the previous Sunday, and a certain number of men dressed in women's clothes, and headed by a distinguished one under the title of "'Becca," proceeded towards the spot with blackened faces, and bludgeons on their shoulders. At their savage and frightful appearance, the constables took to their heels, and all effected their escape, with the exception of one who was lame. He, having run about five hundred yards, was overtaken and immediately knocked down and much abused. The rioters were informed of the day and hour of meeting, by placards, of which the following is a specimen, posted and handed about Dissenting Chapels on the Lord's Day.

1839
Men of Efelwen
Llanboidy!!!—

Let not your feelings, however excited, lead you to blame or injure the native magistrates of your native Country. They have commiserated those feelings. They sympathise with you!!!

Boldly represent to your Sovereign the unparalleled fact that two Sassenachs with scarcely a qualification, and one from a neighbouring isle, have strained your laws to an imprudent tension!

A rara Avis in terris, nigroque simillima Cygno!

An Apostate!! A Fortune Ganger!!!

These support a little Bull in the matter—

Pricilla Top, August 5th, 1839.

'Becca.

The month of November was ushered in by riots at Newport, the leaders being John Frost, Zephaniah Williams and —— Jones. They all received sentence of death on 16th January of the following year.

On 12th December, 1842, a large mob assembled at St. Clears, and destroyed the toll-gates on the main Trust at

Llanfihangel and Tawe Bridge. The same night also a toll-gate on the Whitland Trust, near the Commercial Inn, was destroyed. The leaders of the mob were disfigured, having painted their faces various colours, wearing horsehair beards and women's clothes. The depredators had patrols in every direction, to stop all travellers from proceeding on their journey during the time the demolition was going on. The doors of all the houses in the neighbourhood were locked, and the inhabitants confined within, not daring to exhibit a light in their windows; they had had a gentle intimation from the mob to that effect, and from fear of being ill-treated they obeyed the command.

During the day Narberth Fair was held. The mob stopped all the drovers coming from the direction of Carmarthen, and levied a contribution from them, stating that they had destroyed all the toll-gates, and consequently they (the drovers) had no toll to pay.

Events leading up to 1843

Mob Law Commences

The New Year, 1843, opened with the destruction of Trefechan, Pentre and Maeswholan gates. Rebecca's power increased daily, and it was an open boast that she had the support of five hundred men faithful and true, in the neighbourhood of Haverfordwest. These men actually believed that they had the right to break the law.

In the third week of January, a detachment of the Castle Martin Yeomanry, under the command of Captain Bryant and Lieutenant Leach, received orders to proceed from Pembroke to St. Clears, in consequence of the unsettled state of the neighbourhood, caused by Rebecca and her children. They were served with pistols, carbines, and bayonets, each man carrying twenty rounds of ball cartridge. On February 3rd, the Castle Martin troop of Yeomanry under the command of Captain Henry Leach was also despatched from Pembroke to St. Clears to relieve the one doing duty there in consequence of the disturbances.

Early in the morning of 5th February, the renowned lady Rebecca, together with some of her daughters, all disfigured and disguised in women's clothes, their faces covered, and well mounted, made their appearance at Ganneg Gate, near Kidwelly, which they entirely demolished. The fragments of the gate-posts and toll-board were afterwards found in a river, a short distance from the place. Some of the people living near, asserted that about the time the gate was destroyed, they heard the trampling of a great many horses, but on their approach could not identify any of the parties. This proved that they must have come from a long distance.

The adjourned Quarter Sessions for the county were held in the County Hall, Carmarthen, on 7th February. A discussion took place there, with regard to the police pensioners and cavalry at St. Clears, and an order was made to publish

Mob Law Commences

in the local papers the Address of the representatives of the parish of St. Clears, etc., to those persons who committed the outrages. It is as follows:

Fellow Countrymen,

This address is signed by us who have met this day at the Blue Boar Inn, St. Clears, as representatives of the several parishes of St. Clears, Llanginning, Llandyssilio, Llanboidy, Llangain, Llanfallteg, Llanddewi, Llanfyrnach, Kilmaenllwyd, Llangludwen, Llanfihangel-Abercowin, Eglwyscummin, Trelech, Laugharne, etc., etc., for the purpose of entreating you to co-operate with us in preventing the future destruction of Llanfihangel, Pwlltrap, and other turnpike-gates, and when we tell you that the late riotous assemblies have already cost the ratepayers of the County of Carmarthen little less that £7,000, we are sure you will render us every assistance to preserve the peace of the county, and to bring the guilty to justice.

Our neighbourhood has hitherto been both peaceable and quiet, and the great many religious privileges which we enjoy ought to be a protection against the unlawful assemblies which have now unfortunately brought upon us both shame and disgrace, and our only hope for redress must be this public appeal to the good sense and Christian feelings of our fellow-countrymen, and while we remind them that the penalty for destroying turnpike-gates is no less than transportation for seven years, we trust that the remembrance of the wickedness and evil consequences of such illegal acts will outweigh any other considerations.

The keeping of the police and military at St. Clears must take money out of our pockets, which none of us can afford or wish to pay, but, as long as the laws are disobeyed, they cannot be removed. Let all the county be united in promoting peace and goodwill, and we shall again be a happy people.

We are perfectly satisfied that the magistrates and higher authorities sympathise with the country, and we are sure that they will, as far as in their power, afford us every relief; but at the same time we are convinced that they will, as in duty bound, support and enforce the laws of the country. Dated at St. Clears this 18th day of January, 1843. [Signed by sixty-nine persons.]

A meeting of the magistrates was held at the Blue Boar Inn, St. Clears, on 13th February, to take into consideration the best mode of restoring peace in that district. About fifty respectable farmers came forward, and were sworn in as special constables. The Yeomanry left the same evening for headquarters Pembroke.

The following is a verbatim el literatim copy of a letter[1] received by Mr. Bullin, the contractor for certain gates Carmarthenshire:—

> Take notice I wish to give you notice espesial to those which has sworm to be constabls in order to grasp Becka and her childrens but i can sure you that it will be hard mater for Bowlins and company to finish the job that they began and that is to kep up the gate at Llanfihangel and weinfach gate. Now take this few lines information for you to mind yourselves, you that had any conection with Bowling Mrs. M,c, Les Mr. Thomas Blue boar all their property in one night shall be conflaration if they will not obey to this notice, and that to send them vagabons away which you are favourable to i always like to be plain in all my engagment is it a reasonable thing that they impose so must on the county only pickin poor labrers and farmers pocets, and you depend that all the gates that are on these small roads shall be destroyed, I am willing for the gates on the Queens Roads to stand it is shamful thing for us Welshmen to have the sons of Hengust have a Dominion over us, do you not remember the long knives, which Hengust hath invented to kill our forefathers and you may depend that you shall receive the same if you will not give up when I shall give you a vicit, and that shall be in a short time and now I would give you an advice to leave the place before i will come for i do determine that i will have my way all throught. As for the constables and the poleesmen Becka and her childrens heeds not more of them than the grashoppers flyin in the sumer. There are others which are marked with Becca, but they shall not be named now, but in cace they will not obey to this notice she shall call about them in a short time faithful to Death, with the county—Rebecka and childrens

There were also sent to Mr. Bullin two woodcuts, one of a man without a head, with a written heading "Receipt for the interest I took in the Matter," and the other, of several persons marching with clubs, pickaxes, etc., with the heading "Going to visit St. Clears Gate, when we think proper—Dóroma Buchan."

---

1 *Cambrian*, 17th February, 1843.

Mob Law Commences

The inscriptions over the woodcuts were in a better handwriting than the letter, which was written on ruled paper torn out of a memorandum book. It was examined by some of the Carmarthenshire magistrates, and the signature and handwriting were found to correspond with threatening letters sent to other persons. As intimated in the letter, Rebecca did not object to the gates on the Queen's high road, but destroyed those on roads repaired by the various parishes, upon which the Turnpike Trustees erected gates and demanded tolls. This rendered Rebecca not unpopular amongst some farmers and others, many of whom paid the fine, rather than be sworn in as special constables.

The following night, 14th February, a mob of forty or fifty persons destroyed two turnpike-gates at Trefechan, one leading to Lampeter, the other to Tavernspite, both in the county of Pembroke, and at the same time destroyed the turnpike-gate house, which was levelled, the gate-keeper having left it a little time previously for the night. There can be no doubt that the mob came from the English part of Pembrokeshire, as a person who had hidden himself in a garden just by the gate saw them come up the Lampeter road, watched their proceedings, and heard them converse in the English language only. Three of four of them appeared in disguise. The others seemed to be clad in their usual dress. These gates belonged to the Whitland Trust, and were repaired by the parishes, which seems to have been the principal grievance.

A number of persons tumultuously assembled at dawn on 17th February, and pulled down the toll-bar erected near the village of Llandarrog; not content with that, they actually set fire to the materials and totally consumed them, together with the toll-box belonging to the said bar. A reward of £50 was offered for the detection of the offenders. The day previous, a person had applied to the toll-keeper and offered him five shillings for the passage of a wedding party which was to go that way on the lyth. The toll-collector had refused to accept anything under ten shillings. However, the whole was destroyed as before mentioned, and the wedding party passed free.

Thomas Howells of Llwyndryssi, farmer, and David Howell, miller of Llangain, were examined before the magistrates of St. Clears on February 21st, upon a charge of having, in company with others, destroyed Trevaughan Gate on the

Whitland Trust. Lewis Griffiths of Penty-park Mill, Pembrokeshire was the principal witness against them. He swore that he saw the prisoners in the act of demolishing the tollhouse and gate at Trevaughan. On their committal, his departure was hissed and hooted by a crowd of women and girls who had assembled to witness it.

On 22nd February, two of Rebecca's daughters were taken prisoners and imprisoned at Haverfordwest. They appeared to be respectable men.

About this time the following verses were composed, and their popularity can easily be imagined.

Rebecca and Her Daughters

Where is Rebecca?—that daughter of my story!
Where is her dwelling? Oh where is her haunt?
Her name and her exploits will be completed in history
With famed Amazonians or great "John of Gaunt."
Dwells she mid mountains, almost inaccessible,
Hid in some cavern or grotto secure,
Does she inhabit—this miscreant Jezebel,
Halls of the rich, or the cots of the poor?

With exquisite necklace of hemp we'd bedeck her
Could we but capture the dreadful Rebecca!
Who is Rebecca? She seems hydra-headed
Or Angus-like—more than two eyes at command,
The mother of hundreds—the great unknown dreaded
By peace-loving subjects in Cambria's land.
Unknown her sex too—they may be discovered
To all our bewildered astonishments soon
To be, Mother Hubbard, who lived in a cupboard,
Great Joan of Arc's ghost or the man in the moon.
'T would puzzle the brains of a Johnson or Seeker
To make out thy epicene nature—Rebecca!

Who are thy daughters? in *parties* we meet them,
Which proves them of ages quite fit to *come out*,
Some *Balls* it appears were preparing to greet them,
Which soon would have ended of course in a *rout*.
They are not musicians, though capital dancers,
So puzzled they seem to encounter each *bar*;
But—Shade of Terpsichore! call for the *lancers*,
How fastly they'll step out with matchless éclat;
The wonderful prophet who flourished in Mecca
No heaven could boast like thy daughters, Rebecca!

33

Mob Law Commences

What are your politics? Some people say for you —
Travelling System you always will aid,
And 'twould appear the far happiest day for you,
Throwing *wide open the road to free trade*,
You cannot with Whigs take up any position,
If what I assert here is known as a fact;
That you give decided and stern opposition
To all that *may hinge on the new Postage Act.*
The State is in danger, and nothing can check her
From ruin with politics like yours—Rebecca.

Farewell, Rebecca! cease mischievous planning,
Whoever you might be—Maid, Spirit or Man;
Lest haply your days should be ended by hanging,
And sure you're averse to that sad *New Gate* plan.
Oh no! to the drop you may never be carted,
No end so untimely e'er happen to you:
But change, and be honest, and when you're departed
May have from the Sexton, the *Toll* that is due.
My muse is at fault—I may pinch and may peck her
But all to no purpose—Good-bye then, Rebecca!

March 1st, 1843.

The Evil Spreads

Robeston Wathen Gate, near Narberth, and Canasten Bridge Gate were utterly demolished on 6th March by a riotous mob of Rebeccaites. They assembled in considerable numbers on horseback in the neighbourhood of Robeston Wathen, and immediately proceeded to demolish the toll-gate at that place belonging to the Whitland Trust. The old woman who resided in the toll-house, hearing a noise, went to the door and inquired what was the matter. One of the rioters answered, "You had better hold your tongue and stay within doors; if you come out we will murder you." Having levelled that gate with the ground, they proceeded to the Redstone Gate, also belonging to the Whitland Trust, which shared the same fate as the other. The gang then rode off at a rapid pace.

The rioters threatened that should any harm happen to Howells of Llwyndryssi, and David Howells, then at Haverfordwest Gaol for trial on suspicion of being concerned in these riots, that they would show no mercy to anyone, but would harry the whole country.

A night or two after this, Rebecca and her daughters paid another visit to Narberth, and totally destroyed the two eastern gates at the entrance to the Whitland road. They reached there about 1 a.m., in number from eighty to a hundred, headed by three on horseback in female attire, their horses being covered with white sheets. After the work of destruction had been effectually completed, which occupied them about a quarter of an hour, they marched through part of the town, and then separated, taking different roads and giving off several shots. The night previous they had called at some farmhouses in the neighbourhood, demanding money, drink, etc., which, through fear, in most instances were given to them.

Some of Rebecca's disciples on 13th March assembled at Kidwelly Gate, leading to Carreg mountain, and completely

The Evil Spreads

demolished the toll-house. The gate and posts had been destroyed a month or six weeks previously.

Two nights later six or seven evil-minded persons demolished the Penclawdd Gate in the parish of Conwil, on the turnpike road between the latter village and Newcastle Emlyn. Not content with this outrage, they broke into the toll-house, disguised and armed with guns, threatened the tax-collector and his wife with instant death if they persisted in hurrying out in a state of nudity into the road, and they then proceeded to destroy the house, in which they partially succeeded.

The Spring Assizes opened before Sir W. H. Maule on 16th March. Thomas Howells and David Howells were tried at Haverfordwest for being concerned in 'Becca's disturbances, and both were acquitted.

The Narberth Gate, Plaindealings, and Cott's Lane Gates were entirely destroyed by a lawless mob on 29th March. In a very short space of time the work of demolition was complete, and the perpetrators returned through the town, firing volleys in token of their triumph.

About two o'clock on the morning of 6th April, a second daring and destructive attack was made on Prendergast Toll-gate, near Haverfordwest, by a party of about twenty-four men, some of whom were dressed in smock frocks; they came down in a body from the Fishguard road headed by a tall man in a white mackintosh. The first movement on arriving at the toll-gate was to appoint some of the mob as guards at the doors of the neighbouring cottages to prevent anybody from coming out to interrupt their operations. They advised Phillips, the toll-taker, "to keep in the house if he was not quite tired of his life, because they intended no harm to him." The captain then gave orders to commence the assault, and the mob went to work in good earnest; they did not desist till they had reduced the gateposts and signboard to splinters. They then told Phillips that they had fixed on that night for doing the job because it was bright moonlight, which would prevent them injuring their hatchets! On leaving they gave a hearty cheer, and carried away with them a portion of one of the posts in token of their triumph.

About midnight, on 7th April, Rebecca and a number of her offspring proceeded to Bwlchtrap, near St. Clears, and, after arriving at the gate, the following colloquy took place between the old lady and her youthful progeny. Rebecca, leaning on her staff, hobbled up to the gate, and seemed greatly surprised that her progress along the road should be interrupted.

"Children," said she, feeling the gate with her staff, "there is something put up here. I cannot go on."

Daughters. What is it, mother? Nothing should stop your way.

Rebecca. I do not know, children. I am old, and cannot see well.

Daughters. Shall we come on, mother, and move it out of the way?

Rebecca. Stop; let me see (feeling the gate with her staff). It seems like a great gate put across the road to stop your old mother.

Daughters. We will break it, mother. Nothing shall hinder you on your journey.

Rebecca. No; let us see, perhaps it will open (feeling the lock). No, children. It is bolted and locked, and I cannot go on. What is to be done?

Daughters. It must be taken down, mother, because you and your children must pass.

Rebecca. Off with it, then, my dear children. It has no business here.

With that all the "children" set to, and in less than ten minutes there was not a vestige of the gate or posts remaining. This done, the whole party immediately disappeared. The London police were at the Blue Boar Inn at the time, but they had not the least intimation of what was going forward until their services could be of no avail.

The above *amiable* lady and her *dutiful* daughters were on 13th April at their usual nocturnal malpractices at Bwlchydomen, near Newcastle Emlyn. On this occasion they numbered about fifty, all armed with guns and pistols, besides the tools of destruction they carried with them. In less than a quarter of an hour both the gate and the posts were completely demolished, and a part of the toll-house met with a similar fate. After this the rumour rapidly spread that Rebecca intended very shortly to visit Velindre and Newcastle Emlyn Gates, and that it was her intention to destroy them also.

Rebecca and her children assembled on the night of 18th April at Bwlchclawdd Gate, about three miles from Conwil.

The Evil Spreads

They completely destroyed the turnpike-gate and toll-house. In consequence of this raid, notices were issued to recover the damage sustained by this destruction from the hundred of Elfed.

Trevaughan Gate was once more entirely demolished on the 22nd of the month, the toll-house being levelled with the ground, and the stones of the building carried away and thrown into the river at some distance from the gate.

The Llanvihangel Gate was again destroyed by Rebecca about two o'clock on 29th April. She had four sentinels with loaded guns placed on the bridge to prevent the police from interfering with her followers, and no doubt had they made their appearance they would have been fired upon. When the gate was destroyed, the Rebeccaites fired off their guns, which alarmed the police, who immediately went in pursuit; but it proved fruitless, for by the time they got to the gate, 'Becca and her children had vanished. Why they should again destroy this gate is a mystery, for no tolls had been demanded there after the previous demolition.

A plantation belonging to Timothy Powell, Esq., of Pencoed (a magistrate active against Rebecca), was fired on Sunday, 30th April, and four acres were burnt. The remaining eighteen acres were saved.

Rebecca, with her respectable family, paid a visit on 5th May to the gates in the Llandyssul district. They commenced their work of destruction at Pontweli Gate, then at another gate close by called Troedrhiw-gribyn, the gate and posts of which were entirely destroyed. The band consisted of twenty or thirty, the greater number of whom were dressed in women's clothes; and what appears very extraordinary is that a great number of the inhabitants of Llandyssul were present, looking on at the work of demolition. 'Becca publicly stated there and then that they had several more gates to pull down, and especially named Newcastle Emlyn.

A week later some daring and intrepid depredators of turnpike-gates paid a visit to the quiet little town of Fishguard, and removed the gates and posts in the western part of the town to a neighbouring field. They were completely smashed into pieces. It is but just to say that the Fishguard Turnpike Trust had not repaired any of the roads in the parishes of Fishguard, Dinas, or Newport, through which the Trust led, but all the business of keeping the roads in repair fell entirely on the parishes. The Act of Parliament for the taking of tolls at those gates had expired several years, so that the levying of tolls at the Fishguard turnpike-gates was a very great imposition, and loudly called for redress.

A meeting of the inhabitants of the hundred of Derllys was held at St. Clears on 17th May. Resolutions were passed praying that a rural police be not established, the expense of which would fall heavily on the farmers and ratepayers of that hundred.

The quiet little town of Lampeter was visited about the end of May. The turnpike-gate called the Pound Bar was taken off its hinges and thrown over the bridge into the Teify. Contrary to Rebecca's usual method, very little noise was made on this occasion sure proof that only a small band was engaged on the work.

The Evil Spreads

The Rioters Grow Bolder

The inhabitants of Carmarthen had often read of Rebecca and her doings in different parts of the country, but had not the opportunity of witnessing the depredations committed by this celebrated Welsh outlaw before the end of May, 1843, when she and her sister Charlotte, together with about three hundred of her children, paid a visit to Water Street Gate in that town.

They commenced their work of destruction about one o'clock in the morning, and completed the whole in about fifteen or twenty minutes. About ten minutes before Rebecca's arrival the gate-keeper had been out taking toll for a cart, and he had only just returned and laid himself down in his clothes on the bed, when he heard a thundering noise and ran towards the door; but before he could reach it, it was struck in against him, and Rebecca and her sister came into the passage. He saw it would be useless to make any resistance, and said, in order to save himself from being ill-treated, "Oh! 'Becca is here. Go on with your work, you are quite welcome!" Rebecca desired him not to be alarmed, as they would do no injury whatever to him. The gate-keeper begged of them not to destroy the furniture, as it was his own; and his wife and child were in bed, but they might do as they liked with the gate and toll-house. Rebecca went to the door, and ordered her daughters not to touch anything but the gate and the roof of the toll-house, and not to break the ceiling for fear the rain would harm the woman and child in bed. In their hurry, however, to unroof the house, one of them slipped between the rafters, and his foot got through the ceiling. Rebecca expressed her sorrow at the accident, as it might cause inconvenience to the gate-keeper. She and her sister then told the gate-keeper that they had visited Water Street Gate, in consequence of the information laid by David

The Rioters Grow Bolder

Joshua, keeper of the Glangwili Gate, against a person the previous week; and they would destroy the Water House and Glangwili Gate before August, and would take off David Joshua's head with them.

During the whole of that time the work of destruction was carried on in the most furious manner, with large hatchets and cross-saws; a number of men had taken a ladder, and ascended the roof of the house, which was completely stripped in a very short time.

Before they had commenced breaking the gate, Rebecca had taken the precaution of placing about a dozen of her daughters, with guns in their hands, as sentinels to guard the streets leading into town, and they kept firing incessantly down Water Street, so that it was almost impossible for any person to approach the gate; notwithstanding that, a drunken man, who happened to hear the noise, went up to them and called out, "Hurrah, 'Becca!" They immediately turned him back, saying, "Go about your business, there's a good fellow. You are not wanted here; we are enough already." The gate was broken to pieces; the posts were sawn off about fifteen inches from the ground; the lamp and gas-pipe destroyed; all the windows of the toll-house smashed; the toll-board taken down and split; and Rebecca informed the gate-keeper that had it not been for his civility to them, the house would have been entirely taken down. She then called in her sentinels, and they all left together towards Fountain Hall, making the strangest noises imaginable, apparently trying to imitate the squeaking of pigs; and when they came opposite Green Hall, they stopped and fired ten or a dozen shots.

On this occasion Rebecca and her sister were dressed in long loose white gowns with women's caps and turbans on their heads, and their faces blackened with Richard Rees the blacksmith's small coal, and they had large swords in their hands. Nearly all the rest were also dressed in women's clothes, and the greater number of them were armed with guns. Whilst at work they talked only in whispers, and seemed to use some slang language which nobody else could understand; but Rebecca and her sister talked ordinary Welsh with the gate-keeper.

It was later ascertained that the leader was one Michael Bowen, who lived near Carmarthen.

On their way to the gate, they had entered the smithy belonging to Richard Rees, Moelycwan, and had taken two sledge hammers and a pickaxe, which on their return they put back in the same place. Some of them were mounted on horses, and parties were seen at Cwmduad, Bwlchnewydd, and other places on their return.

They behaved remarkably well to the gate-keeper, and frequently desired him and his wife not to be alarmed, as they would not injure them in the least; but at parting Rebecca desired him not to exact tolls at that gate any more. She also asked him if he had received a letter acquainting him of their intended visit, and when he answered in the negative, the visitors seemed rather astonished and said it had been sent, and that he ought to have received it. The gate-keeper had some presentiment that Rebecca would very soon pay him a visit, as, in the course of the previous month, he had observed several suspicious-looking persons lurking about the place, reconnoitring no doubt; he was therefore not at all frightened when he heard the thundering of the hammers on the gate; and when getting up told his wife that 'Becca was there, and desired her not to be alarmed.

In the course of the conversation Rebecca had with the toll-man she told him that many things besides the gates required to be altered in the country, and as the gentlemen in power refused to do it, they would do it themselves; they would not suffer the poor man in the workhouse to be starved, and they would not allow themselves to be starved either.

The people living near the place got up to the windows and attempted to look out; but they were immediately ordered back, and they could distinctly hear the shots whistling as they passed them. The police, too, were at the corner of Water Street, but they dared not venture farther on. (Afterwards they were severely reprimanded by the magistrates for their cowardice, in not making an attempt to put a stop to the lawless proceedings and capture some of the party.)

The borough magistrates met at the Town Hall on Tuesday, 27th May, when the gate-keeper and several other persons were examined, and their depositions were forwarded the same evening to Sir James Graham, the Home Secretary.

The Rioters Grow Bolder

The following is a copy of a notice, referring to Water Street Gate, which was taken off the door of Bwlchnewydd Meeting House:—

> Hyn sydd i hysybysu y bydd i feddiane y sawl a dalo yn Gate Water Street o hyn allan i gael ei llosgy, a'i bewide i gael ei dwyn oddiarnynt yn yr amser ni thybiont. —'Becca.

("This is to give notice, that the goods of all persons who will henceforth pay at Water Street Gate will be burned and their lives will be taken from them at a time they will not think —'Becca.")

The direct consequence of this notice was that John Harris of Talog, Thomas Thomas, shopkeeper, of the same place, and Samuel Bowen, of Brynchwith, in the parish of Conwil, appeared at the Town Hall, before Edmund Hills Stacey, Esq., Mayor, and W. Morris, Esq., on 3rd June, to answer the charge of refusing to pay the tolls at Water Street Gate on 31st May, the Wednesday after the gate was demolished by Rebecca and her children. The toll-collector proved the case against them, and they were fined 40s. each and 8s. 6d. costs or three months' imprisonment.

On Saturday night, 10th June, a large party of farmers on horseback with their servants and workmen from the neighbourhood of Pantycendy and Talog, in the parish of Abernant, assembled in a field adjoining the Pantycendy racecourse. From thence they proceeded in a body to destroy the walls at the entrance of Trawsmawr Gate, and the plantations which ornamented the same, in revenge of Captain Davies' endorsing a warrant of the Borough Authorities against John Harris, miller, and Mr. Thomas Thomas, shopkeeper, both of Talog, for non-payment of tolls at Water Street Gate.

To bring the guilty parties to justice was out of the question, as no force at the disposal of the magistrates could put into effect any warrant in the hundred of Elvet at that time.

Warrants of distress were issued against the parties fined for defrauding Water Street Gate as detailed above, and the constables proceeded to execute them early on the morning of 12th June. They reached Brynchwith about seven o'clock, where they were informed that Sam Bowen was only a lodger with his father, and had no effects of his own. The constables then went towards Talog; but when on their way there they heard the sound of a horn, and immediately between two and three hundred persons assembled together, with their faces blackened, some dressed in women's caps, and others with their coats turned so as to be completely disguised—armed with scythes, crowbars and all manner of destructive weapons which they could lay their hands on. After cheering the constables, they defied them to do their duty. The latter had no alternative but to return to town without executing their warrants. The women were seen running in all directions to alarm their neighbours; and some hundreds were concealed behind the hedges, intending to appear if their services were required. The entire district seemed to be aroused, and awaiting the arrival of the constables, who were going to levy on the goods of John Harris of Talog Mill for the amount of the fine and costs imposed upon him by the magistrates. There could not have been less than two hundred persons assembled to resist the execution of process, and vast numbers were flocking from all quarters, in response to the blowing of a horn, the signal of the Rebeccaites to repair thither. Various mounted messengers were scouring the country and sounding the trumpet of alarm. They said openly that it was their determination to pay another levelling visit to the neighbourhood that night, for the purpose of demolishing the gate. The magistrates met at the Guildhall at noon to decide what steps ought to be taken in consequence of the failure of the constables to execute the warrants of distress against Harris and Thomas of Talog.

They decided to call out the pensioners in the town and neighbourhood, twenty-eight in number, to accompany the civil force, twelve in number, to execute the warrants of distress. For that purpose they left the town about three o'clock in the morning of the 13th under the direction of David Evans, road surveyor. They proceeded to Talog, where a levy was made on the goods of Harris about half-past five in the morning, which goods were carried away without molestation. Thomas had paid the fine on the Saturday evening previous, as his wife was near her confinement, and he did not wish to have any disturbance about his house. After the levy was made and the force had proceeded about a quarter of a mile on their return to Carmarthen, Thomas of Talog, the person who had paid the fine on Saturday, overtook them, and foreseeing the danger which the whole force would be in if they persisted in retaining possession of the goods, pledged his word that the fine and costs would be paid, and the goods were returned to him. Immediately the party was surrounded by a mob of about 400 in number—105 of whom were armed with firearms—and completely overpowered. They were rigidly searched, and compelled to fire their pistols in the air, and then had to deliver them up to 'Becca and her family, who were all disguised in various dresses. The mob then desired the force to fall into line, and 'Becca inspected them to see if David Rees, constable, and Thomas Evans, police officer, were with them. When she was satisfied that they were not, she said, had they been there, their lives would certainly be taken away. They were then ordered to march to Trawsmawr, the property of Captain Davies of Green Hall, near Carmarthen, who was the county magistrate that endorsed the distress warrants issued by the town magistrates. When they arrived there, Rebecca commanded the constables to break down the wall surrounding the house, which was done. When this act of destruction had been completed, they shook hands with the pensioners, told them to go to their homes, and they would not be molested. They were not so polite to the constables, towards whom they manifested considerable animosity. The arms taken by 'Becca from the constables were returned before she parted company with them.

Penllwynan toll-house and gate were destroyed on the night of 12th June, and the following week Bwlchyclawdd Gate, Llandyssul, was completely destroyed. The Rebeccaites also paid a visit to Pembrey Gate.

The Rev. John Hughes, Vicar of Penbryn, Cardiganshire, received the following letter on 17th June, 1843:

Penyrherber,

Mehefin 16th, 1843.

Yr ydwyf wedi cael achwyniad arnoch gan eich plwyfolion eich bod yn ei gormesu a degwm ac yn awr yr wyf fi yn rhoddi rhybydd i chwi i ddychwelyd beibl y dyn tlawd hwnw a werthsoch yn lie degwm a bod yn foddlon i gymmeryd ganddynt yr un peth ac oeddynt yn dalu o'r blaen gan y rhai sydd heb dalu ar rhai sydd wedi talu'r degwm mawr fel ymaent yn ei alw yr wyf rhoddi rhybydd i chwi i anfon yn ol iddynt y cwbl a dalasant i chwi eleni yn fwy nac oeddynt yn dalu o'r blaen a hyny yn ddioed fel y gallwyf gael gwybod ganddynt dydd gwener yn y Castell Newydd ac os na wnewch fel yr wyf yn gofyn genych nos lun nesaf byddaf fi a rhyw nifer om plant yn dod i ymweled a chwi efallau 3 neu 4 cant a chofiwch ddodi pob peth yn barod mi doraf ddwy och aelodau un glyn ac un fraich a rhoddaf yr hyn oil sydd genych ar dan a chofiwch peidiwch a thwyllo eich hunan y mae y peth uchod mor wired o gymeryd lie a bod bywyd yn eich corph.

D. S. A. ydyw ddim yn beth arswydys fod gweinidog efenyl fel yr ydych chwi yn galw eich hunan yn ymddwyn mor farbaraidd och! och! och! och!

Rebecca.

The following is a translation:

Penyrherber,

June 16th, 1843.

I have had a complaint about you from your parishioners that you oppress them with tithes, and now I give you warning to return that poor man's Bible which you sold in lieu of tithe, and be willing to take from those who have not paid, and those who have paid a big tithe as they call it, I warn you to send back to them all that they have paid this year, more than they paid before, and that without delay so that I shall know from them Friday in Newcastle. If you will not do as I ask you next Monday night I and some of my children will visit you, perhaps three or four hundred and remember to put everything ready. I will break two of your limbs one leg and one arm and I will put all your goods on fire and remember not to deceive yourself the above thing is as certain to take place as there is life in your body. D. S. A. is not the thing awful that a minister of the Gospel as you call yourself behaves in such a barbarous fashion. Alas! Alas! Alas! Alas!

Rebecca.

In consequence of this and other threatening letters, a detachment of soldiers was sent to the Vicar's residence Troedyrhiw. They caught nobody, however, except an old labourer named Wil, who was employed on the place. He was loitering about one night, when the soldiers triumphantly pounced upon him, and marched him into the kitchen. Wil understood no English and the soldiers knew no Welsh, but fortunately Mr. Hughes entered the kitchen at the critical moment, and Wil was set free.

The third week in June a little thatched cottage, in which a woman who received tolls at Pontweli Gate near Llandyssul resided, was burnt to the ground, though no fire had been lighted in it since the preceding day. Shortly after the toll-gate at Pontweli, and that at Troedyrhiw Cribin, both near Lland-

The Rioters Grow Bolder

yssul, with the gate-house belonging to the latter, were completely destroyed by a crowd of disguised Rebeccaites. They compelled those persons whom they met to join them in the destructive work, the toll receiver and special constable not excepted.

On 20th June, a letter signed by "Eliza," and dated at Conwil, was delivered by an unknown man to a certain person at Llandyssul. The writer commanded him to summon all the inhabitants of the village to meet the writer that night at the gate of Llanfihangel-Yeroth. The recipient of the letter, thoroughly alarmed at the consequences threatened should he disobey, hastily sent the Crier to publish the contents of the letter throughout the village. Eliza kept her appointment and passed through Llandyssul with a large party, who were disguised and armed with guns which they discharged at intervals. A great number of the peaceably-disposed inhabitants of Llandyssul, struck with terror at Eliza's threat, joined Rebecca's children and marched to the Llanvihangel-Yeroth Gate, a distance of three miles, where all were "compelled to labour hard in the work of destruction, amid the cheers, howlings, and sometimes horrid screeches of Rebecca and her children." In a short time the gate-posts, etc., were entirely destroyed and carried away by the crowd.

Three gates near Newcastle Emlyn, on the Cardigan side of the river, viz. Adpar, Henafod, and Kerry Gates were pulled down and destroyed on 21st June.

Meetings of the Rebeccaites or farmers of the hundred of Elvet took place on Wednesday night, 14th June, at Trelech, Talog, Blaencoed, and Conwil, when it was proposed and unanimously decided to demand from the Newcastle Trust a debtor and creditor account of the said Trust for the last eighteen years, and if found fair and correct, and the money received from the tolls fairly and honestly laid out on the roads, the gate at Water Street was not to be disturbed; but if unsatisfactory, then the gate was to be immediately demolished. All male inhabitants being householders of the hundred, were to meet at eleven o'clock on the following Thursday, at the "Plough and Harrow," Newchurch parish, to march in procession to Carmarthen—to defy the Mayor and magistrates, and to destroy the gate on their return. Rich and poor were to be compelled to attend, and in case of illness a substitute must be found. All owners of horses were to ride.

All persons absent without a sufficient excuse or substitute were to have their houses and barns destroyed by fire. No disguises in dress or person were to be allowed.

The farmers from each parish had been the previous day to Newcastle to have their demands and grievances put in some order by Mr. Lloyd Hall, a spirited advocate of civil and religious liberty; and the greater number of the Rebeccaites at their various meetings seemed disposed to be guided by his advice. It was proposed at the various places of meeting to pull down and destroy the workhouse. That question was, however, adjourned to their next meeting. The bias on the minds of all present seemed to be to raze it to the ground in the month of August.

The Rioters Grow Bolder

Rebecca and Her Legions at Carmarthen

The magistrates at Carmarthen were naturally much alarmed at the turn events had taken, and after much consultation caused the pensioners and others to be sworn as special constables. All possible means to keep the peace were used.

The rumour now gained currency that Rebecca intended attacking the town on the following Saturday (17th June).

Saturday and Sunday, however, passed by without any hostile demonstration "to revenge on their enemies," as the Rebeccaites put it.

On Monday, the 19th, the threatened invasion took place. The point on which the rioters were ordered to concentrate their forces before entering the town was the "Plough and Harrow," at Bwlchnewydd, about two miles away, and in order to ensure a full attendance of her followers, the church doors in the neighbourhood of Elvet were covered with notices in the dead of night, signed by "'Becca," commanding all males above the age of sixteen and under seventy to appear at the "Plough and Harrow" on the morning of the 19th under pain of having their houses burnt and their lives sacrificed. The time and place of meeting were also published by word of mouth at most of the Dissenting meeting-houses throughout the hundred, and wherever a disinclination was known to exist on the part of any person to join in the procession and to take part in the intended proceedings, he was privately admonished if he wished to protect his property from the firebrand of the midnight incendiary, and to excuse himself from personal injury, that he had better join the procession—"or else." This species of intimidation had the effect of drawing together immense numbers to the place of rendezvous. About ten o'clock people coming into town from Pembrokeshire brought news of the reality of the state of affairs, and after some time Captain Evans, of Pantycendy, came to town and informed the magistrates of their proceedings. As a last effort to arrest the men in their projected visit, Captain Evans and John Lloyd Davies, Esq., both influential magistrates for the county, repaired to Bwlch to expostulate with them on the bad policy and danger of the course they were pursuing. They urged them not to imperil the public peace by a procession through Carmarthen, which could not tend to any good result, but to submit, by memorial or petition, a representation of their grievances to those who were competent to redress them, with an assurance that they should receive every consideration to which they were in fairness entitled. These kind and conciliatory suggestions were, however, rejected, and the most violent of the party threatened to murder Mr. Lloyd Davies if he persevered in addressing them. To this he replied he was in their power, that he was unarmed and defenceless, and that they might carry their threat into execution, adding that a man can die but once. This union of energy and firmness subdued the angry feelings which his benevolent exertions had provoked. Captain Evans's patriotic exertions were equally unavailing to deter them from visiting Carmarthen; neither would they promise that they would not attack the workhouse, nor that they would go into town unarmed. The latter stipulation they observed so far as regards firearms, but they all furnished themselves with cudgels or shillalaghs in lieu. It is said that 150 brought arms to the meeting, but that they were induced to leave them in a house not far from that place until their return. A great many idlers from Carmarthen had gone over to meet them, and now prevailed on them to proceed to town and show their strength. During this time the utmost excitement prevailed in every part of the town. All the shops were closed; business was completely suspended, and the streets were thronged with thousands of spectators waiting anxiously for some information of Rebecca and her proceedings. The police and special constables had received instructions to be in attendance at the Town Hall at eight in the morning, and the Mayor, together with a great number of the county and borough magistrates, soon arrived and held a consultation.

It was determined not to interrupt the procession, should it pass quietly through the town and not commit a breach of the peace.

A little before noon, the immense throng of Rebeccaites was seen coming by Fountain Hall, and in a few minutes they entered the town through Water Street Gate, preceded by a band of musicians playing popular airs, and men bearing placards with the following inscriptions in large printed letters:—

"CYFIAWNDER
A CHARWYR CYFIAWNDER
YDYM NI OLL."

(Justice and lovers of Justice are we all.)

"RHYDDID A GWELL LLUNIAETH."

(Freedom and better food.)

"TOLL RYDD A RHYDDID."

(Free tolls and Freedom.)

The procession consisted of about 4000 men on foot and nearly 500 on horseback, but numbers of women and young men were among them. There were certainly a few respectable persons to be seen in the procession, but the greater part consisted of a motley crowd of countrymen who appeared to be wholly unable to execute deeds which Rebecca and her children had the credit of performing. Several of the town blackguards had settled themselves comfortably behind the men on horseback, and others were seen leading the procession through the town.

Rebecca, the insolent and, up to this point, triumphant dame, was mounted on horseback and ornamented with a profusion of artificial ringlets, which gave her a very grotesque appearance, and she was well guarded by the most resolute and athletic of her mutinous brood. All carried formidable bludgeons. Although in the procession there was much of the ludicrous that was calculated to excite mirth, yet there was also in the apparent spirit of determination and defiance which animated the multitude, in the principle of secret combination and the midnight influence which had distinguished their lawless career, in the dark thoughts of personal injury and loss of property by fire by which they had established a reign of terror throughout the country, much that was calculated to inspire alarm, and to enforce on the mind the inquiry—in what would all this ultimately end?

When the procession had passed through Upper Water Street, Goose Street, Picton Terrace, round the Monument, down Lammas Street, Dark Street, Blue Street, over the Quay, up Spilman Street, and round St. Peter's Church, the mob halted in Little Water Street, and seemed to hesitate whether they should proceed direct to the workhouse or go through the town; but eventually they proceeded down King Street and passed the Town Hall, where they gave three hearty cheers. These were lustily responded to by groups of spectators who had by this time completely filled Guildhall Square, so that the Rebeccaites could hardly pass through.

While the procession was passing through the town an old man on horseback, who appeared to be about seventy years of age, kept crying out in a most doleful voice, "B'le mae mam?" (Where is mother?) "Gweloch chwi mam?" (Have you seen mother?) Others were answering him, saying she was on in front, whereupon he would cast an anxious look at Rebecca, saying, "Ah, I see her!" Several persons had horns, which they kept blowing in different parts of the procession.

It was thought when Guildhall Square was reached that a statement of grievances would be laid before the magistrates who were assembled for the purpose of receiving such a statement, or of hearing one or more of the party detail them, as it was currently reported to be their intention. In this, however, the magistrates were disappointed, for having made the circuit of the town, and having convinced themselves of the fallacy of the report that the military sent by the Government to aid the civil force had arrived, they turned on the right through Red Street, and went direct to the Union Workhouse. When they reached that place, they demanded admittance, which was refused, but when the master saw the door on the point of giving way he opened it. Hundreds of Rebecca's exulting and triumphant daughters immediately entered the workhouse yard, and soon found their way into the house, breaking everything that impeded their progress; whilst the road leading to the building was densely thronged with Rebecca's followers and the sympathisers who always abound in a populous town.

Mrs. Evans, the matron, was seized in the house by one of the mob, pushed against the wall, and ordered to deliver up the keys of the house, or she would be a dead woman in another instant; the children screaming at the same time, "Oh, dear mistress! Don't kill our dear mistress!"

The master was attacked by several of the others, two keys were wrenched from his hand, and he was knocked down. Some of the rioters proceeded to the men's yard, ordered them out of the place, and attempted to enter the bedroom; but they were resolutely opposed, the men saying it was out of their power to better their circumstances. The rioters next ordered the children out of the place, when Mrs. Evans remonstrated with them and said, "Where do you expect the poor children to go? They have no home in the world." They answered, "We will find them a home," and all the women and children were turned out into the road, where a poor old woman was very severely hurt. Others of the Rebeccaites had proceeded upstairs into the children's bedroom (being led by a woman who had lately been discharged from the workhouse), and they immediately commenced throwing the beds, blankets, and pillows out of the windows into the yard; in fact, the whole place was now in their possession. They had forced their way into the Board-room, and were dancing on the tops of the tables and beating them with their staffs in a furious manner; had it not been for the special intervention of Providence the whole place would have been fired or razed to the ground in a very short time.

Mr. James Morse, of the Stamp Office, appearing at that moment, the master entreated him to address the multitude, which he instantly did from one of the bedroom windows, and at some length pointed out the disgrace to the county, and to them, as men, in disturbing the peace that if they had real grievances they should present them by respectful petition to Parliament; that their present unjustifiable conduct would only bring upon them the consequent punishment arising from offending against the law of the land; and that, once the Riot Act was read, their lives would not be safe. He told them that the military were expected, and begged them to go home. This address had a great effect on the most respectable portion of the crowd; they gave him three cheers for his advice, and turned their horses' heads towards the entrance, when they were met at the gateway and shut in by the 4th Light Dragoons.

The latter had come to the "Ivy Bush," in Spilman Street, when the magistrates received information of the proceedings of the mob at the workhouse, whereupon Mr. Thomas Charles Morris instantly headed the military and proceeded to the place. On their way up Mr. Morris cried out, "Now, my men, cut and slash away!" Major Parlby instantly shouted, "Not one of you obey any man's orders but mine!"

When the rioters perceived the dragoons galloping up with drawn swords, a general panic seized the congregated thousands, and they fled in consternation in every direction. The sudden and unexpected approach of the dragoons at top speed, with their bright sabres flashing in the sun, was well calculated to strike terror into the hearts of those who were violating the laws of their country. Seeing that the vengeance of those laws was about to overtake them, those who were fortunate enough to be outside the walls of the workhouse betook themselves to flight with astonishing alacrity, and cut their way through hedges and gardens and over fields of corn towards the country, without once looking back to see what would be the fate of their friends left behind.

The rush of the mounted Rebeccaites up Penlan Hill when the dragoons charged was terrific, and can be compared to nothing but the flight of the French from the plains of Waterloo. "Sauve qui peut!" was the order, or rather *dis*order of the day. Several horsemen, ignorant of the locality, rode up the road leading to Norton's Brewery, where they were cooped up in a *cul de sac*, and in order to extricate themselves were obliged to clear the hedges if their horses were adepts at leaping fences, otherwise they had to abandon them and make their escape on foot. Scores of unclaimed horses without riders, roaming about the fields and roads, afterwards attested the prudential wisdom of their owners and the prevalence of the panic. The mob at first attempted to offer resistance, and some of the gentlemen and constables were rather severely handled, but through the great exertions of the special constables they were soon overpowered, upwards of eighty being taken and placed in confinement in the hall of the workhouse.

As soon as the confusion had ceased, the Mayor, E. H. Stacey, Esq., with the borough and county magistrates, held a meeting on the spot. They sat in the workhouse schoolroom, and the prisoners were brought before them and examined as to their intention in coming into Carmarthen; but they had all the same account to give of themselves, viz. that their houses had been threatened to be burnt and their lives taken. Some of them said that these threats had been published before the churches and meeting-houses on the Sunday previous; and one man said that a notice to that effect had been stuck up on the door of his parish church. Mr. Morris interrupted with the remark: "Oedd dim cywilydd arnoch chwi osod y fath bapur cythraul ar ddrws Ty Dduw?"[1] The matron and the schoolmistress of the workhouse were directed to inspect the rioters, in order to identify any of them as those whom they had particularly noticed when the mob entered the place, but the most prominent had succeeded in making good their escape.

Several of the persons brought before the magistrates were identified as those who had molested the constables in the execution of the distress warrants at Talog, and they were committed to gaol, as were also the persons who had assaulted Mr. Hughes, of Glancothi (who had been most active in his efforts to arrest the rioters), and the master of the workhouse when the rioters were captured. There were nine persons captured altogether. Harris, of Talog Mill, was remanded, for further examination, for sending threatening letters, although bail was offered for his appearance to the amount of £500. The remainder, numbering about seventy, entered into recognisances for their appearance at the Assizes, should a bill of indictment be preferred against them. A great number of horses, as well as several hats, a shoemaker's apron, a hatter's apron, and an immense number of staffs, some of which were loaded with lead, were left in the yard. Others were genteel walking-sticks, and had evidently belonged to respectable persons. The board which showed the placard was left in the workhouse, but the paper with the inscription was torn away.

The workhouse garden was so trampled by the men and horses that everything it contained was completely destroyed, but the injuries done to the building itself were comparatively trifling. Great injury was also sustained by persons holding lands immediately adjoining, as the Rebeccaites in their flight regarded nothing but their own safety.

When all was over, the soldiers were served with refreshments, and the horses fed, of which food they must have been in extreme need. One of the horses had fallen dead on the

---

[1] "Were you not ashamed to put such a devilish paper on the door of God's House?"

road, another died in the workhouse yard from fatigue, and there were several others so knocked up that it took some time to bring them round. The men were also very much fatigued, but performed their duty with alacrity, although with the greatest forbearance. As the work of destruction had commenced before the soldiers arrived at the workhouse, they would have been justified in acting on the offensive without waiting to read the Riot Act; but when they perceived that the Rebeccaites were unarmed, and were expecting no attack, as they immediately fled in all directions, they contented themselves with merely keeping the prisoners within the workhouse walls until the proper authorities should have time to place them under arrest. This was speedily done by the police and special constables on duty. As it was rumoured that the Rebeccaites had gone home for their guns, and would return well armed that evening to make another attack on the workhouse, the authorities thought proper to put a body of special constables to guard the place, and also the several roads leading to the town for that night; but nothing alarming occurred.

Incidents Which Happened During the Attack

When the Rebeccaites, in their attack on the workhouse, saw the dragoons surrounding the place, the terror which prevailed among them was inconceivable, and did not at all accord with the boastings of the lawless heroine in her usual visits. The rabble enclosed within the walls of the workhouse expected nothing but instant death, and one man actually fell flat on his face, where he remained a considerable time, that he might not see the dragoons cutting off his head! Groups of women and boys were seen huddled together, praying fervently for death to relieve them rather than they should fall into the hands of the soldiers and be killed by them.

When the rioters who had been captured at the workhouse were placed in a row, to afford a better means of identification, one of them was so terrified that he asked the person next to him what they were going to do with him. The man addressed, who happened to be a wag, and had seen some service in the Peninsula, answered that they were so placed that the soldiers might kill them all with one shot. The horrified Rebeccaite, with a terrified shriek, jumped out of the line, and it was with the utmost difficulty that he could be again prevailed upon to stand by the side of his companions.

One of the fortunate persons who escaped over the wall made the best use of his legs to reach home; but on the way, when he was nearly out of breath and the terror of the dragoons full in his mind, he heard a tremendous rush through the hedge close to him, and screamed out: "Quarter, quarter! For God's sake, don't kill me!" and fell fainting to the ground, thinking that one of the dragoons had followed him. When he ventured to look up, he saw that the unwelcome intruder was a fellow-fugitive on horseback, by this time nearly out of sight.

Many reached home with scarcely a rag on them, having left their clothes in the hedges through which they had to pass.

Rebeccaite Correspondence

On the eventful day, the history of which is recorded in the foregoing chapter, a notice was sent to the master of the Newcastle Emlyn Workhouse. It read as follows:

Dyhaledd Y Gwaed.

June 19th, 1843.

Ffel mai byw dy enaid, a byw ninau, os na ddoi di allan, ti du a'r tylodion sydd dan di ofal, gin dydd Mercher nesaf, rhydyn yn benderfinol i ddynistrio'r cwbl; ai gwae di gorph tithau oblegid *Ni* a gwmrwm ofal am danat, ffel na chai ddiang! (Gochel!) Nid gellwer rydym bellach.

Rebecca (L.S.)
Miss Brown (L.S.)

To Mr. David Davies,
Master
Workhouse
Newcastle Emlyn.

As thy soul and ours live, if thou comest not out, thou and the poor that are in thy care, before Wednesday next, we are determined to destroy everything; and woe to thy own body, for we will take care that thou shalt not flee! (Beware!) We trifle no longer.

Rebecca (L.S.)
Miss Brown (L.S.)

The Vicar of Llangranog, Cardiganshire, also received a threatening letter the same day. It must be explained that the latter had made himself most unpopular by collecting subscriptions, from "all and sundry" persons, towards a free school, without informing Dissenters of his intention to convert it into a place of worship. The letter was in Welsh and read as follows:

Mehefin 19th, 1843.

Barchedig Syr,

Rebeccaite Correspondence

Bum i ac un o'm merched ar daith yn ddiweddar i Aberaeron ac ymysg pethau ereill clywais lawer am danoch chwi chwi, sef eich bod wedi codi ysgoldy yn rhan uchaf y plwyf, a'ch bod wedi bod yn anonest iawn ynglyn a'r adeiladu, a'ch bod wedi ei ddarlunio fel ysgol rydd i'r bobl, a'ch bod wedi ei droi'n eglwys, a'ch bod yn cael £80 yn y flwyddyn am wasanaeth ynddo.

Yn awr, os yw hyn yn wir, rhaid i chwi roi'r arian yn ol pob dimau, onide dof ft a rhyw 500 new 600 o'm merched i ymweled a chwi, a dinistriaf eich eiddo bum gwaith drosodd, a gwnaf chwi'n destyn gwawd a gwaradwydd yr holl gymdogaeth.

Gwyddoch nad wyf yn malio am y toll-byrth a byddwch chwithau yr un modd a hwy'n union, oherwydd yr wyf yn erbyn gormes.

Yr eiddoch

            Rebecca a'i merched.
            June 19th, 1843.

Reverend Sir,

I, with one of my daughters, have recently been on a journey to Aberayron, and amongst other things have heard many things respecting you, namely, that you have built a schoolroom in the upper part of the parish, and that you have been very dishonest in the erection of it, and that you promised a free school for the people, but that you have converted it into a church, and that you get £80 by the year for serving it. Now, if this is true, you may give the money back, every halfpenny of it, otherwise if you do not, I with 500 or 600 of my daughters will come and visit you, and destroy your property five times to the value of it, and make you a subject of scorn and reproach throughout the whole neighbourhood. You know that I care nothing about the gates, and you shall be like them exactly, because I am averse to every tyranny and oppression.

            Rebecca and her daughters.

Rebecca and a great number of her daughters assembled at Mydrim, Carmarthenshire, about 4 p.m. on 20th June and stopped there some hours. They were nearly all dressed in women's clothes, and Rebecca was on horseback elegantly attired. Having called at "The Wheaten Sheaf," where they cleared the cellars of all the beer and porter, about 10 p.m. they departed for St. Clears. They went to several gentlemen demanding money, saying that they could not carry on their work without having something to eat and drink. More Rebeccaites assembled from all parts of that district at St. Clears, most of them armed with guns and other destructive weapons, and the whole party immediately levelled to the ground the gates leading to St. Clears from both ends.

Mr. Thomas of Clynarthen, having refused to join them, had his wheat-field entirely destroyed before morning, by their turning cattle from the mountain into it that night.

The following address by Mr. Lloyd Hall (see *The Rioters Grow Bolder*, page 41) to Rebecca and her daughters, shows that the lady was by no means modest in her demands:

Welshmen,

You have sent me a letter commanding me to appear on *Wednesday* night at *Blaennant Lane*, armed and disguised. That your object is to obtain redress for some of the grievances with which you are oppressed is evident. But this is not the way to obtain such redress. I have been, as you know, labouring for years to gain you the rights of free men, and now that I begin to see the possibility of doing some good for you, you step in and by your violence and folly hinder me in the good work; and instead of hastening the time when all your grievances will be at an end, your nonsensical extravagance gives an excuse to your oppressors for refusing to listen to your complaints; and the redress you seek is farther off than ever. *Get one grievance redressed at a time*. The magistrates and Trustees of the Newcastle and Carmarthen Trust have appointed *Friday the 23rd instant to overhaul the grievances connected with that Trust*. I have been retained on the part of the men of the Hundred of Upper Elvet to represent their interests at such meeting. *Do you think I will neglect my duty? Do you think it is likely I should flinch from insisting on justice being done to the people? Or do you think that I am ignorant of the means of screwing it out from the Trustees let them be as reluctant as they will?* They have not been accustomed to be brought authoritatively to account. Like young colts not broken, they must be treated at first both gently and firmly.

Do you think I can countenance or join your riotous proceedings? I tell you No. And what is more, though I have fought, am fighting, and will continue to fight your battles, until I can obtain perfect justice and political regeneration for you and your children, I am and will always be the first man to keep the Queen's peace and prevent anything like rioting or disturbance. Enough has been done already to convince the Government of the great and universal discontent which your grievances have caused among you. They have sent down soldiers to keep the peace. *I therefore entreat you not to meet together on Wednesday night.* I have written for the soldiers to come here and prevent your doing mischief if you should. Why will you hinder me from fighting your battles in the only way in which we can be successful, and by your violence and absurdity, which can do no good, turn me from a friend to an enemy? Your conduct is childish and absurd and not like men who have great objects to attain. Why will you exhibit folly when wisdom is required? *The penalty for pulling down a Turnpike-house is Transportation for life.* What good can you get by running such a risk, when you may attain everything you ought to have, in a peaceable and quiet manner, without running any danger whatever? I can only attribute it to your ignorance, which prevents you from being able to guide in its proper course the great and irresistible force which you possess. A hundredth part of your strength properly applied, will do more for you, and without risk, than a thousand times your power wasted in the absurdities you have lately indulged in. Be guided by me. Do what I tell you and *you must be victorious in the end.* Go each one to your own homes on Wednesday night, peaceably and quietly. On Thursday morning let each Parish choose two Delegates to come to me (as the Parishes in the Hundred of Upper Elvet have done) to make me acquainted with your grievances and then follow implicitly the advice I shall give them. If you do, peace and prosperity will be sure to return to you. If you do not, I shall leave you to enjoy the results of your ignorance and folly.

Edw. A. Lloyd Hall
(Barrister-at-Law).

Emlyn Cottage,
Newcastle Emlyn,
June 20th, 1843.

About twelve o'clock on the night of 22nd June, two commercial gentlemen were stopped on the bridge at Newcastle Emlyn by Rebecca and her daughters. They had heard shots fired at intervals for about three miles, and on arriving at the bridge they were surrounded by several hundreds, whom they described as being all dressed in women's clothes, with their faces blackened, and armed with staves and firearms. The leader came up to them, and entered into conversation, relating the grievances of Rebecca and her children. In order to get out of their hands, the gentlemen thought it prudent to give her some silver; she gave the word of command and they were immediately suffered to pass, and indeed conducted to their inns amid the cheers of the Rebeccaites.

Soon after this Rebecca broke down several gates in the neighbourhood, viz. Pontyberem Bar, Castellrhingyll Gate, Pontnewydd Bar, and a great many more in different parts of the country.

A distress for rent was levied on the goods of a man named Lloyd, living at the Albion Inn, Llanstephan, and a bailiff of the name of Rees kept possession of the goods. Previous to the day of sale, Rebecca and a great number of her daughters paid him a visit, horsewhipped him well, and kept him in safe custody until the furniture was entirely cleared from the house. When Rees was freed, he found nothing but an empty house, Rebecca and her followers having departed.

Rebeccaite Correspondence

Cardigan, Newcastle Emlyn, and Carmarthen

The inhabitants of Cardigan were greatly alarmed on 23rd June by Rebecca and her daughters paying a visit to the Pensarne (Rhos) Turnpike-gate, on the Aberystwyth Road, and the Rhydyfuwch Upper Gate, on the Llangoedmore Road.[1]

About eleven o'clock a party of about 150 persons was seen coming down Cardigan Common, preceded by half a dozen horsemen exceedingly well mounted, the rest being on foot; the horses were on the full gallop, and those on foot running after them at a rapid pace. They were all disguised, having their faces blackened, and some wore women's clothes, others smocks, etc. They carried with them guns, swords, scythes, pitchforks, and other weapons of destruction, intended, no doubt, for self-defence, in the event of their being attacked. Immediately on their arrival at the Pensarne Gate (built about two years previous at a cost of £100) the work of demolition began; the sounds of saws and hatchets were distinctly heard, and several shots were fired, followed by tremendous shouting.

The gate and the hedge soon disappeared, but the toll-house being newly and strongly built, the roof and the walls being of the best materials as to stone and mortar, it appeared that it was a difficult task for them to destroy it. However, after considerable exertions, down it came nearly to its foundations.

The rabble then came down through the centre of the town to the Cross, turned down St. Mary Street over Pontycleivion Bridge (Pantylleifion) to Rhydyfuwch Gate, which with the walls thereto attached, being old, immediately vanished. One of the leaders went to the toll-house, kept by a

---

1 See Introduction, page 13.

widow, who remonstrated with him, and expressed a hope that none of her furniture would be damaged or injured. 'Becca replied, "Be not alarmed, shut your door upon you; your house and furniture will not be touched; we only want the gate and walls." After finishing the work, the horsemen galloped away, and the rest dispersed.

It is said that 'Becca herself was not present upon this occasion, but that her daughter "Nelly" was in command.

The magistrates of Carmarthenshire and Cardiganshire held an important meeting at the "Salutation Inn," Newcastle Emlyn, on the same date. It was understood that delegates from several parishes within the Turnpike Trust of Newcastle Emlyn would attend, and large bodies of the farmers and peasantry were congregated in the town. At one o'clock the delegates were introduced into the room, and the Hon. Col. Trevor took the chair. In the course of his speech he read what the magistrates were willing to do:—

> We are willing that every grievance that can be proved to exist, and which can be remedied, should be removed, either in the administration of the funds of the Trust, or by the erection of new gates, or by increase of tolls. For that purpose we will name a committee of trustees and tallyholders to go into all the accounts of the Trust; and at that committee Mr. Hall shall attend, if he wishes it, on your behalf. If any point of law should arise, counsel's opinion shall be taken, by which the trustees must abide until set aside by the decision of a court of law.
>
> The magistrates have had a force of troops put at their disposal by the Government, and though they are willing to redress all that is amiss they cannot give way to force, and must put down all disturbances, the Government being ready to increase the number of troops if necessary.

After a number of speeches, a committee was formed, for what purpose the following address, issued immediately after the meeting, will show:—

> Welshmen,— The trustees of the Carmarthen and Turnpike Trust have met here to-day, and have appointed a committee consisting of John Beynon, Esq., Adpar Hill, Newcastle Emlyn; John Davies, Esq., Guildhall Square, Carmarthen; Capt. Evans, Pantycendy; Rev. Benjamin Lewis, Dyffryn; Thomas Lloyd, Esq., Bronwydd; Rees Goring Thomas, Esq., Llysnewydd; Lewis Morris, Esq., Carmarthen; Edward A. Lloyd Hall, Esq., Emlyn Cottage; to examine and audit the

accounts of the Trust, and to report all other grievances connected with the Trust, and to point out the remedy for them. We meet here next Friday morning, because the Quarter Sessions prevents our meeting before then. The tally holders present have agreed to reduce the interest on their debts to 3½ per cent.

Welshmen,— Here is a glorious beginning! The magistrates have all pledged themselves to see justice done to you. Chwareu teg i bob un. I entreat of you to wait patiently until you see what I can do for you with other Trusts. But I cannot do two things. Give me fair play, or I may not be able to get justice done for you. One grievance at a time. But mind this: if these riotous proceedings continue, I will have nothing to do with you. If you want fair play, give fair play. There is no wrong without a remedy; but if you take the wrong physic for your disease, how can you expect to be cured? Give the medicine I have prescribed fair play, and it will work in time. If you stop it by doing anything contrary to law, you will make your case incurable, and I shall wash my hands of the business.

Edward A. Lloyd Hall.

Emlyn Cottage,
June, 1843.

The large assemblage outside was addressed in Welsh, and informed of the result of the meeting. On being asked by a private individual if the meeting had satisfied them, a person in the crowd replied that it was *not* satisfactory, and that "Rebecca would go on as usual." Another man in the crowd, addressing the magistrates in Welsh, said he was an overseer, and that as such he was obliged to levy the poor-rate on persons who were so poor that they had scarcely a blanket.

Carmarthen was thrown into great excitement about 10 p.m. on 24th June by the sudden departure of the dragoons through Priory Street. Various were the conjectures as to the place of their destination, some asserting that Rebecca and her children were demolishing Glangwili Gate, others that it was Abergwili Gate that was attacked. It eventually turned out that they had been ordered to guard Glangwili House, the residence of J. Lloyd Price, Esq., who had cause to fear an attack from Rebecca. They remained there until one o'clock, when they returned to town. The dragoons left Carmarthen for Newcastle Emlyn on Sunday afternoon the 25th, as news had arrived that Rebecca and her children intended to have a grand procession on the Monday through the town to the workhouse, according to the threats previously made.

On the 26th a detachment, consisting of 120 of the Royal Marines, under Major Whylock, left Pembroke Arsenal in the *Confiance* steamer for Cardigan, to be placed under the command of Colonel Love, Commandant of the district.

Two troops of Castle Martin Yeomanry Cavalry, under the command of Captains Leach and Mansel, were dispatched the same day from Pembroke, the one to Newcastle Emlyn, the other to St. Clears for a similar purpose.

A great number of Rebeccaites attended at Scleddy Turnpike-gate, within three miles of Fishguard, on 27th June, and in a very short time broke the gates, posts, walls, and tollboards into pieces so small that in the morning there was not a piece of the timber larger than would make matches, and those long enough to be dipped at one end only!

The dragoons returned to Carmarthen on the same day, no demonstration having taken place at Newcastle Emlyn.

About four o'clock in the morning of the 27th, Rebecca, with a numerous gang of her children, paid a visit to Penygarn Gate, near Llanegwad. They demolished the gate in a short time, stripped the roof of the toll-house, and left the walls in a tottering condition. They then fired off fifteen volleys, and immediately dispersed in various directions. They were all well armed, and disguised in women's clothes.

Newcastle Emlyn Gate was destroyed next, and on this occasion Mr. Benjamin Evans (father of the late Allen Raine and a prominent solicitor of the town) was forced to be present.

He was staying at Llangranog when he received a letter, signed "Rebecca," demanding that he should meet her ladyship and friends the following night (28th June) at Penwalk, about a mile from the town. If he failed to do so his house and office were to be set on fire.

This threat was too serious to be treated lightly, so Mr. Evans met the Rebeccaites at the appointed place at 9 p.m. Their faces were blackened, but an old servant's voice was recognised, upon which Mr. Evans asked if it was he (mentioning his name). He received the curt reply "that no names were to be mentioned while in their company."

They marched in a body to the town, breaking down the toll-gate on their way. The march was continued, a man leading Mr. Evans by the arm through the one long street the town contained, the rioters shouting to all occupiers of houses to put out their lights if they wished to avoid being shot.

A certain Mr. Titus Thomas declined to put out his candles, but a shot through the window convinced him that Rebecca would not be trifled with.

Mr. Evans was not molested in any way, but was told afterwards that he was made to join, so that if any proceedings were subsequently taken, he as local solicitor might be made a party to them.

On 28th June, an address was issued by W. E. Powell, Lord-Lieutenant of Cardiganshire, to the Rebeccaites, deprecating the present state of affairs, and inviting them to lay their complaints before the magistrates at the petty sessions for legal redress; if no relief were forthcoming that way, he stated he would join with them in petitioning the legislature to remove all their real grievances.

Hugh Owen, Vice-Lieutenant of Pembrokeshire, on behalf of the magistrates, issued an address, reminding the Rebeccaites that the roads must be maintained either by tolls or rates, or a combination of both, and invited all classes to assist in maintaining the law, and preserving peace and good order.

The following day (28th June) the Hon. George Rice Trevor, Vice-Lieutenant of the County of Carmarthen, issued an address as follows:—

To the inhabitants of the County of Carmarthen.

I feel called upon at this moment, when so much of illegal and unanswerable outrage has been committed in some parts of the county, to call your attention to the evil consequences such proceedings are calculated to bring on all those concerned in them. The assemblies that have taken place for the purposes of violence, under the pretence of redressing grievances, are illegal, and though up to this time many of those who are concerned in them have escaped detection, they may be assured that, sooner or later, the law will be too strong for them, and will make its powers felt.

I would also warn you that most serious consequences must follow the assembling of multitudes together, armed and disguised, particularly at night, and that parties so offending will become liable to the infliction of most severe and heavy punishment. For the purpose of restoring order and preventing tumult, there is a large force at my disposal. I am naturally averse to employ it against my fellow-countrymen; but I beg of you to believe me that if it be necessary I shall not hesitate one moment to do so. My duty as Vice-Lieutenant requires this, for I cannot allow the peaceable and well-disposed to be kept in continual terror from lawless violence. At the same time, I invite all who have any cause of complaint and can prove the justice of their cases, to resort to any lawful means of making their grievances known which the Constitution affords.

Lastly, I call upon all such as are willing to support the law to rally round the magistrates, and freely to come forward and offer their services, each in his own neighbourhood, for the maintenance of order and tranquillity, and wipe out the disgrace which their most unlawful and most dangerous proceedings have brought upon the county, hitherto one of the most quiet and orderly in the Principality.

George Rice Trevor.
(Vice-Lieutenant of the County of Carmarthen.)

The same night, Gurrey-fach Gate, near Llandilo, was completely demolished, and the noise of the rioters was distinctly heard in the town of Llandilo; but no one dared go out to prevent the outrageous proceedings. Several other gates and bars were destroyed in the country the same week.

Rebecca and about five hundred of her children also paid a visit to Narberth on the same day, but having learned (probably from some friend in the town) that a troop of the Castle Martin Yeomanry Cavalry, under the command of Major Bowling, had previously arrived and were quartered in the workhouse, they immediately retreated with the utmost precipitation.

The following account appeared in the *Standard* of 29th June. It is a tissue of falsehood:—

Riots in South Wales

Carmarthen, June 27th, 1843.

Never was this part of South Wales in such a disturbed state as at the present moment, when Rebecca and her daughters are demolishing the gates of the county, injuring private property, and threatening the immediate destruction of all the workhouses throughout the land.

Carmarthen was the scene of action on the 19th when the Rebeccaites to the number of 10,000 or 12,000 endeavoured to take possession of the town, armed with bludgeons, pitchforks, and scythes, with banners bearing the following inscriptions: 'Death or Glory,' 'Blood and Revenge,' 'Bread for the Hungry,' etc. The procession reached from one end of the town to the other.

They latterly arrived at the Union Workhouse, where they forced an entrance, and had commenced upon the work of levelling the building to the ground, when providentially a detachment of the 4th Light Dragoons arrived, and dispersed the mob in all directions, with the exception of about 500, who were taken prisoners, and afterwards committed to take their trials at the next assizes. The town throughout the week has been quiet and peaceable, but on Sunday last, orders were given for the immediate departure of the dragoons for Newcastle Emlyn where the rioters had assembled, with their numbers augmented to 15,000 or 20,000. The mob was so well armed and ready for action that the dragoons could not enter the town until Monday morning, and the conflict that took place on Newcastle Emlyn Bridge is beyond description. The soldiers were thrown off their horses, their arms were taken from them and were afterwards thrown into the river Teify, where one of the men named Kearns, the roughrider, met a watery grave, and the others are so bruised from having fallen on the rocks below the bridge pool that they are no more fit for service.

The Union Workhouse had also been entirely destroyed by fire, and it is feared a great many gentlemen's houses will be destroyed in the course of the night. The mob up to the present time is in possession of the town; but a detachment of the 73rd Regiment of Infantry, under the command of Colonel Love, is expected to arrive this evening. They may retake the town, but it is generally believed that a great number must be slain on both sides before the termination of the contest.

The committee appointed at Newcastle Emlyn met on 30th June, and the following resolutions were ordered to be published:—

That the rate of interest on the Tallies from 1838 should be reduced from 5 per cent to 3½ per cent. That the tolls should be lowered to what they were before Michaelmas, 1837, except at Francis Well Gate on the new line of road to Pontwelly, which are to remain as at present.

That Pontwelly Gate to Llanpumpsaint be not reerected for one twelvemonth.

That the gates be so arranged that only two tolls be payable between Pontarselly and Carmarthen.

That Bwlchydomen, Nantyclawdd, and Velindre Gates should not be re-erected.

That the Newcastle Gate be re-erected beyond Pontbrengwyddon.

A. Goring Thomas,
Chairman of the Committee.

Newcastle Emlyn,
June 30th, 1843.

Rebecca's Tactics Continued

A visit was paid by Rebecca and her children to the village of Llanddarog, about six miles from Carmarthen, on the same day (30th June). They mustered about five hundred, and were armed with guns, swords and pickaxes. Notice had been previously given that Rebecca intended paying a visit to the above-mentioned gate, and accordingly about midnight this renowned lady and her daughters fulfilled their promise. When they arrived, they inquired of the toll-collector what was to pay, to which that frightened gentleman replied instantly, "Nothing to you, ma'am!" Rebecca having acknowledged his politeness, desired him to go into his dwelling, and shut himself in, which he immediately did, and her orders were given for the destruction of the gate. In a short time it was levelled with the ground, amid the exultation of the family and the firing of guns. They then proceeded to Troedyrhiw Gate, which met the same fate.

On 3rd July, Frances Evans, the girl who led the Rebeccaites through the workhouse, was apprehended at Kilgwynuchaf Llannewydd. She was brought up at twelve o'clock, and bail was taken for her appearance at the Assizes, to answer any bill of indictment which might be preferred against her. A reward of £300 was issued, signed by Colonel George Rice Trevor, for the apprehension and conviction of the chief ringleader of the riot at Talog, with his four accomplices on the 12th June, the reward to be paid by Her Majesty's Government.

Colonel Love formed a military cordon round the disturbed districts on 5th July. A detachment of the 4th Dragoons arrived the same day at Llandovery from Brecon.

About a quarter to twelve on 6th July, a party consisting of about two hundred men on foot, headed by a Rebecca dressed entirely in white and who rode a white horse, were

Rebecca's Tactics Continued

seen approaching Goppa-fach Bar near Pontardulais on the main road and from that direction. The object of their visit was soon surmised, and the inhabitants of the few houses in the neighbourhood, apparently apprehensive of danger, retired within doors. Rebecca having advanced to the toll-house demanded admittance, which, having been given, she directed a few of the troops to carry out the toll-collector's goods and chattels to the side of the road, and to protect them from all injury till they had completed the object of their mission. She then gave the word of command for the total demolition of the house and bar, and actually within five minutes the bar was completely cut to pieces, the house in ruins, and the whole party in full retreat. During the time they were engaged at work a portion of their gang kept firing guns, etc. They took the Carmarthenshire road, and separated, going in different directions. The farmers of the surrounding district strongly condemned this outbreak, and stated their willingness to have abided by the decision of the turnpike trustees whom they had memorialised the previous day.

On Thursday, 6th July, a detachment of the 4th Light Dragoons arrived at Llandovery from Brecon, under the command of Captain Halket. The same day, a troop of Rebecca's children entered the district, to commence a campaign against turnpikes and toll-bars.

That night an attack was made upon Pumpsaint Gate, midway between Llandovery and Lampeter, the gate, posts, and rails being completely destroyed, and levelled to the ground with Rebecca's usual celerity.

The following Saturday the dragoons received orders to march to Llandilo on the Sunday—a most unusual command, Sunday marches only being resorted to in cases of great emergency.

Rebecca was not dismayed though, for the same night (Saturday), about 11 p.m., the turnpike-gate and bar at Bronvelin, five miles from Llandovery on the Llanwrtyd road, were completely destroyed.

John Lewis, commonly called John Pengelly, fisherman, Steam Mill, Carmarthen, surrendered himself on the 7th, and was brought up before the Mayor, etc., to answer the charge of taking an active part in the riotous proceedings at the workhouse on 19th June. He was held to bail to answer the charge at the next Assizes.

A great number of gates were demolished at this time in the Three Comotts district, amongst others being Pontyeates, Minke, Pontyberem, and both gates at Kidwelly. The gate-keeper at Castellyrhingyll, seeing a cart coming up, the horses being at full trot, threw a chain across the road, which made them stumble. The chain was instantly destroyed, and the gate-keeper soundly thrashed. At Fanissa a private gate which secured a limekiln belonging to J. E. Saunders, Esq., of Glanrhydw, was destroyed and burnt in the limekiln. The Bridgend Gate near Llangennech was destroyed, and the toll-house much damaged; and the Forest Gate between Pontardulais and Llanelly was destroyed and afterwards burnt.

On 7th July Rebecca and family, numbering about one hundred strong, mustered in the neighbourhood of Nantgaredig, about five miles from Carmarthen. They were on this occasion thoroughly disguised, and had their faces blackened, and wore something designed to imitate a turban. They were all dressed in smock frocks, and carried with them various implements of destruction. Their first outrage took place at Llandilo-rwnnws Gate, which was attached to a bridge called New Bridge, over the River Towy. This bridge had been erected by a certain John Jones, M.P. for Ystrad, for the convenience of the neighbourhood and his private property. At the time of their approach, two gentlemen from Carmarthen were fishing in the Towy, on the meadow immediately contiguous to the bridge, and they were at once directed to leave the place, or remain at the peril of their lives. The appearance of the mob was so alarming, and their threats being expressed in language both violent and determined, the two anglers (perceiving discretion to be the better part of valour) immediately coiled up their lines and departed. At the same time, a respectable young farmer of the name of Nicholas, happening to be on the spot, was placed under examination, and charged with having on some former occasion volunteered to become a special constable, with a view to aid in quelling the riots and depredations committed. He, however, did not escape so well as the gentlemen of the rod and fly, but had to endure a very serious horse-whipping before he was allowed to depart. A man named Lloyd, from Carmarthen, attempted to escape, but they pursued him, and he shared a like fate. Lloyd and a person named Evans had been placed at the gate, to enter the names of all persons who refused to pay

Rebecca's Tactics Continued

tolls, and to take care that the gateman did not raise more toll than he was authorised to do. At the first appearance of Rebecca, Evans started off at full speed towards Carmarthen, and being a remarkably swift runner, succeeded in making his escape from the clutches of Rebecca. He was so frightened at the appearance of the old lady, who was at least six feet high, had her face blackened, and brandished a large hay-knife in her hand, that he protested he would have nothing more to do with turnpike-gates.

The course being clear, Mr. Lewis, the lessee of the tolls, was the next object of the attack. On the previous Saturday week, Mr. Lewis had summoned a number of persons for refusing to pay toll in passing the gate in question, and this strongly excited their wrath. Lewis was brought out from the toll-house, and he was at once overpowered. Unfortunately he was armed with a horsewhip, and this was used to administer a violent beating. Rebecca, however, was not content with this, but compelled him to swear on his bended knees three successive times, by all that he held sacred, that he would never again have any connection with the tolls or turnpike-gates requiring the payment of tolls. Then followed the scene of destruction, pickaxes, hatchets, crowbars, and saws were set in operation, and the gate completely destroyed.

An express was, with difficulty, sent down to Carmarthen for the dragoons, and about six o'clock they were mounted, and went off at a rapid pace through Abergwili to the scene of Rebecca's movements. Passing under Merlin's Hill, which commands an extensive view of the vale of Towy, a shot was fired, which, it is supposed, was the signal of the approach of the soldiers, and for the dispersion of the mob. At all events, on the arrival of the military, and although an active pursuit was made by them, nothing was discovered beyond the destruction that had taken place. After the lapse of some hours, the dragoons made their way back to Carmarthen. Spies must have been placed in all directions, because the Rebeccaites, nothing daunted, proceeded to destroy the "Mansel's Arms" bar and toll-house (the latter being a very strong building), also Llanfihangel Gate and part of the toll-house which was situated on the main road to Llandilo, immediately under Golden Grove, the seat of Earl Cawdor.

The toll-bar and house at Bolgoed, near Pontardulais, were completely levelled with the ground about 7th July. The furniture belonging to the house was carried out, and placed on the side of the road.

The following letter, from the pen of Edward Lloyd Williams, is evidently a reply to certain threats:

To the person calling himself Rebecca, and others in unlawful connection with him, and calling themselves the daughters of Rebecca.

I have just received a notice to threaten if I give not back to my tenants on next rent day 5s. in the £1, that you will attack my possessions, my farm and my lands; and it is probable that some of my neighbours have had a like notice.

Now, I am willing to believe that *you* had nothing to do with such an act, and that it is no part of your policy, nor *your* desire to interfere with the *personal affairs* of others; but that some cowardly wretch ventured to send such notices thinking to frighten us.

I am telling everyone to keep them carefully, because their writers and those who caused them to be sent are certain to be brought soon to answer for such actions in the Court of Law, and those found guilty shall spend the rest of their days in a degrading occupation in a foreign land. Transportation for life is the punishment proclaimed by law for *writing or causing to be written* a threatening letter of such like nature. And if *you* sent to me the notice, I am informing you now that I **will not** *conform with it*, and if I had not informed my tenants a month ago that I would give them two shillings in the pound next rent-day without *being asked*, I would not *now* do so. *So much for your* interference.

What damage soever you can do to my property will fall in the long run on many of those whom *you pretend* you are benefiting. According to the Act 7th, 8th Geo. IV. it is stated that the inhabitants of the Hundred in every case where such damage is done, must *make full compensation* to the person that is injured, therefore, *not only* for the damage done in such a manner, but also for any damage at the same time by any of the evildoers to any immovable goods, furniture, *or any manner of possessions whatsoever.*

The Act of Parliament gives me the right to the direct payment for the damage from *all* the inhabitants of this parish, and many of the adjoining parishes included in the large Hundred of Troedyraur; and I would take upon me not to spend a *shilling* of them in this country; therefore instead of *bettering my tenants* you will throw upon them an addi-

Rebecca's Tactics Continued

tional burden. And also, you can make up your minds if you are determined to try, that you shall have a *pretty warm welcome*, and the law says whoever commits such an act "and is proved guilty is to suffer death as an evil doer."

Any attempt of the kind threatened, would kill all my faith in the character of the Welsh, and would cause me to stop living amongst my tenants, but appointing some solicitor to collect my rents, to be spent in another district, instead of giving daily work to from 30 to 40 persons, as I have done up to now, to help them to earn their living in an honest way, at all seasons of the year.

The rates and taxes that I pay as one of the foremost in the parish, would fall heavier *on others* through the number thrown out of employment by my not living here; and thus you will *harm my tenants again* by depriving them of a friend to whom they have never appealed in vain for counsel or help.

If you persist in your unlawful acts, you will cause the gentry of the county to absent themselves until you make the country like unto Ireland. You will bring the working class to poor and needy circumstances, when it is clear they are better off than they have been for many years, when they can buy their bread and their butter for nearly half the prices of 1832 and the previous year's cheese for two pence per pound and all necessaries for a corresponding price.

Many of the common people have been induced by your followers to join with you in your unlawful habits, by threatening to burn their houses should they refuse, but they know now that for any such loss two *Justices* can order *full compensation* to them, taxed on all the inhabitants of the Hundred, so that they need not be afraid to *refuse* to join you in that respect; but *if they join with you, they make themselves open to transportation for life*.

Now they know how to act correctly, and may God lead them to do so; they can place full reliance in the *Magistrates* for help.

It is said that you are deceiving the ignorant by taking that part of the Scripture which is found in the 60th verse of the xxiv chapter of Genesis, which is as follows:

> *And they blessed Rebekah, and said unto her, Thou art our sister, be thou the mother of thousands of millions, and let thy seed possess the gate of those which hate them.*

What crooked rendering of the Holy Scripture!! All the learned divines agree that the meaning of the words is that the mother and brother of Rebecca were praying on God for her to be fruitful, and that her seed should overcome her *enemies*. Rebecca *was a female certainly, a good and godly female* fearing the Lord and respecting all his commandments, taking care not to transgress them by "*doing evil unto others.*" But if you persist in your literal explanation of the text, it is necessary to take the *next* verse also in the same way: "*And the servant took Rebecca and went his way,*" which means that *Rebecca had been taken*, and that the servant was not hindered in the work.

And this will be to you, you will be caught, and the peasants whom you have wrongly directed and forced to help you, will return to their peaceful homes. They ought not to trust in strangers whom they do not know and *who dare not show their faces*, to go against those amongst whom they have spent their lives; they may have looked upon attacking the toll-gates as a small evil without one desire to commit a serious evil action as many did.

It is to be hoped that the Clergy and Ministers of all denominations will feel their responsibility and duty to urge their congregations and their friends to *withstand* such evil examples to the best of their ability, to point out the evil results that must follow such conduct, and to join together to end that which has brought such discredit on the country. And it is also to be hoped that you and your followers will leave your evil ways before the law overtakes you, which is certain to take place, and your lives will end in misery and disgrace.

Edward Lloyd Williams.

Gwernant,
Near Newcastle Emlyn.
July 9th, 1843.

On 10th July Rebecca and her family mustered about 200 strong in the neighbourhood of Llanybyther and New Inn, and destroyed the Gwarallt Gate, not far from the latter place on the Carmarthen and Lampeter Road, and also another bar. Rebecca on this occasion was gaily dressed, and sported a parasol. When the work of demolition was complete, the party quickly dispersed over the hills. A bridge near Cross Inn was also destroyed, and the scaffolding of a bridge about to be erected at Cwmgwili; but it appears that Rebecca did not confine her enmity to turnpike-gates and bridges, as about

Rebecca's Tactics Continued

this time she demolished three gates leading to a Dissenting chapel in the upper part of Carmarthenshire.

The dragoons, at a minute's notice, were ordered off to Tyllwyd Gate, near Carmarthen, as news had arrived that the Rebeccaites were mustering in the vicinity, and it was feared they intended to destroy that gate. When they arrived there, no person was to be seen, and in a few hours they returned to town. The Rebeccaites had timely notice of the approach of the military, and lay concealed in the hedges and fields adjoining, during the time the soldiers were there. The arrival of the dragoons, however, deterred them from committing any depredations at that place on the night in question, and they departed peaceably to their homes.

Eight persons were taken up on suspicion, and were kept in custody at Llandovery one night, but were discharged the next day, as there was not sufficient evidence to convict them. While these persons were in custody at Llandovery, some others completed the work of destruction at Bronyfelin Gate, by taking down the toll-house and setting fire to the materials. The toll-house to Bethel Dissenting chapel, Carmarthen, was also attacked, and its destroyers took particular care to remove the materials of the roof, etc., to a sufficient distance, so as not to endanger the chapel by the fire. A reward of £100 was offered by the trustees for the discovery of the delinquents.

A detachment of the 14th Dragoons, under Captain Halket, returned to Llandovery on 10th July, where the soldiers remained until replaced by another troop on the 17th.

Rebecca paid a visit to the Porthyrhyd Gate, the one placed on the road that leads from the main road towards Middleton Hall and Llanarthney, on the evening of 14th July. The rioters were on this occasion, as heretofore, all disfigured, and the majority on horseback. Several hundreds assembled, and began their work at twelve o'clock. Effort succeeded effort—change of hand, and change of power in quick succession, until the point was gained, and the gate destroyed. They then proceeded towards the ruins of Llanddarog Gate, and on their way smashed the windows of Evan Thomas, a parish constable of the hundred. Unchecked and bent upon mischief, they arrived at the spot where, some week previous, had stood Llanddarog Gate, but which had recently been destroyed by Rebecca's mandate. It would seem that their work on a former occasion was incomplete, as they had only destroyed the gate, leaving the house undisturbed. After this visit not a stone was left upon another.

The same evening another division of the firm proceeded to Minke, for the purpose of destroying the toll-house, the gate having been previously destroyed. On this occasion Rebecca's visit seems to have been anticipated, and three pot-valiant constables of the parish were in attendance to protect the toll-house from the threatened intrusion.

John Mami, David Davies, and, last but not least, "Will Llwynpatria," had, frequently, over their cups, expressed their determination to oppose 'Becca's invasion, and that they would stick to the toll-house, whatever the consequence might be. When the lady arrived, and her family surrounded the toll-house, the valiant protectors of the public peace would fain have beaten a retreat, but this was not allowed. Weapons of destruction were placed in the hands of the constables, who were the first to commence operations. With the assistance of the Rebeccaites, the toll-house was soon a heap of ruins. The party, as usual, departed after firing a signal of joy.

Pontyberem Gate, in the very centre of the village of that name, was destroyed on 15th July. This gate had cast-iron pillars, which had been manufactured at the Gwendraeth foundry. The Rebeccaites on this occasion were not numerous, being about fifty in number. They commenced work about one o'clock, and effected their object about five minutes past two. The mob came down from the neighbourhood of the limekilns, walking two abreast, three being in advance, and three bringing up the rear, all the party being disguised. They had fifes, horns, guns, pickaxes, crowbars, and sledges, and had well prepared for the enterprise, as from the time they were occupied, it would seem that they had a more than ordinary task to perform. Considerable excitement was consequent on this visit to Pontyberem, and the women frightened, and but half-dressed, were anxious spectators of the scene.

The same night also Pompren Gate, about two miles from Llandilo, on the Llangadock road, was demolished by a party of Rebeccaites, who at the same time warned the gatekeeper, on certain pains and penalties, never again to demand tolls from persons travelling on that road. The belligerent party arrived at the gate from the direction of Llangadock, and their

Rebecca's Tactics Continued

approach was announced by the occasional discharge of firearms, notwithstanding the danger of their position, there being military situated both at Llandovery and Llandilo.

A Rebeccaite Conference

Glamorganshire was visited for the second time by Rebecca on 15th July. Between one and two o'clock in the morning, a man on horseback arrived at Pumfry Gate, near the Three Crosses in the Gower district, about six miles from Swansea, and asked the tollman to open the gate. The man complied, and the horseman passed through, shortly after blowing a loud blast with a horn, which was the signal for the appearance of about sixty men, disguised, and having their faces blackened. When the party arrived at the gate, the collector had gone into the toll-house, and the mob informed him, that if he opened the door, or drew the curtains of the window, they would shoot him. They then fired off their guns and began to destroy the gates, which were soon smashed to atoms. The posts were cut close to the ground with hatchets. A chain which was stretched across a by-road, and supported by two strong oak posts, together with several perches of wall on each side of the road, were levelled with the ground. While the destruction of the gate was going on, a farmer named William Eaton, residing near the spot, came from his house towards the toll-house, but the moment he was seen, the mob threw pieces of broken gate at him, and fired off their guns; and he was compelled to retire within his house. When the destruction was complete, the mob returned in the direction of Cadoxton and Three Crosses, and dispersed.

Three days later, Rebecca visited the neighbourhood of Llechryd, in Cardiganshire, with the intention of destroying the weirs in the River Teify in that locality, or possibly Rhydyfuwch Gate; but on learning that some marines from Cardigan were awaiting their arrival, they dispersed.

On Thursday, 20th July, several of the Rebecca rioters appeared for the purpose of entering into fresh recognisances for their appearance on the following 30th October, to answer

A Rebeccaite Conference

to a bill of indictment preferred against them at the Assizes, before our Sovereign Lady the Queen, in any part of England where she might be pleased to call them on. John Harris of Talog was ordered to give bail, himself in £200 and two sureties in £100 each, several others in £100, £50, and £25. In consequence of the non-attendance of one of the rioters called Job Jones, nor his sureties, the sureties forfeited their recognisances, and a Bench warrant was issued for the apprehension of the said Job Jones.

A large meeting of Rebeccaites took place on Thursday, 20th July, at Cwmifor, five miles beyond Llandilo.

Cwmifor is a picturesque dell in the heart of the mountains, remote from the high-road, the only buildings at that time being a house and a chapel. As soon as dusk began to close in, the Rebeccaites were seen approaching in twos and threes and fives down the mountain sides, and by every path which led to it, till about 9.30 there must have been from 300 to 400 present. Proceedings commenced in the burying ground of the chapel, and were afterwards continued in the schoolroom adjoining, which was crowded, as well as the steps leading to it.

The Times reporter succeeded after considerable parley in getting admission, and was in time to see a chairman appointed and the commencement of business. The meeting was addressed by several speakers, in the Welsh language, who all complained of the grievances under which they suffered and which they declared they would endure no longer. They described the tolls as most oppressive; the tithes had been increased enormously; they declared the Poor Law to be a wicked and most unjust enactment. At length a speaker laid a series of resolutions in Welsh and English as follows:—

> To the conductors of the Convention appointed to be held at Cwmifor, in the parish of Llandilo, in the county of Carmarthen, on Thursday, the 20th day of July, in the first year of Rebecca's exploits, A.D. 1843.
>
> To concur, and inquire into the grievances complained of by the people, and to adopt the best method of avoiding the surprising deprivations that exist, and the external viligance of our superintendents, which is the price of our liberty.
>
> We wish to reduce the price (taxes), and secure our blessings. An army of principles will penetrate where an army of soldiers cannot. Power usurped is weak when opposed. The

public interest depends upon our compliance to examine the cause of the calamity and unveil the corruptions to Rebecca, etc.

The following resolutions agree and intend to recommend to your future aspect by us, whose names are here subscribed at foot, being householders within the above heretofore mentioned parish:

1. To level all petty gates and gate-posts connected with by-roads and bridle-paths, or any roads repaired by the parishioners. Also coal, lime, and grains taken to market, to be exempt from tolls.
2. The motive is the abolition of heavy tithe and rent charge in lieu of tithe.
3. The abolition of church rates.
4. Total alteration of the Poor Law.
5. An equitable adjustment of the landlord's rent.
6. Not to allow or grant any Englishman the privilege of a steward or governorship in South Wales.
7. If any man rents his neighbour's farm treacherously, we must acquaint the lady, and endeavour to encourage her exertions whenever she wishes to execute our phenomena and combat.
8. To request the farmers not to borrow money on purpose to pay unlawful demands; and if the result be that some person or persons will annoy anyone by plundering, and sacrifice their goods to such charge, we must protect them, and diminish their exploits of agonism.
9. That a Committee of Privy Council must be held when necessary, and all persons under the age of eighteen years are not admitted into it. Neither women nor any of the female sex shall be introduced into this select assembly except Rebecca and Miss Cromwell!!!!

These resolutions met with the unanimous approval of the whole meeting, and were received with considerable applause. It was also agreed that there should be a committee in each county; without whose sanction no farmer was to take any farm which had been vacated by another, and if he did so in opposition to the committee, he was to take the consequences. Four persons were then appointed to frame rules, which were to be agreed to, and signed by all the persons constituting what they called their Society or Lodge.

The meeting then closed, and in five minutes the whole of the parties present had so completely dispersed themselves

A Rebeccaite Conference

by the various by-roads, that no one could have imagined any such meeting to have taken place.

About one o'clock on the morning of 20th July a great number of Rebeccaites paid a visit to Ystradfeiris Gate, about a mile beyond Llangadock, which they completely destroyed, and afterwards burnt. They also smashed in the windows of the toll-house, and the gate-keeper making some resistance, they carried him off; but at his wife's intercession, Rebecca allowed him to depart, after cautioning him to be more careful in the future to obey her mandate. The rioters next loop-holed the front doors of Church House, Llangadock. They were nearly all well armed and fired several salutes; they also had several musical instruments, with which they made a most discordant noise.

In consequence of the continued unsettled state of affairs, orders were received at Woolwich on Sunday, 16th July, to have in readiness four six-pounder field-guns, and two twelve-pounder howitzers, which were selected from the field-train department. At 10 a.m. they left Woolwich under the command of Captain Taylor, whose orders were to proceed to Bristol by G.W.R., and from Bristol to Carmarthen with the least possible delay.

The cavalry and infantry stationed at Carmarthen patrolled nightly the different parts of the neighbourhood in certain directions, by which means town and country were kept quiet during the following week. The Assizes on 17th July went off without any of the disturbances anticipated, which may be attributed to the circumstance of the military having been retained in the town, a most unusual procedure on these occasions. On 21st July a detachment of the 14th Dragoons marched under the command of Lieutenant Kirkman from Carmarthen to St. Clears, to relieve the Castle Martin Yeomanry, who were on the march to Newcastle Emlyn. A troop of the Castle Martin Yeomanry arrived at Carmarthen the same evening from Lampeter.

Two hundred of the 75th Regiment of Foot reached Swansea on 21st July, by the Bristol steamer. Billets were taken for three days.

On 22nd July, about two o'clock in the morning, Cenarth Gate on the turnpike road between Newcastle Emlyn and Cardigan was entirely demolished, and the materials thrown over the bridge into the river Teify. The rioters, about sixty in number, had not given previous notice of their intentions.

The same evening, a meeting of colliers took place in the neighbourhood of Pontyberem. It is said that all the workmen employed in the different collieries of the Carmarthenshire valleys, excepting the Cwmmawr men, were present; and the resolutions passed or proposed at this meeting were precisely similar in import to those suggested at the meeting at Cwmifor, near Llandilo two nights previous. They created no disturbance on this occasion, and dispersed quietly after passing the resolutions.

On 22nd July, the farmyard of Mr. Howell Davies, a respectable farmer living in the village of Conwil, and an Anti-Rebeccaite, was set on fire. With the assistance of the neighbours the fire was ultimately got under, but not until two ricks of hay and three stacks of corn or straw had become a prey to the devouring element.

Rebecca in North Wales. On Sunday night, 23rd July, the turnpike-gate of Brynefal near Tremadoc was destroyed. There were between twenty and thirty rioters present, some of whom spoke with the South accent, and others in English.

They told the toll-keeper that, unless he kept silent, they would make him so, and tried to effect an entry into the house. The man had had the presence of mind to place four sacks of salt against the door, which prevented this.

Having pulled off the posts, etc., they carried the gate about a mile, then cut it in pieces, and left the fragments by the riverside. No clue was obtained as to the perpetrators.

Abergwili Toll-bar, at the entrance of Abergwili village, was totally demolished by Rebeccaites on 24th July. They mustered very strong at this place, and commenced their work of destruction about twelve o'clock, having previously placed a body of men, with guns in their hands, on Abergwili Bridge, and also sentinels on all the roads leading to the bar. The gate and posts, as well as the walls adjoining, were completely destroyed in a very short time. Several inhabitants of the village were witnesses of the activity with which Rebecca carried on her work, but dared not approach the place nor even leave their houses. The gate on the main road close by was left uninjured, which plainly indicates that this lady's

A Rebeccaite Conference

antipathy was principally directed against bars and side-gates.

The riots were not without their humorous aspects, as the following incident will show.

On 24th July, a party of workmen, while returning from haymaking above Mount Pleasant, Swansea, amused themselves by pushing before them one of their party, a mason named Williams, who covered his face with his apron, at the same time crying out, "'Becca for ever!" The mayor, who was accidentally passing at the time, immediately seized him by the collar, and gave him into custody to two soldiers. Mr. Morris, a joiner, meeting them, told the mayor that he would answer for Williams's appearance on the next day. He was accordingly set free; but on the following morning entered into recognizances to appear before the magistrates on 1st August.

Both toll-house and gate at Tyllwyd, Carmarthen, were demolished by a gang of about thirty Rebeccaites, on 25th July.

On 25th July, the Quarter Sessions took place at the Town Hall, Carmarthen, twenty-six magistrates being present. Colonel Trevor (afterwards Lord Dynevor), proposed the establishment of a rural police throughout the county, the chief constable at £300 a year, with an allowance of £150 for two horses and residence; six mounted superintendents at £154 per year; ten sergeants at 22s. per week; twenty first-class policemen at 20s. per week; and twenty more at 11s. per week. It was carried.

About two o'clock the next morning, Croeslwyd Gate, which had for some time been threatened with destruction, was visited by the followers of Rebecca and totally destroyed. A party of the 4th Dragoons rode up about one o'clock in the morning, and, all appearing quiet, they returned, and proceeded up to the St. Clears road, being attracted thither by the blowing of horns on the hills, which appears to have been done purposely to decoy them away. Two constables were left to watch the gate, and were comfortably smoking their pipes at a neighbouring smithy (which commanded a view of three roads and three turnpike-gates), when a loud whistle was heard, and about thirty Rebeccaites jumped over the hedges. They proceeded at once to demolish the toll-house and gate, which work they completed in less than half an hour. The toll-keeper, who had a wife and family to support, was severely kicked in the groin, which, being a serious injury, quite laid him up. The rioters threatened to pull the house about his head, and only allowed him and his family to go out when the roof was falling in. The constables no sooner saw what was going on, than they valiantly turned tail and peppered away down to Carmarthen at Newmarket speed, and they ought to have the credit of coming off victorious in the fray, for—

> When the fight becomes a chase,
> They win the fight who win the race;

and it is an undoubted fact that they first reached Carmarthen!

Early on the morning of 26th July, the house of John Thomas, Esq., of Cwmmawr, was surrounded by a large party of Rebeccaites and colliers from the neighbourhood, who greatly alarmed the family by blowing horns and firing guns. The visit was the direct result of Mr. Thomas having been requested to direct the dragoons on their road on the previous Tuesday night when in that neighbourhood. A threatening letter was left pinned against the front door requesting him to dismiss one of his work-people, telling him that his son was a marked man, and saying that the next time they visited his house they would raze it to the ground.

At the end of July, Mr. Hall, chief magistrate of Bow Street Police Office, left London by the direction of the Government for Wales. His orders were to institute a rigid and searching inquiry and examination into all the circumstances connected with the Rebecca Riots. He was accompanied by one or two legal gentlemen, who assisted in the inquiry.

On 28th July, he passed through Swansea, bound for Carmarthenshire .

A Rebeccaite Conference

Rebecca at Swansea—Capture of some Rebeccaites

On Saturday, 29th July, a countryman, known as John Jones, of Lletty Llangefelach, went to the Swansea Inspector of Police, and made a statement, which induced him (Mr. Rees) to believe that he could give full information as to the names and residences of the men engaged in the destruction of the bar and toll-house of Bolgoed. Mr. Rees at once conducted the man to a place of safety, where no person had access to him, until he (Mr. Rees) had procured the attendance of two magistrates of the county. They, having heard the man's story, issued warrants for the apprehension of the individuals against whom he informed, on the charge of being concerned in the outrage at Bolgoed on 7th July. Four warrants were placed in the hands of Captain Napier, chief constable for the county, for the apprehension of William Morgan, and Henry Morgan, of the parish of Llandilo-Talybont, also Mathew Morgan and David Jones, of Tymawr, of the parish of Llangefelach. At twelve o'clock on Saturday night a party consisting of Captain Napier, Inspector Rees, and P.C.'s William Jenkins and Henry Davies, proceeded, well armed with swords and pistols, to execute the warrants. About two o'clock on Sunday morning they arrived at Pontardulais, where they put up their horses, and about half-past four they succeeded in apprehending Mathew Morgan in his house. At five o'clock they apprehended David Jones. They then returned to town with their prisoners, whom they lodged in the borough station, and took the precaution of placing a sentinel at the door. At half-past seven the party again left Swansea for the purpose of apprehending William and Henry Morgan, the sons of Morgan Morgan, a freeholder. The former they succeeded in taking, and Captain Napier and Mr. Rees left him, ironed, with the two P.C.'s, while they proceeded to apprehend Henry Morgan. Upon arriving at his residence,

Rebecca at Swansea—Capture of some Rebeccaites

Cwm Cillefach, near Velindre, he instantly suspected the nature of their visit, and feigned illness. The warrant was produced, shown to him, the nature of it explained, the cause of its being issued stated, and the signatures of the magistrates pointed out to him. He again feigned illness, protested he was unable to move, and could not apparently be brought to understand that it was necessary he should accompany them to Swansea. "Some other time would do quite as well!" Captain Napier, in a firm and decided manner, requested him to submit, and to accompany them peaceably, otherwise they would be reluctantly obliged to use force. The scene at once changed. The invalid who had previously been unable to stir without pain, suddenly sprang up, his family surrounded him, and expressed their intention of resisting his capture to the utmost of their power, at the same time making use of bloody threats, desiring the officers of justice to stand off, at the peril of their lives. Captain Napier and Mr. Rees then laid hold of the man they sought, and endeavoured to drag him out of the house. Two men and two women instantly laid hold of the inspector, felled him to the ground, and, in spite of his efforts, kept him there. The rest of the family, four in number, attacked Captain Napier. He again laid hold of Henry Morgan, and succeeded in dragging him out of the house, but the instant he got outside the door he was violently thrown to the ground. Henry Morgan's father stood over him on one side, with his foot on his stomach, and one of the sons stood over him on the other side, father and son having firm hold of Captain Napier's pistol, and endeavouring to turn the muzzle towards his stomach, and to fire it off. Fortunately, the pistol was not cocked. After a lengthened struggle, Captain Napier succeeded in turning the pistol towards them, and, conceiving his life to be in the utmost danger (his assailants being armed with hatchets, sickles, and hammers), he fired and hit John Morgan. The latter, finding himself wounded, started back for a second or two, and then advanced again, attacking Captain Napier with the utmost fury. A third brother, armed with a mason's hammer, advanced towards Captain Napier, and aimed a blow at him, which he avoided, in return knocking the fellow down. He sprang up in an instant, and again struck out with his hammer. Captain Napier then closed with him, wrenched the hammer from him, and finally threw him. Mr. Rees, in the meanwhile, had a hard and hot engagement with his opponents, who, having thrown him down, endeavoured by tightening his neckcloth to strangle him. Being a powerful man, and accustomed to defend himself, he succeeded in regaining his feet, when he was in a position to cope with them to better advantage. He had pistols with him, and presented one of them frequently at different individuals, but did not fire. The women during the whole of the time fought with the most frantic violence. One of them attacked Captain Napier with a sickle, and inflicted a very severe wound upon the side of his head. The other woman seized a saucepan of boiling water, which she threw at the officers, but fortunately missed them. The struggle had now lasted several minutes, and both Captain Napier and Mr. Rees, having to contend against such odds, were becoming exhausted, when succour arrived in the person of P.C. William Jenkins. He, finding Captain Napier bleeding at all points, and Mr. Rees's condition much the same, drew his sword, forced the crowd back, and rescued his superior officers from certain death.

Two constables had been left by Captain Napier with their prisoner, upon the road within a field or two of Cwm Cille. Some time after Captain Napier and Mr. Rees entered the house, Jenkins having heard a pistol fired, set off, and arrived just in time, as stated above, to be of the most material service.

The prisoner, who was then in Henry Lewis's custody, began to cry out, "Help, help—Lladdwch hwynt!" so as to cause the whole neighbourhood to turn out. After a great deal of trouble, difficulty, and danger, the officers of justice succeeded in securing John Morgan, the young man who was shot. They brought him and the other prisoner to Swansea, and lodged them there about half-past ten in the station-house.

The news soon spread that several of the Rebeccaites had been taken, and vast crowds surrounded the station-house during the remainder of the day, who expressed the liveliest sympathy with the young man who had been wounded. Dr. Bird and Mr. Rogers, surgeon, were sent for, and, after examining the wound, succeeded in extracting the ball, which had entered the abdomen on the left side, lower than the navel. It had then crossed, touched the upper edge of the haunch-bone, took an upward and backward course, finally remain-

Rebecca at Swansea—Capture of some Rebeccaites

ing over the third lower rib on the left side of the body, where it was found and extracted. Captain Napier was taken to the residence of Mr. Bird, who dressed his wounds. The captain was able to attend the meeting on the following day.

On the afternoon of the 31st a party of police fully armed, accompanied by a detachment of the 73rd Regiment, and three vehicles, proceeded to the neighbourhood of Pontardulais, for the purpose of apprehending the men and women who had assisted in the attack upon the police in the morning. About eight o'clock in the evening the whole party returned, having in custody a man and two women one of the latter being the person who had wounded Captain Napier with a sickle. The father of the wounded man, having come to town to make inquiries respecting his son's health, was recognised, arrested, and placed in custody.

During the morning the space of ground in front of the station-house and the streets leading to it were crowded by persons of all ranks and conditions, their excitement being evidently intense. A rush of the crowd gave notice that some event had taken place. It proved to be Superintendent Peak and Sergeant Bennett, advancing with two prisoners in custody Mr. Griffith Vaughan, landlord of the Pontardulais Inn, and Mr. David Lewis, of the same place, weaver, both of whom, it was alleged, had been engaged in the Bolgoed affair.

At nine o'clock a meeting of the magistrates took place in the Town Hall. The proceedings were strictly private, no person, with the exception of Mr. Thomas Attwood, being allowed to enter the room.

About ten o'clock the prisoners, strongly guarded, were marched down to the room where the magistrates were sitting. Vast crowds accompanied them, and in expectation of hearing the examination, rushed into the large hall, which in a few minutes was crammed. After some time the Rev. Samuel Davies entered, and, standing in the Judge's seat, said:

> I suppose you have assembled here for the purpose of hearing the examination of witnesses in the case which now occupies the attention of the magistrates. I have to inform you that it will be a private hearing, and therefore you may all depart; but before the investigation is brought to a conclusion, when the prisoners are brought up for final hearing, the public will be admitted.

This announcement was received with expressive marks of disapprobation.

Mr. Powell (of *The Times*), on behalf of the reporters, applied for permission to be present, but was refused. The solicitors who had been engaged to defend the prisoners, made a similar application, and in reply received the following:—

> Resolved unanimously—That all meetings with a view to the investigation of charges relating to the demolition of turnpike-gates in this neighbourhood be strictly private, until the parties are brought up for final hearing.

The friends of the parties in custody asserted that Captain Napier did not show the warrant at Cwm Cille that he and Mr. Rees abruptly entered the house, seized the man named in the warrant, and with the greatest violence proceeded to drag him out, stating that he must go with them, dead or alive.

With respect to Mr. Vaughan and Mr. Lewis, the chairman of the magistrates, in reply to their attorney, stated that the magistrates themselves were unacquainted with the charges to be preferred against the parties in custody.

About thirty Rebeccaites on 1st August attacked Alltfawr Gate on the road from Llannon to Pontardulais. They had sent a notice to the toll-collector (an old man of eighty) of their intention of visiting the gate on 22nd July.

This engagement they did not keep, but came on 1st August, destroyed the gate, and burnt the toll-house to the ground. They certainly tried to save the man's furniture, but the flames were too much for them. Previous to leaving, and when nothing remained "save a little smoke curling from the ruins," the Rebeccaites cried out in malignant triumph, "Gate ahoy! gateman!" fired a few shots, and dispersed.

The trustees of the Kidwelly Trust held a meeting at Llangendeirne on the same date, and after a full investigation resolved to abolish thirteen side bars out of the fifteen then established on that Trust.

During the night a wall, which had been recently erected in the village of Llandebie, across a portion of the common or waste lands, and said to be an encroachment on the Commons Rights of the Villages, was levelled with the ground, and the field which it enclosed was again thrown open, and made part of the common, as it originally stood. The same night, the side-bar on the road leading from Llangadock to the

Rebecca at Swansea—Capture of some Rebeccaites

limekilns, called Pontarllechan Bar, was set upon by a party of Rebeccaites, and completely destroyed in the short space of ten minutes. The same night also a number of the sisterhood appeared in the village of Llannon, where they demolished the gate, and also burnt the toll-house. They then proceeded towards the mansion recently built by Rees Goring Thomas, Esq., and smashed in all the windows, after which, having given three cheers as a token of success, they immediately dispersed. There were no less than eight gates taken down between Lampeter and Aberystwyth that selfsame night.

On 3rd August, very early in the morning, a party of men attacked and completely destroyed the Red Lion Turnpike-gate within a hundred yards of the town of Swansea. This outrage was attended with circumstances of peculiar aggravation, one of the men having been a toll-collector.

The same morning, between two and three o'clock, Rebecca and a great number of her children, well armed with guns and other destructive weapons, made their appearance at Llanelly, and proceeded to destroy the Furnace Lodge, and sandy limekiln gates, and the toll-house belonging thereto; which they accomplished in a short time, afterwards burning the materials. They also attacked Williams, the gate-keeper at Furnace Lodge, and beat him severely. One of them discharged his gun at him, and shot him in the face. After completing the work of destruction, they fired several more shots, by way of intimidation, and afterwards separated in various directions.

The farmers met at Llanfyrnwyd on 3rd August, and agreed to petition Colonel Trevor, protesting against being taxed to maintain the rural police, also praying for removal of toll on lime in the Three Commotts district; for the removal of Llandilo Walk Gate, and the heavy burden caused to the parish by Abergorlech Bridge. The petition was signed by many persons, and was entrusted for presentation to Sir John Mansel, Bart., and J. W. Phillips, Esq., who attended the meeting.

The same day Rebecca visited Aberayron, with about a hundred of her followers, and destroyed two gates; five only of the Rebeccaites were on horseback. They made the toll-keepers begin the work of destruction, and in a short time the gates, posts, and boards on the walls were smashed to atoms.

A number of Rebeccaites also assembled at Burton Gate, near Pembroke Ferry, which they destroyed in a very short time.

On 3rd August also, the Tycoch Toll-bar in the borough of Swansea was destroyed by a party of men, who came from the direction of Llansamlet. Not content with destroying the bar which was situate on the old road leading from Neath to Swansea, and only separated from Swansea by the river Tawe, one of the rioters brutally assaulted the female who filled the office of toll-collector, with an iron bar, striking her upon her right forearm. He inflicted a severe wound, and threatened to "smash her brains out" with the same instrument. By the activity of the borough police one of the chief offenders was taken into custody the same evening; he was committed to take his trial at the Assizes.

Another Important Conference

About this time an address to the farmers of Carmarthen was published under a nom de plume. It is as follows:—

Fellow Countrymen,

I have long watched the growing discontent that prevails in your minds at the existence of what you deem insufferable wrongs and grievances; and I will not for a moment conceal my opinion that you have a fair and undoubted cause of complaint, and that if you went the right way to work you would without doubt very soon have your burdens removed.

The first cause of complaint is the frequency of Turnpike Gates, and high rate of toll demanded on the carriage of Lime and Coal, and the conduct of Trustees in allowing Toll Collectors to persuade them to make Bars and Side Gates which harass the neighbouring Farmers without any reason or pretext whatever.

There is no man, gentle or simple, who will have the hardihood to deny that both the above complaints are grounded in truth; but the question is how they can be legally remedied according to the existing state of the Trusts.

I know that many people say, *"Knock down all Turnpike Gates, and let us have a free passage without any payment."*

Now, suppose this was to take place, how are the Roads to be repaired? I do not think that any man can be found to stand up for this plan if he thinks for a moment that the consequence would be to throw the repair of all the Roads upon the parishes through which the great Roads run; in fact, that those parishes between Cardiganshire and the Lime and Coal district would have to repair the Roads, at their own expense, for all the other parishes in Carmarthenshire and Cardiganshire, which would amount to many thousands a year. I am told that the rental of all the Gates is £10,000 a year, and that the calculation is, that six out of this ten are paid by Cardiganshire and other Counties and

Another Important Conference

Travellers. If this be true, we should lose £6000 a year by doing away with the Gates. This would never do.

You may then well ask what is to be done? for if I admit a grievance, I ought to point out a remedy; otherwise I do nothing but inflame the present excited state of the public mind.

The vast number of different Trusts in this County is the great difficulty that stands in the way of an immediate adjustment; and I must confess I do not see the possibility of getting over the obstacle without the assistance of our good and benevolent Queen, who will not allow the meanest of her subjects to be oppressed, if the matter is properly laid before her and her Parliament, for I fear it would be time thrown away to endeavour to get the Trustees of the different Trusts in the County, as they have not the power, to arrange for the position of the Turnpike gates that no Gate should be nearer than a certain number of miles to the other: *or that the Government should take upon it the management of all the Trusts in the Principality and raise a fund by a Toll or by a Tax.*

If you think, as I do, that the plan I have suggested would be just and fair, I would advise that every Parish in the County should get up Petitions, first to the Lord Lieutenant, and if he cannot do anything for us, then to Parliament, and I have no doubt whatever that we shall find men there who will fight our battles for us upon having a fair and unbiassed case, capable of proof, set before them.

If you were to be as active and energetic in petitioning Parliament upon your present grievances as you were upon the Education Clauses in the Factory Bill, you would soon find that injustice would be redressed; for there is no man or body of men in England that dare withstand justice backed by the voice of the people, for "The voice of the people is the voice of God."

It is to be regretted, although not wondered at, that many Gates and Bars have been removed by force; but this is perfectly useless and very wrong, for in doing so, the law of the land is violated and parties subject themselves to very severe punishment, and do no good whatever to the cause they wish to favour, for they may be again put up, and the Parishes are liable for the damage, and worse than all, we Welshmen, who have been always proverbial for loyalty, and peaceable and religious conduct, are now looked upon as being riotous and irreligious, and cannot be trusted without having Regiments of Horse and Foot Soldiers, and Artillery stationed among us.

The object of my addressing you is to endeavour, with the little ability that God has given me, to convince you that it is not by force of arms but by peaceable and firm assertion of our rights—by the constitutional means of petitioning Parliament we can expect to arrive at what we have in view.

We have had the credit hitherto of being a peaceable and religious people, all members of some congregation; and I have determined, by means of your respective ministers, to make my sentiments known; and I trust, through God, that I shall not do so in vain. I make your ministers the channels of communication, as they are known to you, and entrusted with the care and instruction of your souls' good.

I address myself to your good sense and not to your passions; I know you are a reasonable people, and if you believe my arguments, I am quite sure that the power of the arm will give way to the power of the mind.

I am aware you have other grievances, and I know that the Farmer, and consequently his Labourer, are labouring under great difficulty, and such as we cannot at this moment contemplate without lively fears for the result; but through God's assistance I trust that those who have the power to alleviate our sufferings, by means entirely in their power, will not slumber and shut their eyes to the real state of things until we are so far reduced in circumstances that the boon will be useless.

Let me entreat you and those under your authority to avoid private meetings and secret societies; no good ever resulted from them, but much mischief. If our complaints and objects are just, why should we fear to meet in open day? We have a right to do so, and no Government or Authorities will ever trench upon that right so long as we are peaceable and quiet and respectful to the authorities, and ask nothing dangerous to the Constitution. We have nothing to ask that we are ashamed of, therefore why seek the shadow of night or secrecy? I am one of yourselves toiling for the support of my wife and family. Personally I have little or no power in this county; but I tell you boldly that if you seek to redress your grievances peaceably and lawfully, and allow your minds and not your strong right hands to be your instruments, I pledge myself to find you powerful friends in this County and in the House of Commons, who will not allow you to be wronged, but carry your Petitions to the foot of the Throne should it be necessary.

Another Important Conference

> After I wrote the above I heard with pleasure that the Government have appointed a Commissioner[1] to investigate the alleged grievances as to the Turnpike Gates and abuses said to exist in the different Trusts. Now you have an opportunity of laying what you complain of before a Gentleman who will pay every attention to what you have to say, and it will be your own fault if you allow this Gentleman to close his labours without mentioning everything to him, so that he may report thereon to Government, and if his report is favourable to your views, I am quite certain that your grievances will be removed without delay. The means of redress are now in your power, and you have nobody but yourselves to blame if you neglect the opportunity offered; therefore be vigilant and select some person in your respective Districts of Turnpike Trusts, and furnish him with materials to go before the Commissioner. Go about it in earnest, and like men of business as if you were preparing for a trial; for if you do not, you cannot hope for success, nor will you deserve it.
>
> I do not put my name to this paper, because I seek to convince your judgments by the arguments I use, uninfluenced by any particular set of political opinions or views which I may entertain.
>
> A Lover of Peace.

The following is an extract from *The Times* of 4th August, 1843:—

> Having heard that there was to be another meeting of the Rebeccaites at Penlan, a small village on the hills, off the roadside, between Llangadock and Llandilo, and not far from Cwm Ifor, where the Rebeccaites held a meeting a fortnight ago, on Thursday, August 3rd, I proceeded to Llandilo, determined, if possible, to be present. I then got an intelligent young Welshman, the son of the innkeeper of the town, who spoke both Welsh and English fluently, and proceeded in a gig to a roadside house within a mile of the place. I here learned that the meeting was to take place in a solitary farmhouse barn at nine o'clock. The night was windy and stormy, with occasional heavy showers of rain, and the uninviting aspect was calculated to keep all indoors whom business or necessity did not compel to go out.
>
> The country around the place of meeting is the most romantic and beautiful in Carmarthenshire. On all sides are lofty

---

1 Mr. Hall, Chief Magistrate of Bow Street Police Office.

hills, verdant, and clothed with wood to their summits, with deep and luxurious valleys between them. From the smallness of the farms (and they rarely exceed 50 to 60 acres) the landscape is dotted over with the white-washed cottages of the farmers, and the country for an agricultural district is thickly populated.

My Welsh guide and I made our way for about a mile along some lanes, and then we struck into a path across some fields, and in a short time arrived at the place of meeting—a solitary farmhouse in a sequestered dell, not visible until within a field's distance from it. All was silent, save the rushing noise of an occasional blast through the trees. The dark clouds, intercepted by the hill-tops, hung among them, and rolled down their sides like curling smoke.

To this centre, the farmers from the surrounding farmhouses kept coming by the different pathways.

I addressed one or two who appeared to be leaders among them, and shortly explained my object. I was evidently viewed with caution and distrust. My young guide, who appeared known to most of them, was called on one side and questioned about me. At length, after much whispering and consultation, one who appeared a leader amongst them again approached me, and to him I produced one of your printed Parliamentary Circulars to your reporters, which I happened to have in my pocket. This served as a sufficient credential, and I was then told I might be present at their meeting. The farmer led the way, and I followed him into the barn. In the centre was a small round table, with one candle burning upon it, throwing a feeble light over the figures of about 70 men, all seated around on chairs or benches, or on the straw, while numbers whom I could not see were lying about in every corner amongst the bundles of straw. Many of those present were evidently respectable farmers. On my entering and seating myself on a chair, a dead silence prevailed, which continued for some minutes, and no one appeared disposed to speak. Thinking that my presence might have caused this, I briefly addressed them, and told them my object in coming amongst them; that as your reporter I sought only to ascertain the truth, and to make it known to the public, and with that simple object and honesty of purpose, I trusted myself, fearless, among them; that I did not wish, nor would I name, nor make any of them known; but would merely give an account of what they said, which I did, and they appeared to be more satisfied.

Another Important Conference

Having requested my interpreter to repeat to me in English what was spoken, as well as he could, as the speaker went on, I now proceed to give you a report of the proceedings.

The farmer who had addressed me outside was appointed to take the chair. He then said, with the permission of the meeting, he would read to them some resolutions, which it was their object that night to consider. The following resolutions (of which I obtained a copy) were then read:

The Farmers' Union.

1. That all farmers and others wishing to support this Union shall be members.
2. That a Chairman, Vice-Chairman, and Secretary be elected by the majority of the members present to fill their offices gratis, and to be re-elected every six months.
3. That each person wishing to be a member of this Union shall enrol his name with the Secretary of the Union.
4. That the amount of rent of each member be entered, and every change in amount to which he as a tenant shall become liable, shall be from time to time entered by the Secretary on his book for that purpose.
5. That during the sitting of the Union, if it should happen that a member should enter the room at all intoxicated, his expulsion for the time of the sitting shall be determined by the majority present.
6. That no wanton oath be taken, nor cursing, swearing nor intemperate language used by any member during the sitting under a penalty of ———

7. That discussion shall be carried on in the Union by motion put to the majority, pursuant to notice given to the Secretary at the previous meeting.
8. That this Union shall be competent to enter into communication and correspondence with any and every other Union formed upon the same principles and guided by the same views.
9. That this Union do meet on ——— at ——— or at any such place and time as the vote of the members present shall from time to time appoint.
10. That all meetings of the Union be held for the purpose of taking into consideration all griev-

ances that shall affect the Agriculturists and the country in general, and to pass resolutions thereon.

These resolutions were proposed, seconded, and agreed to, and the chairman proceeded to take down the names of the other parties present, who were willing to join the Union.

After a short discussion it was determined that it should be the last public meeting, that in future all meetings should be held in private, and that none but those whose names were enrolled should be admitted.

A resolution was agreed to that the resolutions just passed might be amended afterwards as occasion might require.

It was then resolved "that no person after the present meeting should be admitted to their meetings who was under the age of eighteen years."

A farmer spoke in strong commendation of the Rev. Mr. Pugh, the Rector of the parish, for having returned to them half the amount of his tithe; and also Mr. David Pugh, a gentleman of landed estate and Chairman of the Quarter Sessions, for having returned 20 per cent of their rents, and hoped that their example would be followed by others.

A farmer highly commended all present for meeting in secret. They could express themselves more freely among themselves than in a public place.

A farmer said they were not afraid of anyone coming to hear them; what they did, they did above-board. They came there to get the burden shaken off their shoulders He proposed that those who held this opinion should raise their hands.

A farmer hoped all those now present would give in their names so as to be able to meet together at a future time.

A farmer thought something ought to be added to the resolutions, so as to state their grievances plainer.

Another farmer: "You must not move any amendments upon the rules till you have become a member."

A farmer: "All those who wish to become members give your names to the Chairman. If the objects of this meeting do good to any, they will do good to all."

The Chairman wished to make known a circumstance which might not be known to all—That the Government had sent down Commissioners to look into the way in which their Trustees managed their accounts, and to ascertain where the fault lay; and what the Trustees had done with

Another Important Conference

the money, that the country might know how the accounts stood.

A farmer: "It is one of the best things that ever came into the country to see persons well off in the world come to try to take off the grievances of the poor. This Union among us is a very excellent thing if all join. When they elect members of Parliament they do just as they please, and we have no voice, but here we have. There is no way of putting things to rights till we get up this Union, and then we can do as we please and think best. If we had had this Union many years ago we should be better off than we are now!"

A farmer: "I should not wish any person to think our cause is bad in consequence of our meeting to-night. Had the times been a little better, we might have met in the daytime. But it is not the fear of making known our grievances that causes us to meet at night. The country being in such a state, has caused us to come now, because we cannot meet another time. Our grievances are too numerous to mention, but here we talk to each other and make known to each other things as they really stand. The privilege given to man over animals is to speak, not to fight, and we ought to speak to our landlords with regard to rents being very high, and we ought to speak in consequence of tithes being so very high. We ought to become members of a Union, and by speaking as such to our landlords we can get a remedy. We ought to speak of the poor rates that oppress us so very much, and of those Union Officers' Salaries that are so very high. And we ought to speak to our landlords about the tolls."

A farmer: "My friend has said remarkably well, and has spoken according to my own wishes. There are grievances that we have all together. The aristocracy of the County do not see this; we are enough oppressed now, but in addition they are going to fix upon us a rural police. There is a great deal of the poor rates that goes to fill the bellies of Union Officers. My belly is large enough, but there are larger than mine [a laugh—the speaker was a very stout man]. With the addition of the rural police, instead of paying 7s. 6d. in the in rates, we shall have to pay 20s. in the £."

Another farmer: "If the poor rates were properly expended, it would be very much better for the poor in the Unions. The overseers receive no pay for collecting the rates. They put the money into a cashier's hands, who is paid for receiving it, and then another person is paid for distributing it to the poor!"

Another farmer: "We are obliged to repair our roads, and if we go only a short distance on them, they make us pay toll."

The Chairman: "You all have heard of the rural police, and you know where the money comes from to pay them with. It comes from the poor rate. I want to change the term, and instead of calling it the 'poor rate,' I will call it the 'Aristocracy Rate' [very good]. The Inspector of Police is to have £450 a year—£300 for himself and £150 for house and horse. I fancy £300 is quite sufficient for him and his horses. Let us just look how many working-men this £450 would maintain for a twelvemonth at 7s. per week. It would keep 25 at 7s. per week. Then there were 50 policemen to be placed about Carmarthenshire, which will make it cost us £4000 a year, and our rates will be raised 3d. in the £. Special Constables had been sworn in, as they all knew, but he wanted to know what they were good for [a laugh]. One man who had refused to be sworn in, had been distrained upon by the magistrate for a £5 fine, and two of his cattle had been taken. The magistrates afterwards told him to drop all, but he was afraid this constable would not drop all, as the magistrate wished.

"Mr. Neville and Mr. Chambers of Llanelly had proposed to pay the amount of the public rate levied upon their tenants. This was very creditable to them." (Hear, hear.)

A farmer: "Don't you think it proper that we should ask those present who refuse to sign their names to the Union, to state the reason why they will not sign?"

The Chairman: "They will understand that they will not be admitted into our future meetings unless they give their names to-night."

A farmer: "I wish to know if all present have their names down on the list."

Another farmer: "I suppose this Union will become general throughout the country, and that everyone will join; but before I give you my name, I should wish to know if the resolutions are legal."

Another farmer: "I should wish counsel's opinion taken upon them."

The Chairman said that another branch of this Union was being established in the parish of Llansadwrn. Some further matters would be decided upon that night week.

A place of meeting was then arranged, business to commence at eight o'clock and finish at ten.

Another Important Conference

A farmer: "Would it not be a good thing to see whose names are down to-night?"

A farmer: "Any person here who does not choose to give his name must give the reason why."

A farmer: "I have given my reason."

The meeting was then dissolved.

The Chairman said to me they had only spoken of some things that night, as they had discussed others before, and that upwards of 200 farmers had given their names before that night to join the Union.

I then scrambled my way back across the miry fields in the dark, till I reached the lane. I stopped a moment to listen, but there was not a sound to indicate that nearly a hundred men were dispersing themselves in all directions within two hundred yards of me. All was darkness and silence. I reached the roadside in about ten minutes, and found it to be past eleven o'clock. The landlady said the dragoons from Llandilo were expected every minute to patrol past. I ask, of what use, in such a country, and with a people like this, are dragoons?

Further Riotous Proceedings

Newinngate, ten miles from Cardigan, was attacked by a mob of Rebeccaites, and the gate destroyed, on 4th August. The toll-collector's wife, on looking through the window, was fired at, wounded in the face, and blinded for life. Seeing the toll-man's coat hanging inside the toll-house, another, under the impression that it was the toll-man himself, fired at it, and thirty slugs were next morning found in it. Hearing the woman groan, they asked if she was hurt; the toll-man answered that he was not, but that they had murdered his wife. They said that was a pity, ordered him out of the house, and made him go with them to the chapel-keeper of a neighbouring Dissenting chapel. The keeper was knocked up and compelled to give to the toll-man a bottle of the communion wine, which they told him to take back to cure his wife.

The Rev. Eleazer Evans, of Llangranog (already referred to), received another menacing letter on 5th August. It was not very intelligible, being written in bad Welsh. It contained a request that he should return the advance in tithes, and the law expenses, by a certain day. If he did not do so 'Becca had found a place for his body, and desired him to find a place for his soul—the place for his body was to be at the end of the National Whore (i.e. the Established Church). That he had been a great oppressor since he had been in office; then followed a reference to Judges vi. 27, 28, which is the account of "Gideon taking ten men of his father's house, and throwing down the altar of Baal. Because he was afraid of doing it by day, he did it by night, and when people got up in the morning the altar of Baal was cast down, and the grove was cut down that was by it, and the second bullock was offered upon the altar that was built." (The meaning was that the Rebeccaites would destroy his house, and he was the "second bullock," his curate having been previously

Further Riotous Proceedings

attacked.) 'Becca further desired him to read much of the Old Testament, to see whether his conduct was like that of Pharaoh—that he had doubled the tasks of the people. The letter wound up: "Do not you suppose that I am an idle old woman. I have not been brought up in idleness, and I am determined to have justice done, in spite of the world, the flesh, and the devil. —'Becca."

The Vicar, in consequence of these threats, was obliged to sell his farm, stock, and everything he had except his household furniture. His wife was almost worried into the grave. They dared not retire at night without having a wardrobe moved to the window, as a protection against firearms.

In the early hours of 5th August the long-looked-for attack on the Porthyrhyd Gate was carried fully and amply into effect by Rebecca and her daughters. This renowned lady and her companions arrived there about five minutes past midnight, the force numbering about 300. They came from five different directions, seemed to be well organised, and arrived simultaneously on the spot.

The gate in question was strongly built, and the pillars made of Welsh oak, twenty-seven inches in diameter. There were several special constables keeping a look-out, who over their cans and pots were remarkably valorous, and had even gone so far as to express their determination not to be driven into flight by any visit which Rebecca might think fit to make. On the arrival of the party, or rather their approach towards the gate, away bolted these sworn protectors of the peace. Ianto'r Gwehydd, Jacob Thomas, and two or three others at once made off, and the toll-man, one Dick Morganwg, also deemed it prudent to follow the example set him, for he, as well as the constables, made himself scarce with all possible dispatch.

Rebecca arrived with her daughters, and at once commenced operations. Saws, hatchets, and crowbars were set to work, and the muscular power of the men, with the way in which they exchanged work, enabled them to demolish the gate, toll-bar, and toll-house by one o'clock on the Saturday morning. The wall in front of old Mother Powell's house, "The Nelson," was partially destroyed, and the poor old lady was obliged to get out of bed to supply the Rebeccaites with ale, the money being returned to her in the different cups. The leader, who was on horseback, with his face blackened, intimated to Mrs. Powell that she need apprehend no injury, as they would neither molest nor wrong her. She, on this, requested that the wall in front of her house might not be further destroyed; when Rebecca with uncommon sympathy intimated, that had she made the request a little sooner, not a stone belonging to her wall should have been removed.

Their next visit was to a shopkeeper named Davies, who resided near the gate. There they requested to be supplied with powder and percussion caps. Davies sent down his servant, but Rebecca issued her mandate requiring the presence of the girl's master, and gave him one minute only to make his appearance. He obeyed, and supplied them with what they required, on which he was again allowed to retire to rest, without any further interference. They then attacked the house of the blacksmith, who had previously said he would face fifteen of the best Rebecca boys, and who also had been sworn in as a special constable; according to his own statements he was a man devoid of fear.

The smith—fearless man of Vulcan—had, however, departed; but smash! went in his door and windows, and his deserted smithy was practically destroyed. At the outset of these proceedings the toll-man "Dick" contrived, by running over ditch and dell, to warn a parish constable, one Evan Thomas, otherwise "The Porthyrhyd Lion," of his own mishap, as well as the peril to which he thought him exposed, Evan being somewhat unpopular in the neighbourhood.

On receiving this hint, away bolted "Ianto," scampering over the ditches and fields until he found a cow-house where he lay concealed in anxious suspense the remainder of the night. Notwithstanding the retreat of "Ianto," about seventy of the tribe visited his domicile, smashed in his windows and doors, destroyed his shelf and dresser, and all his crockery, as well as the spokes of a new cart, put a cheese on the fire, cut down some of the trees in the garden, and then simultaneously raised the cry, "Alas! poor Ianto!"

A gentleman of the name of Cook, a steward of Mr. Adams, of Middleton Hall, was returning to his own house, and passed through a division of about forty persons. He was enabled to give warning to the toll-collector, and also Evan the constable, the latter of whom, if found, was to have his ears cut off. In the course of this riot the Rebeccaites damaged the windows of the Coburg Inn at Porthyrhyd; but later

Further Riotous Proceedings

enclosed in a letter sufficient remuneration, at the same time making this apology—"that it was the error of some of the younger branches of the family."

These riotous proceedings caused considerable excitement and alarm, although intimation had previously been given that the destruction of this gate had been contemplated. The different persons in the neighbourhood who were sworn in as special constables for this particular hundred, on the following Monday (7th August), gave up their staves, with the determination of refusing on any future occasions to interfere with the movements of Rebecca or the protection of the toll-house. The following doggerel verses, composed by some country poet near Porthyrhyd, may not prove uninteresting:—

> Poor Ianto the Lion they all failed to find,
> His cheese and his butter were left too behind,
> Farewell to his crockery, and spokes of the cart,
> His life he thought sweetest, and then made a start.

> The Lion, though frightened, lay still among cows,
> And now well ashamed has made many vows,
> If 'Becca will pardon his former offence,
> He'll not meddle with Toll Gates on any pretence.

> Yn mysg y Constebli 'roedd Constab lied smart,
> Hwn 'ddwedai'r ymladdai a'r hen Bonaparte:
> Ond pan ddaeth Rebecca at Gate Porthyrhyd,
> 'Roedd Dick o Forganwg mewn llewyg yn fud.

> The smith had thought proper to make his retreat,
> Good-bye to the Tollhouse, farewell to the Gate,
> 'Roedd udgorn Rebecca yn swnio fel cloch,
> A chwatodd y chwiwgi yn gymysg a'r moch!

On Monday night, 7th August, Llandilo Walk Gate, about a quarter of a mile from Llandilo and immediately under Dynevor Castle and Park, was completely destroyed by the Rebeccaites, and the toll-house almost entirely demolished. These worthies took the Llandilo folk completely by surprise; it was presumed that because a troop of the 4th Dragoons was stationed there, and the gate and toll-house narrowly watched, they would hardly have ventured their lives, on the chance of capture, in the hazardous attempt of destroying the gate. They, however, arrived at their usual hour, and proceeded with the work of destruction with less noise and hubbub than on any former occasion. The force was considerable, for in the short space of fifteen minutes the gate was entirely demolished, the toll-house unroofed, and the walls practically destroyed. The Rebeccaites then quickly dispersed, leaving the ruins of the toll-house and gate as evidence of their daring and lawless proceedings. It is to be regretted that the dragoons, who were so near the spot, had not proper intimation of this boldest move of the 'Becca family, as in all probability the leaders would have been captured.

A troop of the Castle Martin Yeomanry marched from Newcastle Emlyn to Cardigan on 9th August.

The same day witnessed the destruction of Penygarn gate a *third* time. This gate, about seven miles from Carmarthen, had been visited by the Rebeccaites about six weeks previously. They destroyed it, and pulled down the toll-house. Subsequently the house was substantially re-erected, and a new gate was put up. A month afterwards, the gate was a second time visited, and was again completely lestroyed; owing, however, to the gate-posts being lined with iron, the Rebeccaites had so much trouble with the work of destruction, that they did not interfere with the toll-house that night. On 9th August, however, they, for the third time, paid this place a visit. The toll-keeper, having heard that the Rebeccaites had threatened to destroy the toll-house that night, removed his furniture to the roadside, hoping that it would be allowed to escape. About twelve o'clock, 'Becca and her daughters, true to their threat, surrounded the house. The toll-collector, fearing their approach, concealed himself in the neighbourhood. The Rebeccaites took the furniture again into the house and set fire to it, and the collector, hearing them say they would burn him too, took to his heels and escaped. The toll-house was completely pulled down, and was left a mass of ruins.

On 10th August a troop of the 4th Dragoons marched from Llandovery to Lampeter, and a troop of the same regiment marched from Llandilo to Llandovery.

The Carmarthenshire adjourned Quarter Sessions were held in the Town Hall, Carmarthen, on the same day. Colonel Trevor proposed that Captain Richard Andrew Scott be appointed Chief Constable of the Rural Police of the County of Carmarthen. This was agreed to without a dissentient voice.

Further Riotous Proceedings

The following morning a company of the 75th Regiment marched into Carmarthen from Llanelly.

William Davies of Pantyfen, farmer, was apprehended on the same day by David Rees, constable, at his own house. He was supposed to be one of those who burnt Penygarn Gate, and underwent examination in the County Gaol.

Rebecca and the Black Footman. About two years previous, a respectable freeholder of the county of Carmarthen had taken advantage of the condition and weakness of one of his female servants, who subsequently gave birth to a boy. The unfortunate girl had no means of proving the paternity of the young one, according to the provisions of the Poor Law Act. She was consequently obliged to shelter herself at Newcastle Emlyn Workhouse, where she was confined, and where she had to remain for a considerable time. Even when she was discharged, she was under the necessity of maintaining the child herself.

The facts of the case reached the ears of the now renowned outlaw Rebecca, who at once resolved to befriend the betrayed girl, and to correct the evil under which she groaned in a summary but ingenious way. About midnight on 11th August the deceiving freeholder was awakened from his slumbers by a rattling noise which intimated the approach of a carriage, and which was soon driven up his farmyard to the house he occupied. A thundering rat-tat at the door gave him to understand that his presence was at once required. He jumped out of bed and proceeded to answer the call of his visitors. Opening the front door, he saw a black footman taking down the steps of the carriage, and opening its door. A lady, very gaily attired, emerged, with a child in her arms. She entered the house, and introduced herself to the farmer by the name of Rebecca, saying that she had brought with her his own child, to which his servant girl had two years before given birth, and which child he was required henceforward to take care of, and bring up respectably as he had been brought up himself; further adding that she, Rebecca, would keep a sharp eye upon his conduct to his child. Should she find him wanting in the duties and obligations of a parent, a second visit would be paid him, when he would be taught to rue his disobedience to this imperative direction. The astounded farmer at once promised obedience in the most implicit manner. Rebecca delivered up the child to the father, who fondled and affectionately caressed it. Rebecca then expressed herself as satisfied, shook hands with the farmer, stepped back into her carriage and rapidly drove off. The father subsequently carried out his promise honourably.

On 14th August, Mr. Francis M'Kiernin, innkeeper, and George Laing, publican, both of Llanelly, were apprehended and brought up before the Llanelly bench, charged with having taken part in the destruction of the Sandy Turnpike Gate, Llanelly, on 2nd August. They were committed to take their trial at the next Assizes, but admitted to bail.[1]

---

[1] Vide *Commissioners' Report Rebecca Riots*, p. 358.

Further Riotous Proceedings

An Address to the Inhabitants of Conwil Caio in the County of Carmarthen and the adjacent Parishes

Printed by William Rees, 3 Market Street, Llandovery, MDCCCXLIII.

Address

My dear Friends,

I have for many years resided amongst you, during which period I can truly state that I have not intentionally been guilty of any act of tyranny or injury towards any of you, nor have I at any time offered you advice which I did not conscientiously believe to be for your future advantage. I do not make these statements in order to elicit from you any praise, but as an apology for the course which I, as a private individual, take in thus addressing you, in the hope that the recollections of the reciprocal good feeling which has hitherto existed between us, will induce you to view in a kind spirit this slight effort which I make with sincerity for your benefit, and to believe that I am actuated by no other motive in making it, than an ardent anxiety for the common good of our common country.

The notoriety of the destruction of property, to a large amount, by the hands of considerable multitudes of people illegally assembled under the shelter of night, is such that I need not remind you of it; I sincerely hope that none of those whom I address have been induced to lend their aid in the conduct of those criminal proceedings; the punishment which the law awards to those who may be found guilty of the crime which now so generally disgraces our country is well known to you; but it may be, that it has not been considered by my misguided countrymen, that, however artful

An Address to the Inhabitants of Conwil Caio in the County of Car-

may be the means which they have taken to secure themselves from immediate discovery, their crime ceases not to exist legally, save with their own existence, or until it be expiated by legal punishment; that in years yet to come, anyone in the hope of reward, or to avenge some fancied insult, or some unintentional injury, may lay information against those who have joined these illegal assemblies, cause them to be torn from their homes, arraigned at the Bar of their country, and if convicted, to be exiled from that country to undergo a term of abject slavery, where no friend can condole with them of their ignominous sufferings by one kind word of consolation; but if they do escape punishment, is it a matter of small moment to lead a life of endless apprehensions; of constant dread that the messengers of justice are about to seize them as their victims, and of continual thraldom to those whom they know to be cognizant of their crime? Can any threat of present danger, which is said to have been offered to compel the presence of the otherwise well-intentioned at these unlawful meetings, be compared to the life of terror which must ensue from your attendance at them—or to the unceasing anxiety consequent on your participation in their guilt?

The consequence of these riotous proceedings must also be attended with considerable pecuniary loss to us all; already it has been deemed necessary, for the preservation of peace within the county, to apply to the Government to establish a rural police, a measure which will materially add to the amount of our local rates; already have applications been made to the magistrates of some of the hundreds of the county, to compensate the injured parties for the loss they have sustained by the illegal destruction of their property; and hereafter, unless the existing riotous proceedings are suppressed, all the expenses incidental to the repair of the roads must fall on the occupiers of the land, an expense which, with regret (for I am equally interested with yourselves) I state, must be great and constant; whereas if any grievances had existed, and a proper representation had been made to the Trustees of the different districts of roads, I feel satisfied that it would have met, and will still meet with attention, and where redress could, it would have been given. But on this point I must call to your recollection that the Trustees have a double duty to perform, a duty to the persons who make use of the roads, and a duty to those who have advanced money, either to form those roads, or to render them of greater utility to the country; they must hold the scales of justice even between these two parties, every disposition has been evinced to give you an opportunity of judging whether they have acted fairly between the public and the mortgagees of the toll. If you have not availed yourselves of the opportunity afforded, you ought not to condemn them without enquiry; if you have made use of the means of judging placed within your reach, and can find no cause to accuse the Trustees of partiality, you should endeavour strictly to protect the property entrusted to their care from lawless and riotous depredation, and even should you, on investigation, suppose grievances to exist, and that the Trustees have been led into error, let me entreat you to prevent, by all your influence and your persuasion, any attempt to redress such supposed grievances by force, and to represent to the Trustees the grounds on which you have arrived at such a conclusion; I think I may promise you a patient hearing, and if all you require cannot be granted, that reasons founded on the principles of strict justice, will be laid before you to justify the refusal.

The ostensible cause of the riotous proceedings which have taken place in the country, seems to have been the exaction of toll at the various gates placed on the turnpike roads, Now I do not believe that you, nor yet any of my fellow countrymen who have so disgracefully transgressed the law by the illegal destruction of property, are actuated by motives of dishonesty; but should these proceedings be successful, they must have a dishonest result. I am fully aware that there is an apparent hardship in calling on those who pay turnpike tolls to aid in the repair of the turnpike roads, still if the revenue derived from the tolls be shown to have been fairly administered, and yet to be insufficient to pay the interest due to the mortgagees, and to repair the roads, the Trustees have no other mode of keeping those roads in repair than that of calling for assistance from the occupiers of land in the different parishes in which the roads are situate, else they must allow the roads to get out of repair, the effect of which would be an indictment and a consequent increase of expense to the parishes; but I am addressing some whose memory can extend so far back, as to recollect the state of the roads to have been such that scarcely a waggon, or even a cart, was kept by any farmer in the neighbourhood. Within my own recollection, I think I may fairly state that the same weight which was formerly conveyed by three, if not four, can now be conveyed by two horses, let me then seriously ask you; is this of no advantage to you? Whether in diminishing the number of horses you were formerly obliged to keep, or if you still keep the

An Address to the Inhabitants of Conwil Caio in the County of Car-

same number, in enabling you to use some of them on your farms, instead of sending them to the road to convey lime or coal, or in enabling you with the same number of horses, in a much less space of time, to carry an equal supply of lime, and if it be an advantage, of which there can be no doubt, that advantage you have obtained, from the capital laid out in the formation and improvement of these roads, and from which capital the owners rightly expect a fair return. But is it just, is it honest in those persons who travel over those roads, now to turn round to the Trustees, and say, "It is true that you have vastly improved these roads, and we must confess that they are advantageous to us; but that advantage we can grasp, you cannot prevent us, and we will do all we can by force and by cunning, to obstruct in levying the tolls required to pay the interest of the capital expended, although we reap the benefit of that outlay." I am very much deceived, if any one of those I address would not agree with me in branding such a proceeding with the stamp of dishonesty, fraud and injustice. I hope, too, that I am not wrong in believing that those who have violated the law, would have abstained from such a course had they considered the subject with that reflection which it deserved.

There are also reasons which I might deduce from the truths of our holy religion, and urge to induce you not only to preserve the peace yourselves, but also to use your exertions to excite a similar feeling in others: but I am satisfied that the Pastors of the different congregations of Christians, of which you are members, will not fail in that duty, which bids them impress those Divine Precepts strongly on your minds.

I have now endeavoured to direct your attention to the personal risk which those persons incur, who associate themselves with the illegal assemblies prevailing in the country; to the pecuniary loss which we must all sustain by their proceedings, and to the dishonest result which must arise from their success. I therefore earnestly request you for your own sake, for that of your families, and should these considerations not be of sufficient weight, I entreat you, as you would wish to preserve unsullied the character of our common country for honesty, and justice, not to be induced by any persuasions or threats, to join the illegal meetings of these misguided men; but on the contrary, to use your best exertions to repress, and by your utmost influence to dissuade others from attending them, by which course, believe me, you will not only perform your duty to yourselves, and to your neighbour, but also to the community at large.

> I am, my dear Friends,
> Your sincere well-wisher,
> John Johnes.

Dolau Cothi, August 16th, 1843.

An Address to the Inhabitants of Conwil Caio in the County of Car-

A Farmers' Meeting

It being known to the authorities that a meeting of the Colliery Rebeccaites was to take place at Llangendeirne, the dragoons were ordered out on 15th August, and Doctor Bowen, the magistrate appointed for the night, accompanying them, they proceeded thither. On arriving at the place, the dragoons found everything quiet, and were unable to discover the place of meeting. After remaining there between two and three hours, the dragoons returned. The meeting was held at a field's distance from the road. About 250 persons were present, and were seated in a circle, under the shade of some trees—thus escaping detection. They came to the resolution that inasmuch as they had assisted the farmers in the reduction of rents and turnpike tolls, they should now call upon them to reduce the price of butter, and other agricultural produce, and insist upon the publicans reducing the price of beer. It would thus appear that the Rebeccaites were now splitting into sections, according to their different class interests.

The detachment of the 73rd Foot, which had been stationed at the workhouse in Carmarthen for three months, marched from that town at four o'clock on the morning of 16th August, and arrived at Llanelly about twelve o'clock, after a hard walk in the rain, and, of course, well drenched.

Since the destruction of the gate at Bwlch-clawdd, a chain had been put across the road at the place where the old gate stood, and a person was appointed to receive the tolls there. Rebecca could see no difference between a gate and a chain, as both took money out of the pocket, and she determined to get rid of the chain also. Therefore, on 16th August she collected her forces, about 200 in number, all mounted on horseback, and well armed with cutlasses and guns. About twelve o'clock they arrived at the place, and the chain, posts,

A Farmers' Meeting

etc., were immediately destroyed. Then, to divert themselves, they had a sham fight, and the charges they made on each other were truly terrific; guns were discharged in all directions, and fire flashed from their swords as they met in combat, so that nothing was to be seen but fire and smoke. Some people, who had assembled to watch their proceedings, actually thought that a conflict between them and the dragoons had taken place, and they were much frightened at the spectacle, fully expecting to have the dead and wounded carried off the field in a few minutes. But in this they were disappointed, for Rebecca and her troops suddenly wheeled about, and were immediately out of sight.

As they were all dressed in white gowns, girded round the middle with sword-belts, and large straw hats on their heads, they presented rather a warlike appearance. The gateman decamped at their approach, or he would probably have been compelled to take the oath never to receive tolls again.

Destruction of Porthyrhyd Gate. Some of Rebecca's scouts were sent to reconnoitre this gate on the next evening. Finding that workmen had been employed in replacing the gate and re-erecting the toll-house, they, according to ancient custom, "smote upon their thighs," vowed by their mistress' shoe-tie that toll should no longer be collected there, and cautioned "Dick Morganwg," the toll-collector, to beware of them; for if he continued to take toll, dire vengeance would assuredly be taken, and he would be made to repent his contumacy.

Dick (the deceitful rogue) promised compliance, but apparently, having perfect confidence in his light heels, which had so well served him on a former occasion, remained at his post, and exacted toll as usual. Of course, the audacity of this subordinate of the lessee could not be borne the majesty of Rebecca's mandates was not thus to be insulted. Accordingly, on Saturday morning, the 19th, at a very early hour, a strong party of "Grey Coats" made their appearance at the spot, seized Evan, the constable (an official rather unpopular with these gate-levellers) in his bed; compelled him to turn out in his shirt take a pick in his hand march before them to the gate and begin the work of destruction with his own hands! which they soon completed. Thus was this gate a third time destroyed. The poor constable, *alias* the "Lion of Porthyrhyd," was kept in custody for some time longer by the party, and made to swear upon his knees that he would never more, directly or indirectly, meddle with, or interrupt, Rebecca and her daughters. The party soon afterwards fired off their guns, huzzaed, and dispersed.

A public meeting of freeholders, farmers, and farm labourers was held on 21st August at the schoolroom in the parish of Llannon for the purpose of taking into consideration the distressed state of the country and the best means to be adopted to restore confidence and prosperity. The curate of the parish, the Rev. —— Rees, was unanimously called to the chair. Rents were declared to be much higher than they should be. The new Poor Law, the salaried officers and the poor houses were particularly condemned. The meeting lasted for a considerable time, and all the proceedings were conducted in a most peaceable manner.

Late on the same evening a special messenger brought information to the local authorities of Swansea that Rebecca and her multitudinous offspring had assembled in alarming numbers on Fairwood Common, Gower, and requiring the presence of the military *instanter* to prevent the destruction of the whole peninsula! The detachment of the 4th Light Dragoons stationed at Carmarthen was accordingly brought into requisition, and mounting their neighing steeds dashed off, as they thought, in the direction in which they were needed; but after proceeding for some miles, and finding they had mistaken the place of meeting, they halted. In a short time the officer in command, accompanied by Mr. Grove, a county magistrate, overtook the party, and put them in the right direction. Upon reaching the Common, all that they learnt, or saw, or heard, was that about 200 persons had been seen in the neighbourhood late that evening; whether they were gone, or whether they were disposed to imitate the mad pranks of Rebecca's followers, were points upon which no person was able to give satisfactory information. Some of the county police, who had arrived at the common a full hour before the dragoons, said they found nothing "to obstruct their passage across the heath," all being quiet, and the rain descending in torrents. The officer in command gave orders for returning to Swansea, where they arrived about three o'clock in the morning, thoroughly drenched. A dragoon, who was somewhat late in joining his comrades, owing to the darkness of the night,

A Farmers' Meeting

got bewildered among the heath and bog, and with the utmost difficulty extricated himself, and proceeded along the road.

On 23rd August a meeting of freeholders, farmers, and farm labourers was held in a schoolroom in the parish of Llanedy, Carmarthenshire. They resolved to petition the tithes-owners for a reduction in the tithes, the present amount being oppressive. They condemned the Poor Law and the existing Corn Laws, and, indeed, any laws which tended to cramp and fetter commerce. They decided also to beg landowners to reduce rents. Everything passed off peaceably.

A deputation of farmers of the Conwil district, having waited upon *The Times* correspondent, stated that owing to the rapid progress of Mr. Hall, the Commissioner, through the country, they were unable to state their grievances before him, and requested that gentleman (the reporter) to appoint a time for meeting the farmers, in order that their complaints might be laid before the public through the columns of *The Times*: 23rd August was appointed for the meeting in the village of Conwil. There were present deputations from each of the parishes of Abernant, Llangeler, Conwil, Trelech, and Newchurch, in number about a hundred persons. The meeting was held in the long room in the inn, capable of holding one hundred, and it was quite filled. The proceedings commenced with a request to the reporter of *The Times*, that as the inquiry was to be made before him, he would take the chair.

Mr. Hugh Williams, the attorney, briefly stated the grievances of the farmers, as comprising oppressive tolls, objections to the new Poor Law, high rents, increased county rate and tithes, oppressive fees, and contumacious behaviour on the part of the magistrates of the county. At the request of the chairman, each farmer then stated his opinion of their existing grievances under the above heads, without any leading or prompting questions being put to them, and Mr. Williams took no further part in the statement, Mr. Edwards, the landlord of the inn, having volunteered to act as interpreter. The farmers then proceeded to state a number of most oppressive extortions of tolls on the Newcastle Emlyn Trust—that those who cut turf on the mountain in passing through the Wernfach Gate to Newcastle, were compelled to pay one toll on passing through the Gate with their turf, and if, on their return, they brought any article whatever in their carts, they were compelled to pay double toll for a fresh load. One farmer said he had been compelled to pay again on his return for having a kettle in his cart. Another, who carried two loads of turf to Newcastle, had paid 6d. toll for one cart, drawn by two horses and two bullocks, and 4½d. toll for another cart drawn by three horses. Having had ten bundles of thatch given him at Newcastle, in value about 1d. or 1½d. per bundle, he divided them between his two carts, and on his return was again compelled to pay 1s. for one cart, and 9d. for the other, thus paying 1s. 9d. toll for a load not worth at most more than 1s. 3d. Others complained that if they went the straightest roads from their farms to the market, they were fined for not going through turnpikes, which it was out of their way to go through. This had been repeatedly the case at the Bwlchclawdd Gate. With regard to the new Poor Law, the farmers said generally, that in the country districts it was more expensive, and fewer poor received less relief. The poor looked on the workhouse in the same manner as they (the farmers) did on prisons. After much to this effect, the chairman put it to them, through the interpreter "whether if they had the power, they wished to return to the Poor Law as it formerly existed, in preference to the present law."

The meeting rose, and raising their hands said, "Yes, to-morrow, if we could."

With regard to county rates, the farmers complained that though the price of agricultural produce was less, the county rate was nearly double what it was five or six years ago. This they attributed to the building of walls and other improvements, to please particular individuals. With regard to tithes, they complained that the Tithe Commutation Act, instead of being a relief to them, had doubled the amount of tithe, and stated that it would be a great relief to them if they could pay their tithe in kind.

With regard to rents, the farmers stated that the present amount of rent was based on the prices given some years ago for agricultural produce. Formerly a farmer could get £10 for his beast and 1s. a lb for his butter. Now he could only get £6 for his beast and 6d. a lb for his butter, and yet rents remained the same. The farmers, many of them, after working hard, could not get the necessaries of life, and not one shirt to change for another.

A Farmers' Meeting

With regard to magistrates' and their clerks' fees, the farmers stated that fees were most oppressive, that when they had business with the magistrates they were treated with the greatest indignity. One farmer said "they were treated by the magistrates more like brute beasts than human beings." It was better to go before a lawyer to settle their differences than to go before the magistrates. The lawyers cost them a good deal, but going before the magistrates cost them much more.

The chairman then put it to them, if any political grievances had anything to do with their dissatisfaction, and if they were enabled to live comfortably, and had the grievances complained of redressed, would the present disturbances be continued? The whole meeting again rose, and holding up their hands said, "Redress these grievances we have complained of, give us simply justice, and not a soldier or policeman would be required to protect property." Votes of thanks were then given to the chairman, for his attendance, and the meeting separated.

Rebecca and her Black Footman again. On 23rd August another instance of Rebecca's care for bastard children occurred at Carmarthen. David Moses of Ffynondeilo, a respectable farmer in the vicinity of Cothy Bridge, had had an illegitimate child a few years previously, and it had been put to nurse with a woman called "Shan Ionath," wife of John Evans (Skippo), of Carmarthen, where it remained till 23rd August. On that date the child's mother called on Skippo, and desired him to take the child to her father's house; the father also lived near Cothy Bridge. Her instructions were carried out immediately. When they arrived at that place, they were joined by Rebecca and about 200 of her children, who accompanied them to the house of the farmer; they were told that he was not at home, but after searching, they found him hiding in a field close by. They took him back to the house, and delivered the child to his care, with a strict injunction that he should look after it henceforth. This he promised faithfully to do, and after caressing the child in the most affectionate manner, he delivered it to the charge of his wife, who seemed highly amused at the adventure. Rebecca expressed herself as quite satisfied that she would take proper care of the child. He was then desired to pay Skippo for conveying the child home, and to give him some meat and drink, which he did cheerfully. Afterwards Rebecca and her companions departed, and Skippo was left to wend his way back to Carmarthen.

About 8 a.m. on 23rd August a great number of Rebeccaites suddenly made their appearance at Croes-lwyd, within two miles of Carmarthen. The gate and the toll-house at this place had been demolished a few weeks before, and a chain had since been put across the road. A person had also been stationed there to receive tolls, attended by his men from Carmarthen to guard the place. At the approach of Rebecca and her children the guards fled, and left the toll-man to shift for himself. One of the guards hid in a potato field till all danger was over.

The chain and posts were soon destroyed, and the rioters, who were all disguised, then dispersed.

The same day a meeting of the farmers of Llanarthney parish was held in the village of Llanarthney, at which the Rev. H. Williams, the minister, consented to take £100, in lieu of the £150 due from the parish to him.

Mr. Price, of Neath, and several ladies of the Society of Friends from Darlington, visited Carmarthen about this time, in order to endeavour to pacify the county. They held a meeting at Water Street Chapel, when the ladies addressed a numerous congregation on the benefits of peace and the horrors of civil war.

A great number of rioters assembled on Llandebie Common on 23rd August, and completely destroyed the enclosures which had been made there, and which they considered to be encroachments on the rights of the people. This was the second time for these enclosures to be levelled.

Another common—Crugebolion—in the parish of Trelech, Carmarthenshire, had been enclosed by some of the adjoining farms (Tretoisaf, Treto-uchaf, Cwmblewog, Ffynonwen, and Blaen-gilfach).

Rebecca and some two hundred of her assistants assembled there one morning, armed with mattocks, pickaxes, spades, and shovels, and in a few hours all the long and high hedges on the common were pulled down and made level with the ground. The gang on this occasion was led by several men, well attired, on horseback.

(The Common of Crugebolion has been in the possession of the parish ever since.)

Attacks on Private Houses

The Rebecca outrages, which had been practically confined to the destruction of gates, now spread to that of private property, and the endangerment of human life. On the morning of 23rd August, the village of Llannon (Carmarthenshire) and the surrounding neighbourhood was the scene of an outrage of the most daring character. Between eleven and twelve o'clock on Tuesday night (the 22nd) the inhabitants of Llannon were alarmed by the shouts of an immense body of the Rebeccaites, consisting of about 500 persons, who were passing through the village. The majority of them had on women's clothes, or shirts over their dresses; all of them were disguised by having their faces blackened, the leader, or "Rebecca," being mounted on a horse, which, contrary to the ordinary usage, was not a white one, but a bay or some dark colour. Rebecca was dressed in white. Nearly all the party were armed with guns, which they repeatedly fired in their progress through the village. Several horns were also in full play, and a number of rockets fired. There was also a kind of carriage in the procession, the lamps of which shed a lustre over the crowd, and lighted the apartments of many of the villagers, who were afraid to leave their bedrooms, thus to obtain a better view of the procession. When the party arrived near the end of the village, where one road leads to the Pontardulais highway, and the other towards Llanelly, Rebecca, who had previously given several orders, cried out, "Silence!" The party immediately left off firing guns and blowing horns. They then decided to take the Llanelly road, which also led to Gellywernen, the house of Mr. Edwards, the agent of Mr. Rees Goring Thomas, who was lay-impropriator of the tithes of the parish. Mr. Edwards had for some time past had the management of the collection of tithes. When the party had proceeded as far as Morlais Bridge, they halted, and remained

Attacks on Private Houses

there for about an hour and a half, waiting for another division which was to come from Mynydd Selen. During the whole of the time the blowing of horns and firing of guns and rockets were kept up without intermission. 'Becca, thinking the party to be rather behind time according to their engagement, accompanied by several others on horseback, proceeded for about three-quarters of a mile on the road along which the second party was expected to come, until she met them. A third party, from some other direction, also joined them. They afterwards proceeded towards Gellywernen House, the party by this time amounting to 700 or 800 persons. Their vehicle remained on the bridge.

Upon the arrival of the rioters before Gellywernen House, they repeatedly fired off their guns. Mr. Edwards, who had for some days been confined by illness, was in bed in one of the rooms upstairs, in which there was a light. Hearing the firing, and being greatly alarmed at seeing so large a crowd, Mrs. Edwards asked what was the matter. What did they require? At this a shot pierced the window, several panes of which were broken. Mrs. Edwards, who had cautiously avoided standing immediately in front of the window, fortunately escaped injury. She went to the window a second time, and received a similar answer. Another shot was afterwards fired towards the door of the room near which Mrs. and Miss Edwards stood, both of whom fortunately escaped unhurt, although the marks of shot were very thick upon the door. Several gunshots were then fired in succession into the bedroom, the evident aim of the rioters being to injure seriously, if not indeed to murder, Mr. Edwards, who, as before stated, was in bed. Happily their endeavours were not attended with success, for, although parts of the walls were so thickly marked with shots and slugs that scarcely a square inch was free from them, while the windows and curtain were thickly perforated, Mr. Edwards escaped untouched, the rioters standing too low to enable them to fire into the bed. Some guns, however, must have been discharged by persons standing on the court wall, as there were marks of shot at a distance of half a yard from the pillows on which Mr. Edwards lay, while those which were fired from the ground of the yard could not take effect much lower than the ceiling. Another window in the back part of the house was also broken by gunshots which had passed through the front window. There were in all fifty-two panes of glass broken in five windows.

Greatly alarmed at the dangerous position of her father, Miss Edwards, at considerable personal risk, came downstairs and went to the door, at which there was a kind of porch. Several large stones were immediately thrown at her through the glass, but none of them struck her.

Some of the party called out in Welsh that they would not injure Miss Edwards or her mother, but that "they would not set a greater value on her father's life than a feather thrown before the wind, and they would have their tithes lowered." Miss Edwards appealed to their humanity, and told them her father was exceedingly ill, and confined to his bed, but that they might see him on any future day. This had its effect, and having fired a few additional charges, they left the house. While these outrages were carried on at the house, several of the mob forced open the door, and entered the beautiful walled garden adjoining the house, where they committed devastations of a most disgraceful character. Nearly all the apple trees and wall-fruit trees of different kinds, were entirely destroyed, being cut to pieces or torn up from the roots. The various plants and herbs with which che garden abounded were all destroyed, and a row of commodious greenhouses, extending from one side of the garden to the other, was attacked, and a large quantity of glass broken with stones.

A party of the desperadoes proceeded to the house of William Barrett (or Bassett), the gamekeeper, who resided in a woodland cottage, a short distance from Gellywernen House. On hearing their approach the gamekeeper, against whom they had sworn vengeance, fled for refuge in the wood, leaving his wife and children at home. The Rebeccaites, on entering the house, discharged a gun or pistol containing powder only, nearly into the face of the wife, who had a child in her arms at the time, and who was by the shot slightly wounded.

They then broke the clock, a very good one, an old pier-glass which had been handed down for several generations, the chairs, table, and all the little furniture the poor people possessed. They also carried away the gamekeeper's gun, and 10s. or 12s. worth of powder and shot, and previous to leaving took from the drawers all the clothes of the family, which were torn, trodden upon, and partly burnt. They then left the

Attacks on Private Houses

place, after firing several times. Several of the painted doors, leading from the road to the plantation, were destroyed by the Rebeccaites. When they returned through Llannon it was two or three o'clock on the Wednesday morning. A proclamation was afterwards issued, offering a reward of £500 for information that would lead to the conviction of the offenders.

A meeting was held by Mr. Price, of Neath, and Lady Friends from Darlington, in the Magistrates' Room, Carmarthen, on 25th August, when several magistrates were present, who listened attentively to their exhortations. They visited that part of the country on Rebecca's account, as a deputation from the "Society for the Promotion of Universal Peace."

The following effusions, together with a printed paper, headed, "The Perfect New Government, by the Second Moses," were received on the 25th by the keeper of the Sandy Limekiln Gate, near Llanelly, enclosed in a letter, bearing the London postmark:—

Behold!

Oh Sir, place this[1] as we implore,
Upon the Church and Chapel door;
And honour thus Jehovah's name,
When all the Jews adore the same:

By whose almighty blest decree
The poor are set for ever free;
Or hereof at your peril fail
Where blood and fire fools assail:

Amen!

Alas! Alas! poor Jenkin Hugh,
We see your Gate is broken through,
But there's great work for all to do,
And if you think in jokes we deal,
A wound may come which none can heal,
We never take God's name in vain,
And He alone shall prove it plain.

Amen!

No wonder you did not understand our last letter; and still less wonder if you are quite blind to this letter. Nevertheless take it, and pray God to give a little bit of Christ's eye-salve,

---

[1] Alluding to the printed papers.

if you believe the 3rd chapter of Revelation and the 18th verse, and if not, you may die, and deplore it for ever, and you can never say it was our fault. No, no, but the fact is, the world is blind. "The blind lead the blind, till they all tumble together into the ditch," and the ditch is nothing but Hell according to 15th Matthew 14.

John and Daniel,
Brothers.

About one o'clock on the morning of the 25th, the toll-house of Glangwili Gate, near Carmarthen, was surrounded by about 200 Rebeccaites, who began shouting and yelling. They compelled the gate-man, David Joshua, to commence the work of destruction. The gate, being very strong, resisted their efforts for a considerable time, but ultimately the posts were sawn through and the gate smashed to pieces. They then attacked the toll-house, which was speedily brought almost to the ground, the roof and walls being thrown in upon the furniture and stock-in-trade of David Joshua, who was a bookbinder.

The house soon presented a ruinous appearance, and the furniture and tools were buried beneath a heap of rubbish. Joshua was attacked by the Rebeccaites, struck several times with a hatchet, and otherwise severely abused; while some country constables who were with him guarding (?) the gate, took to their heels, and made the best of their way towards the town! An express was sent to Carmarthen for the military, and the dragoons were instantly called out, and went off at a dashing pace for the scene of the riot. The sisters seemed to have taken measures very well, taking every precaution to avoid surprise, two of the party being placed as sentinels—one on the main road to Carmarthen, and the other upon an elevated site, from which he had a view of the road leading to Abergwili. The passage along the main road to Carmarthen was obstructed by the destruction of Glangwili Bridge by a recent flood. When at some distance from the place of their destination, the dragoons heard the report of a gun, which was probably fired by one of Rebecca's sentinels as a signal of the approach of the military. When the latter arrived on the spot, they found the gate and toll-house destroyed, but no trace of Rebecca or her children. In the course of the day the gatekeeper was examined before some of the county magistrates, when he stated his ability to identify four of the party,

Attacks on Private Houses

against whom warrants were issued, viz. David Thomas, of Penlan, Llanllawddog (farmer), Benjamin Richards, Llynydd Styfle, Carmarthen (carpenter), William Jones and Arthur Arthur, of the village of Abergwili (labourers).

A letter published about the end of 1843, from D. W. Joshua, Glangwili Gate, contains the following:—

> Behold! disastrous days have come; yea, days are these when men are traitors, hot-blooded, and bombastic, loving to commit outrages during the dark hours of the night. Hardly a night passes without hearing of the destruction of toll-gates here—possessions fired there—and—what is much worse—treacherous attacks on the lives of those who venture a word of protest against the Rebecca movement. Among others who have been the object of sinful attacks by the thieving workmen of the night, I have become at last an object of visitation.
>
> Between one and two o'clock on the morning of 25th August the destructive goblins descended on the toll-gate of Glangwili, and in a short time they completely destroyed everything; they stole from my house £9 19s. 5d.; they burnt many of my valuable books, in order to have light with which to carry out their thieving actions—not only that, but when I escaped from their clutches, one shouted, "Shoot him! Shoot him!" and another attempted to strike me with an axe.
>
> Yours—
> rendered a pauper because of the above circumstance,
> D. W. J., Glangwili.
> September 9th, 1843.

A great public meeting was held on the summit of Mynydd Selen, a mountain in the parish of Llanelly, on 25th August. Upwards of 3000 men attended the meeting, and William Chambers, junior, was elected chairman. The declared objects of the promoters of the meeting were to take into consideration the dreadfully depressed and retrograde deterioration of the people in the neighbourhood, with a view to remedial measures; to specify the particular grievances which pressed most severely upon them; to make known their wants and wishes in a legal and peaceful manner; to denounce the course pursued by ministers as too futile to meet the exigencies of times requiring firm and honest measures; and, lastly, to memorialise the Queen for a dissolution of Parliament. The meeting was very peacefully conducted; it lasted four hours. At the conclusion, three cheers were given for the chairman; another three for Hugh Williams, who took an important part in the meeting, and "three cheers for the Queen," which were given in a style worthy of Welshmen.

Attacks on Private Houses

"Some Exciting Incidents"

The following address was issued by the "London Peace Society" to that portion of the Welsh people known by the name of "The Rebeccaites," about the end of August, 1843:—

> Brethren,— It is with serious concern we have heard of recent acts of violence perpetrated in Wales, and it is now in a Christian spirit of affection and of sorrow that we venture to address you. We inquire not here into the causes that may have led into those acts; we do not here seek to point out the penalties of the law to which you are exposing yourselves, but we appeal to you on a higher principle, and would place before you the spiritual, the eternal dangers you incur by such conduct. You, in common with ourselves, propose to be followers of the Prince of Peace; but how can the work of violence and destruction be reconciled with the meek, gentle, and peaceable spirit of Christianity? No two things can be more opposed. You have set at defiance the laws, by obedience to which social peace and order are preserved—you have forcibly opposed yourselves to the constituted authorities—you have violated the laws of God—whatever the end may be that you propose to yourselves, know you not that we are forbidden to do evil that good may come? The moral power with which men have been endowed may be exerted in strict conformity with the Christian religion; and if it be directed to a true and good object, it will, by the blessing of God ultimately prevail—Pause and reflect, we beseech of you—"Consider your ways"—Remember that in an attempt to gain the things of a day, you are risking the welfare of eternity.

A rumour reached the magistrates of Haverfordwest that the spirit of Rebeccaism was spreading rapidly among the inhabitants of the neighbouring district. Some wiseacres in the vicinity of little Newcastle and that neighbourhood, thinking themselves sufficiently powerful, made arrangements for a demonstration of their united forces to take place on 25th

"Some Exciting Incidents"

August. Each village and farmhouse sent forth its aspirants for the cap of their venerated mamma. The tributary gatherings of this stream, having met at a small roadside pot-house, called "The Three-Cornered Piece," distant four miles from Haverfordwest, placed sentinels to prevent any lights being brought to the door, outside of which they were drawn up, "for they loved darkness rather than light, because their deeds were evil." Having been regaled with sufficient swipes to screw their courage to the sticking place, they boldly marched forward; but little did these feather-bed warriors think that a *spy* was in their camp! In the midst of their carousals and consultations, this "chiel" was taking notes, and having made himself acquainted with their numbers, he forthwith proceeded to Haverfordwest in sufficient time to give the Mayor notice of their approach.

That worthy functionary instantly repaired to the Prendergast Gate (accompanied by the constabulary force), the gate being the object that this predatory band intended to destroy.

Onward they came—'Becca leading the way, some fifty yards in advance, with a "twice-barrel" in her hands, and dressed in a fantastic style. When she reached the gate, the mayor, deeming it prudent to prevent the main body coming up, gave instructions for an immediate attack, and the gun of this modern Jezebel, like the gates of Somnauth, became the object of their capture. Williams, the police officer, instantly laid hold of the weapon, for which 'Becca struggled *manfully*, keeping her seat on horseback all the time; but the officer being the stronger man, succeeded in wresting the gun from her grasp. One of the barrels was, however, discharged by accident, and killed a horse of one of the daughters.

The courageous matron deeming discretion the better part of valour, made a scrambling retreat, being fully convinced that

> Those who fight and run away
> Will live to fight another day

the truth also flashing across her mind that

> Those who are in battle slain
> Will never rise to fight again.

Away she scampered with her motley crowd both on foot and horseback amounting to nearly 300 men, not so quickly, however, but that two of her offspring were taken prisoners.

142

Their countenances were very black; their headgear—composed of an "ould cawbeen," as Paddy would have called it—was firmly secured on their heads by means of firm lashings. They were, after divers examinations and cross-examinations, bound over, to render themselves up for trial at the next Assizes, in securities of £50 each, the prisoners being under age.

Time discloses almost all things. The owner of the gun which Williams captured, proved to be one Thomas, a gamekeeper, residing not far from Ford Bridge. As the day of destruction to the feathered tribe drew near, its want was most unpleasantly felt. For a gamekeeper to be seen in search of coveys without his gun was indeed most laughable. But how did Thomas lose his gun? Through sheer indiscretion while endeavouring to be discreet. He was appointed the Rebecca for the night, and having with the rest got as far as Colby Scott, he there halted, and signified the necessity of his going across the fields into the Cardigan road, and thence to Prendergast to espy what strength opposed him. He handed the gun, for safe custody, to a neighbouring farmer's son, by the name of Davies, with strict injunctions to remain there until his return. These orders were unheeded. Davies, having the gun, urged those around him to follow. They obeyed, and Davies armed and mounted on a splendid charger, thought to earn and wear the laurels himself. How he marched—how he was stopped—how he lost his gun, and how he galloped away crestfallen and disgraced, have already been chronicled.

On 25th August some Rebeccaites paid a visit to a gentleman in the parish of Llanegwad, who had a large quantity of old corn in his possession, and told him, unless he immediately sent the same to the different markets to be sold, they would soon find a way to dispose of it.

The same night a visit similar in character was paid to an old gentleman farmer, who was intensely eager to make as much money as he could, and who resided near Haverfordwest. In his mode of amassing wealth, he had thought fit to retain in his haggard the produce of two harvests. Now it is well known the poor want bread, and that as cheaply as they can get it. To hoard up, unnecessarily, bread which gladdens man's heart, was, according to Miss Rebecca's ideas, a most heinous crime, and completely against her peace and the statutes of her realm. She therefore *in propria persona*, in her best robes, yea, even with golden droppers in her ears and drawn in her carriage, with the usual retinue of servants, waited on the aforesaid farmer on 25th August, and was admitted to a *tête-à-tête* with him. Her mission was dispatched in a few moments. She informed him that her desire was that all the corn in straw should be threshed, and the clean grain brought to market the following Saturday, that the poor labourer might have a chance to purchase it at a moderate price, or she would, in a few days, assist in the removal.

The farmer promised implicit obedience to her commands, and fully carried out his promise to Miss Rebecca.

The next evening David Joshua, the toll-man of the Glangwili Gate, having put together the fragments that remained of his household furniture, prevailed on a countryman with whom he was well acquainted to assist in removing the same to a room he had taken in a yard, called "The Round House Yard," near the Guildhall, Carmarthen. He arrived near the square about nine o'clock, when the town mob surrounded the cart, and were about to cut the horses' traces, and deal out "Lynch Law" on the poor countryman for merely assisting the toll-man, when Mr. Nott kindly interfered. With difficulty he assisted the poor carter in saving his cart and horses from the vengeance of the people. Joshua's troubles were not yet ended, for his furniture was nearly all destroyed, his books and papers were strewn throughout the square and Lower Market Street; and had he not by some means escaped to a place of concealment, he undoubtedly would have been severely ill-used. The police interfered, and assisted in removing the ruins that were left of his already destroyed furniture, but were unable to disperse the mob, or to persuade them to go home for more than an hour after the first outbreak.

A temporary shed had been erected for the purposes of the collector Joshua soon after the destruction of the Glangwili Toll-gate; but on 27th August, although the Sabbath Day, some of the Rebeccaites set to work chopping up the remaining fragments of wood, which they at once set on fire and burned to the ground. The dragoons were soon on the spot, but they saw nothing of Rebecca, although the embers of the fire and the destruction of the shed bore evidence of her visit, or rather *visitation*.

David Thomas, of Penlan Llanllawddog, was apprehended on Friday evening the 25th, Richards on the Saturday, and William Jones and Arthur Arthur on 28th August. One of the prisoners, proved by witnesses, whose veracity could not be doubted, that he was in his house the whole night of the 24th, and that in the early part thereof he went to fetch a midwife, afterwards remaining at home, his wife being confined at the time.

On Saturday Richards was committed to take his trial on the capital charge; Monday he was committed to bail. Tuesday the 29th the other three were fully committed to take their trial at the next Assizes on the charge of felony.

On the night of 29th August, a part of the grove of fir trees belonging to Mr. Howell Davies of Conwil, on the farm at Blaenffrwd, was cut down and completely destroyed.

The same night, Rebecca, and about 400 of her family, paid a visit to the farm of Penybank, in the parish of Llanarthney, and compelled the person who was in possession of the furniture and farming stock for her attorney under a bill of sale to leave the place. They then made him promise never to make his appearance on the premises again, giving possession to the person owing the money.

On 30th August some miscreants set fire to two mows of wheat. These were in a field near King's Lodge, on the road to Llandilo, and were the property of Lord Dynevor. They were entirely consumed.

On 30th August Rebecca also visited the farm of Kencoed, in the parish of Llanegwad, the property of Seymour Allen, Esq., of Cresselly, but then in the possession of Mrs. Davies. She had another farm under lease from the same landlord called Penyrhoel, which she underlet to Charles Davies, who was in arrears of rent. In consequence she put in a distress through her attorney, Mr. Popkin of Llandilo, who sent down two of his bailiffs to execute it. This they did, removing the cattle to Kencoed for better security. About half-past twelve o'clock Rebecca and her family arrived at Kencoed, and called at the house. Mrs. Davies appeared and asked them what they wanted. They said they wished to know where the cattle were.

Mrs. Davies, out of fear, sent the servant to show them the cattle, when they at once removed them, returning them to their different owners, for they had been placed at Penyrhoel to graze.

David Joshua, the Glangwili gateman, had evidently incurred Rebecca's unending displeasure, for on 1st September he found the following notice stuck on his gate:—

> I'll be damned if I will not be with you, and send your soul to the infernal crew —'Becca.

Green Castle Side-gate was destroyed some time before, as was also a chain which had been subsequently placed there. On 1st September the toll-house was taken down and entirely demolished, the gate-keeper being allowed to remove his family and furniture, as Rebecca did not wish to injure him.

David Joshua, and a person whom he had attacked with a sword for refusing to pay toll, made their appearance at the Town Hall on 6th September, 1843. The plaintiff alleged that David Joshua snapped a gun at him three times, and when he found that the load would not go off, he fetched his sword and cut him severely on the head and arm, his wounds being visible at this time. David Joshua denied having used a sword, and said he had only a constable's staff in his hand. One of the magistrates, in the course of a conversation, observed that it was useless for him to attempt denying that he had used a sword, for he had examined the wounded man himself, and would swear that he had been wounded with an edged instrument, and that the man had also a surgeon's certificate to testify as to the nature of his wounds. The magistrate also observed to Joshua, that they had every desire to protect him in the discharge of his duty, but that he had taken the law into his own hands, and must abide the consequences.

He was indicted at the Assizes, under the "Cutting and Maiming Act." This man David Joshua was the person who had figured some time previously in Carmarthenshire as a hired Chartist orator; and had delivered a most treasonable speech at the celebrated Chartist Lamplight Demonstration in Carmarthen, about the year 1840.[1]

---

[1] David Joshua was by trade a bookbinder. He was at one time employed by D. M. Jenkins, chemist, Newcastle Emlyn, in connection with "Cyfaill y Werin," and also by Josiah Thomas Jones, Aberdare. I believe he died at Aberdare. —H.T.E.

The previous evening Rebecca and four of her daughters, all dressed in white, and otherwise disguised, had paid a visit to a respectable farmer in the parish of Abergwili, who had committed a faux pas with one of his servant maids, and afterwards neglected his offspring. Rebecca addressed him in a very friendly manner, but insisted upon his taking the child home, under pain of her (Rebecca's) displeasure. She said that unless he complied with her request, she would certainly pay him a different visit the following night. The farmer faithfully promised to obey her orders, and very early on 6th September he fetched his child home.

A meeting of the ratepayers of the parish of Llandeveilog was held at Raymond's Lodge on 6th September. Mr. Edwards of Gelli took the chair. The following grievances were submitted:

Grievances.

1. The Highway Act ought to be reformed.
2. The Gates are too numerous, and the tolls too high.
3. *Poor Law*:
    i. The overseers ought to pay the poor.
    ii. This is to be done under the directions of the guardians.
    iii. The guardians ought to choose and pay all the Officers connected with the Workhouse.
    iv. There ought to be no separation of man and his wife.
    v. The old law was better in the cases of bastardy than the new.
    vi. The accounts ought to be passed before Justices as before.
    vii. The Chaplain ought not to have any salary.
4. *Tithes*:
    i. The meeting wish that the tithes go towards keeping the poor and the Church.
    ii. The tithes ought to be paid according to the annual value of the land.
    iii. They ought to be reduced at least 3s. or 4s. in the pound.
5. Church rates ought to be amended.

6. Church and State:
    i. They ought to be separated.
    ii. The laws should defend religion the same as in Madagasgar and Haheite.
7. County Stock:
   This meeting thinks the same with regard to this grievance as the Mynydd Selen meeting did.
8. The Corn Law ought to be repealed for a year or two to try how it can be done without.
9. There ought to be no Bye-laws in the Highway, the Gates, the Poor, the Tithes, and the Income Tax.
10. Every parish to choose its own Minister, as in Germany.
11. The Archbishops and Bishops have better work to do than to be in the House of Lords.
12. No Clergymen nor Preachers are wanted in the Workhouse, if the Guardians do their duty faithfully.
13. The Law of the Land to be amended in many other particulars.
14. Income Tax:
    It is a great folly to raise a Tax with this name to it.
15. The D.V.J. Tax:
    The meeting thinks Sir Robert Peel will take off this tax, if asked to do so.
16. Soldiers are serviceable where they are wanted, but they are not wanted here.

The meeting was adjourned to the 27th instant, to be then held at Alltcynadda.

Destruction of Pontardulais Gate— Capture of Rebecca and other Rioters

The Swansea Authorities having received secret information that an attack would be made by Rebecca and her daughters upon the Pontardulais Turnpikegate on a certain night, arrangements were made by Captain Napier for the purpose, not of protecting the gate itself, but of capturing the ringleaders while in the act of destruction.

A small police force—one superintendent, two sergeants, and four constables—left Neath on the afternoon of 6th September, and proceeded across the country to Lougher. Upon Lougher Common they were met by Captain Napier (chief constable), and shortly afterwards by Mr. Dillwyn Llewellyn, Mr. Lewis Dillwyn, Mr. William Chambers, of Llanelly, Mathew Moggridge, Esq., and Mr. Attwood.

About 11.30 p.m. they saw a rocket explode in the air, and at the same moment heard firearms discharged in various directions. Bugles were also sounded, being probably the signal of the Rebeccaites for gathering.

The magistrates and policemen moved on silently and unperceived, halting within a short distance of Pontardulais Gate, the bugles and firearms of the Rebeccaites continually sounding. Within a few minutes of one o'clock a.m. a large body of men, principally on horseback, was seen advancing towards Pontardulais Gate from the direction of Llannon; as they approached, they repeatedly fired their guns and cheered. When they got opposite the Red Lion Inn, where Mr. Griffith Vaughan resided, they fired a general volley, and gave three loud cheers. They then advanced, firing and cheering, to the gate, which they knocked to pieces in about ten minutes, and then instantly commenced tearing down the tollhouse. By this time the magistrates and policemen had reached the spot, and called upon the rioters to desist. The appearance of an imposing force seemed to astonish, but not to alarm the rioters, who instantly called upon each other to be "true till death," and fired at the police, who were not long returning the salute. The rioters then fired away at their opponents as fast as they could, without method or order, by which, fortunately, they did no injury, but by their unskilfulness several of their own party were wounded. The police then fired a second volley; and the rioters scampered off in all directions, leaving their wounded companions upon the ground. The police pursued them and captured several.

To capture the ringleader was the aim of the magistrates, consequently the person who acted the part of "Rebecca" on this occasion was particularly marked—his horse shot under him, and he himself taken after a desperate resistance. He had one arm broken, and sustained other injuries. His name was John Hughes, a respectable farmer's son and a resident of the village of Llannon in Carmarthenshire.

After the fight was over, and the prisoners secured, an express was sent off to hasten the arrival of the military, as the reassembling rioters were again firing off their guns and blowing their horns, apparently with a view of reassembling their scattered party, and attacking the police at the gate, but fortunately no further attack was made.

About half an hour after the express had been sent off a party of eight dragoons arrived at the gate. Mr. C. H. Smith, Mr. V. P. Cameron, and Mr. William Cameron were shortly afterwards at the place. The sound of horns was heard incessantly in all directions among the surrounding hills, but no Rebeccaites were to be seen.

It was then found there were seven men in custody, three of whom (including Hughes) had been taken in Glamorganshire, and four in Carmarthenshire. The first-mentioned three were taken to Swansea, and the four were conveyed to Llanelly, escorted by the dragoons. Three horses were also captured and conveyed to Swansea.

There were upwards of 150 men engaged in the attack on the gate, the majority being on horseback.

On the arrival of the prisoners at Swansea great excitement prevailed among the townspeople. In the fight Hughes had received a ball on the outer side of the elbow-joint, which crushed the lower end of the bone of the arm, and, passing upwards, was extracted at the back part of the arm, midway between his elbow and the shoulder. David Jones, one of the other men, had received some shot or slugs in the back, and three sword-cuts on the head. He was in a very precarious state.

Dr. Bird immediately attended the wounded prisoners, and did all that skill and humanity could suggest to alleviate their sufferings. He extracted the bullet from Hughes's arm, and then very kindly conveyed him in his carriage to the Infirmary at the House of Correction. In the pocket of the leader, Hughes, were found a quantity of percussion caps, powder, etc., about £3 in money, and the following 'Becca notice:—

Daniel Jones of Brynhir—

Meet us at Llan on Wednesday night, if you don't this shall be your last notice —'Becca.

Shortly after, the third prisoner, dressed in most fantastic manner, having an old straw bonnet trimmed with a red ribbon upon his head, was led down to the House of Correction by two policemen, followed by some hundreds of persons. Some of the weapons with which the rioters were armed were taken to the Swansea Police Station House, and most formidable ones they were—heavy bars of iron, hedge sticks, pitchforks, in fact, everything that was available, either as an instrument of offence or defence.

Armed with such weapons, even without firearms, so large a body of men must have been a formidable enemy; and when it is considered that the majority of the rioters were on horseback, and armed with guns, the cool and steady valour displayed by the magistrates, Captain Napier and his half-dozen men must be admired.

Some persons, supposed to be part of the mob that attacked the Pontardulais Gate, later in the day, set fire to a stack of corn, the property of William Chambers, Esq.

A great number of Rebeccaites attacked Sanders Bridge Gate, near Kidwelly, on the morning of 8th September. They completely demolished it in a short time. They were all disguised and well armed.

That night a stack of straw near Mr. Chambers' pottery was burnt to the ground.

A large party of Rebeccaites also visited Fishguard, and completely destroyed the Fishguard and Parcymorfa turnpike-gates; scarcely a vestige was left, and on the departure of the rioters they warned the toll-collector not to levy any more toll at those gates.

Destruction of Hendy Gate, and Murder of the Toll-Collector.

About 2 o'clock a.m. on 9th September a party of men, disguised in white dresses, came to Hendy Gate, about half a mile from Pontardulais, carried out the furniture from the toll-house, and told the old woman, whose name was Sarah Williams, to go away, and not to return. She went to the house of John Thomas, a labourer, and called him to assist in extinguishing the fire at the toll-house, which had been ignited by the Rebeccaites. The old woman then re-entered the toll-house. The report of a gun or pistol was soon afterwards heard. The old woman ran back to John Thomas's house, fell down at the threshold, and expired within two minutes, without saying a single word. She had received several cautions to collect no more tolls.

11th September. An inquest was held before William Bonville, Esq., Coroner. Two surgeons, Mr. Ben Thomas, of Llanelly, and Mr. John Kirkhouse Cooke, of Llanelly, gave evidence that on the body were the marks of shot, some penetrating the nipple of the left breast, one in the armpit of the same side, and several shot-marks on both arms. On the external end of the left clavicle there were two shot-marks, one on the left side of the windpipe. There were several on the forehead, and on the external angle of the right eye. Two shots were found in the left lung. In spite of all this, the jury found *"that the deceased died from effusion of blood into the chest, which occasioned suffocation, but from what cause is to this jury unknown!!!"*

John Hughes (chief of the Rebeccas), David Jones, John Hugh, William Hughes, and Lewis Davies, were on the 11th committed for trial at the next Assizes for Glamorganshire for the riots at Pontardulais Gate. Thomas Williams and Henry Roger—his farm servant—were admitted to bail, and liberated (see further on).

A Petition to the Queen

At Maesgwenllian near Kidwelly, several bailiffs were put in possession for arrears of rent to the amount of £150, but about one o'clock on the morning of 11th September, Rebecca and a great number of her followers made their appearance on the premises, and after driving the bailiffs off, took away the whole of the goods distrained on. As soon as daylight appeared, the bailiffs returned, but found no traces of Rebecca, nor of the goods which had been taken away.

The following day the tax-collectors at Parcymorfa and Fishguard gates, not heeding Rebecca's warning on the 9th instant, took toll as usual. This exasperated the lady to such a pitch that she sent notices that they should remove their furniture from their houses, as she would visit them on Monday night (the 11th instant). Accordingly she did, about midnight. From 400 to 600 arrived at Fishguard Gate, went to work at once, and completely destroyed the toll-house. They then proceeded to Parcymorfa Gate, and ordered the collector to remove his furniture in five minutes, and then instantly pulled the house down, razing it to the ground. They next proceeded to pay a visit to Mr. John M'Kennel, the road surveyor, and in going fired several rounds of musketry opposite Mr. Henry Collins' house, warning him to behave properly, otherwise they would visit him also. They levelled a piece of wall which Mr. M'Kennel had built around his garden to the ground, after which they departed at 3 a.m. By this time there could be no less than from 2000 to 3000 assembled in Fishguard, but not a single person dared to go near, or face this renowned lady and her numerous offspring during the time the work of destruction was being carried on. Mr. Mortimer, a surgeon, made himself rather too free by going very near the party. The lady advanced towards him and fired off a

A Petition to the Queen

pistol in his face; but as it contained powder only, he was not injured.

About midnight on 12th September, Rebecca and three of her companions paid a visit to the village of Felinwen about three miles from Carmarthen, to correct what she called the evils of the new Poor Law. A young woman of that place, of the name of Jane Jones, had had the misfortune to have a bastard child from a person who resided somewhere near Wernderlwyd, Llangunnor. The father had contributed nothing towards the maintenance of his offspring. The woman resided at the home of David Morris, smith, at that place, and when Rebecca called, the smith was in bed. Rebecca knocked at the door, and was admitted. As soon as she and her companions entered the house, she awoke the smith, putting him on his legs, and jocosely asking him if he knew her; to which the smith answered "No." Rebecca and her companions were elegantly attired in women's clothes; and Rebecca herself had a beautiful gun in her hands, to which she put a cap, after turning herself round so that the smith might have a fair view of her person. The girl was then called, and was desired to lay her right hand on the lock of the gun, and make her oath most solemnly as to the father of the child. This having been done to the satisfaction of Rebecca, the girl was desired to put herself in readiness against a future night, when they would call to convey the child to its father, the mother also to accompany them. She wanted to excuse herself, and said she could not walk so far, but they told her they would find a cart to convey her—that there were plenty of carts in the village, and if any of the owners showed unwillingness to lend one of them, they would make him come back with them and be the driver himself. To this the girl replied that she would accompany them with the greatest pleasure.

The Rebeccaites then left the house, proceeding up the road towards Llandilo, and in a short time fired two shots. Notwithstanding that Rebecca behaved so civilly, the smith was so frightened that he was wholly unable to resume his occupation the following day.

Some miscreants the same night set fire to two ricks consisting of about sixty tons of hay, valued at £200. They were the property of Ed. Adams, Esq., of Middleton Hall, and were entirely consumed.

An express was dispatched to Carmarthen for the military, but it was too late for their services to be of any avail in stopping the conflagration or in arresting the offenders.

An attack was expected to be made on the mansion itself the following night, and an express was again sent to Carmarthen for the military. A troop of infantry was conveyed in carriages to the Hall with the greatest dispatch. A troop of the 4th Dragoons also went over, but returned in a few hours. Mr. Adams and the whole of his family left Middleton Hall the same evening for Carmarthen.

On 13th September a great meeting was held on Bank Llyn Llech Owen,[1] on the mountain between Swansea and Carmarthen, to consider the various local grievances, under which the county had long suffered, and the course it would be best to adopt to seek redress. About 2000 individuals attended. At the end of the meeting there were between 3000 and 4000 present.

A petition to the Queen was voted, the chief points in it being:—

1. Turnpike Tolls were complained of as being very heavy. Prayed that all Turnpike Trusts might be consolidated and placed under one management, which would regulate the distances that Gates were to be placed from each other.
2. New Poor Law bitterly complained of. Prayed that the old Law might be with certain modifications re-enacted.
3. Tithes to be as formerly, either in kind or in money, according to option.
4. County Stock greatly added to the burdens of the farmers.
5. Legal and magisterial fees were exorbitant.
6. Stipendiary Magistrates prayed for, to prevent any suspicions being attached to the administration of Justice. At present Magistrates were indiscriminately appointed, regard being taken only of the income of the

---

[1] N.B. The "Cambrian" gives the place of this meeting as "Carnfig," about a mile on the Llandilo road from Cross Hands, Carmarthenshire.

party appointed, and not of his qualifications to fill the office.
7. Assessed rental prayed for, also all tithes, local taxes, etc., should be charged on the land and not on the tenant.
8. Petitioners expressed themselves convinced that no good would be done the country by the existing Parliament, and prayed Her Majesty to exercise her prerogative, and dismiss it, and call another which would evince greater sympathy with the people.

When put to the meeting, every hand was held up enthusiastically in its favour, and on reversing the question not one appeared. After returning thanks to the chairman, Mr. J. Morgan, for his able conduct in the chair, and giving three hearty cheers for the Queen, they separated.

The same night Mr. Chambers' farm at Mansant was set on fire by the Rebeccaites. All the farm produce and outbuildings were apparently ignited simultaneously. A body of dragoons arrived there from Carmarthen at 11.20 o'clock, having galloped all the way; but they found they were, as usual, too late to be of service in preventing the conflagration. An intelligent non-commissioned officer of the detachment sent on this service, said that, on arriving on the spot, they found all but the dwelling-house enveloped in flames, which had reached such a height as to defy all human efforts to subdue them. From hence he could plainly discern the flames of the still burning ricks which had been set on fire on Saturday the 9th instant at Mr. Chambers' farms at Tynywern and Gellyglynog, and he described the scene as awful and painful in the extreme. Rebecca, having threatened to burn the house at Tynywern, some soldiers were also stationed there, but no attempt was made to carry the threat into execution. Mr. Chambers also had a valuable horse shot on Sunday night, the 10th instant, the one which had been rescued from the burning stable at Tynywern.

LLECHRYD WEIR was destroyed on the night of 13th September. An alarm had been given that it was Rebecca's intention to pull down a small weir near Felingigfran. Consequently the marines, about ten o'clock, marched down to protect the weir, and during their absence the Rebeccaites embraced the opportunity, and succeeded in demolishing Llechryd Weir. Though the weir had stood for ages, and braved many a mountain flood, yet it was destroyed in about fifteen minutes. There were about 300 Rebeccaites present. While the marines were returning from Felingigfran, the rearguard were three in number, two of whom were a little in advance; the third, who was behind, fell in with a party of Rebeccaites on a crossroad. He was asked if he had a musket. He said, "Yes." "Is it loaded?" "Yes." "Capped?" "Yes." "Take off the cap," Which was done. He was then marched off to a neighbouring public-house, treated to some ale, and discharged. He arrived at Cardigan about two hours after his comrades.

Llechryd Weir was the property of Thomas Lloyd, Esq., of Coedmore, held by a royal grant, and at this time leased to A. L. Gower, Esq., of Castle Maelgwyn.

Carregsawdde Gate, in the parish of Llangadock, was also destroyed on the same morning by a party of Rebeccaites, armed, as usual, with offensive weapons of every description. Instant death was threatened to the toll-collector if he dared to open the door which they had fastened on the outside, with instructions to two sentinels to guard. The gates and posts, toll-tablet and lamp were destroyed in the usual way, and the windows of the toll-house were smashed in. It was at first intended to pull down the toll-house, or set fire to it, with the inmates inside, but this was abandoned, supposing the military were not far off. By this party on the same night, and in the same parish, three other gates, Waunystradfeiris, Pontprenaneth, and Pontarllechan were destroyed for the third time.

17th September, Pontardulais Gate, or rather Bar, which had been erected to serve the purposes of a gate, was knocked down. On the night previous it had been watched with the most jealous vigilance, but 'Becca was too wary. The next night it was levelled.

It had been previously rumoured that for some weeks past a number of disaffected persons were in the habit of holding nightly meetings on various hills in Cilgerran parish, at which they were regularly trained in Rebecca's tactics, but for what purpose was a mystery, as there was not a single turnpike-gate in the parish. However, about midnight, on 18th September, the mystery was solved, by the march of a great number of men in disguise through Cilgerran village, well armed with saws, guns, etc., on their way to Porthyrhyd Gate,

A Petition to the Queen

about five miles from Llandovery, on the road to Lampeter. This gate was soon destroyed, leaving only about nine inches of the stumps of the posts above the ground. From this place they proceeded towards Dolau hirion Gate, about a mile from Llandovery, clearing as they passed every vestige of the posts of some bars which had fallen into disuse some years before. When they arrived at Dolau hirion Bridge, they waited for a short time, either for the purpose of taking rest, or to ascertain whether all was right. At the word given by their leader in the English language, they fell to work, and both gates shared a similar fate to that at Porthyrhyd. There were several houses near the gates, before which stood sentries with loaded guns to prevent the egress of the inhabitants. Several shots were fired into the toll-house, through the windows, which were thereby completely shattered. Next morning the thatched roof of a neighbouring cottage was observed to be strewn over with burnt wadding from the number of guns which had been fired.

A notice was fixed on the door to apprise the toll-collector that his gates were destroyed because the trustees had reerected some other gates, and if he or anyone else presumed to raise any new tolls at the place he should be shot.

The Rebeccaites then moved off along the road leading to Cilgerran, and soon disappeared. Mr. Richards, collector of the tolls, received a notice from 'Becca through the Post Office on the following morning, ordering him not to demand any more tolls at the gates which he had rented, otherwise his life would be endangered. The whole of Lord Paget's troop of 4th Light Dragoons was during the above occurrences snugly reposing only a mile distant from the scene of action.

On 21st September a party of Rebeccaites assembled and set fire to a house and premises near the Black Mountain, in the hamlet of Gwynfe, Llangadock, and the property of John Bevan, Esq. Dwelling-house and buildings were burnt down. The premises had only just been leased by a person in the neighbourhood, and it is reported the outrage was committed because the man had taken it *without the knowledge and consent* of the Duffryn Union. £100 was offered for such information as would convict the perpetrators.

The corn and hay in the haggard at Dolhaidd were set on fire on 22nd September.

The Law in Motion

First Appearance of Rebecca in Radnorshire. On 18th September a night attack was made on the turnpike-gate leading from Builth to Rhayader, about a quarter of a mile from the former place. The gate was taken away, and very much damaged, and the windows of the toll-house completely destroyed. If an alarm had not been given by some persons who were coming at a late hour from their work in the neighbourhood, serious damage would most likely have occurred.

A bailiff to Mr. James Thomas (Jeremy Genteel) of Llandilo, who, it would seem, was down on 'Becca's *black list* of the law, being in possession under an execution against a farmer living at Ffosgrech, Llanfynydd, was on 22nd September suddenly called to his account. This, not being satisfactory, he was himself levied upon under 'Becca's mandate—tied up hands and feet, and committed to the next common pound at Brechfa. There he lay till the dawn of next day, when 'Becca ordered his discharge from custody, on payment of a fee of 4d. to the pound-keeper (the ancient common law fee on releasing animals), and on making a morning's meal of the process of the law, and entering into his own recognizances to keep the peace towards all her children for twelve months. Sufferings and associations sometimes beget extraordinary sympathies, even in such as had been callous to merciless inflictions—even in the bosoms of bums; for the one in question became a strenuous advocate against cruelty to animals and solitary imprisonment!

About one o'clock on the morning of 29th September Rebecca's sister, Charlotte, with about 250 followers, presented themselves at the turnpike-gate at Cwmdwr, a short distance from Llanwrda (Carmarthen). They summoned the old woman who collected the tolls out of bed, and gave her the choice of removing her furniture out of the toll-house, or of allowing it to be burnt, as it was their intention to make a bonfire of the gate-posts and house. The articles of furniture were accordingly removed by the old woman and her son who lived with her, during which time the gate and posts were broken up sufficiently small to make the requisite firewood; which, being placed inside the house on the straw of the old woman's bed, were set on fire. The party then marched off to Llansadwrn village, where they purchased some gunpowder and flints from Mr. Davies, the shopkeeper, and with this fresh stock of ammunition they surrounded the Vicarage house, the residence of the Rev. J. Jones. He and his family were roused from their slumbers by a volley. This was followed by incessant striking at the door and a demand for the presence of Mr. Jones to speak to Miss Charlotte, as she had a particular message to convey to him from her sister Rebecca.

When Mr. Jones appeared she gave him the alternative of removing his furniture out of the Vicarage within ten minutes, that the house might be set on fire; or that he should pledge his word that he would not take into his possession a few fields which he had bought some months previous, and which adjoined the Vicarage; as it was contrary to 'Becca's law that he as a clergyman should hold any lands. Either the *barn* or the *Church*, but not *both*, was the peremptory fiat of Queen 'Becca; and backed, as her vicegerent was, by some hundreds of well-armed attendants, ready to perform her commands, Mr. Jones was compelled, as a matter of personal safety (not wishing to have his house burnt over his head) to comply with 'Becca's commands. He therefore engaged that the tenant who had occupied the fields should be allowed to retain possession of the same at a reduced rent, the amount of which was then stipulated. After having extorted these terms from the worthy vicar's just fears, the party left the place, not one of them being recognised.

The same night a body of the A division of the Metropolitan Police, under Inspector Tierney, succeeded in capturing two of the most daring characters in Carmarthen concerned in attacks on private property. The circumstances were as follows: A few nights previous, an attack had been made upon the Gwendraeth Iron Works, at Pontyberem, by a number of men. They surrounded the house between one and two o'clock in the morning; and having fired several shots, commenced battering at the door, demanding to have the managing clerk, Mr. Slocombe, brought out to them. His wife presented herself at an upstairs window, demanded who they were, and what they wanted with her husband. The answer of the leader was: "I am Rebecca, and we demand to see him instantly." The wife, however, firmly refused, stating that her husband was not there. Finding that they could not gain admission, they said, "Mr. Newman" (the proprietor of the works in whose house Mr. Slocombe resided) "has behaved well, and we will not hurt him, but if Mr. Slocombe is not out of the country within a week, we will make him a head shorter."

They then fired some more shots and made off.

Several persons who were present at the outrage had been forced from their houses to join them, and consequently information was given to the magistrates that the ringleaders were two men of notoriously bad characters, named John Jones, *alias* "Shoni Scuborfawr," a man about thirty years of age, who had been a prize-fighter, and David Davies, *alias* "Dai y Cantwr." Before they proceeded to Mr. Newman's house, they had met on the Bryn Dyleth Mountain, and having separated, they had gone by the way of Pontyberem and Trimsaran, pressing men to join them. After arriving at a house called the "Stag and Pheasant," they disguised themselves, and proceeded to Mr. Newman's. In consequence of this information, warrants were granted, and placed in the hands of Inspector Tierney, who, with eighteen men of the A division, and accompanied by a person who was familiar with the country, scoured the mountains, searching every public-house, and near the Five Roads they succeeded about midnight, 29th September, in apprehending David Davies. He was immediately handcuffed and conveyed in a cart to Llanelly, where he was placed in the custody of the military at the workhouse. The next day further efforts were made, and about eleven o'clock the ruffian Jones was apprehended at a place in the mountains called the Tumble. Both the prisoners were then conveyed to Carmarthen for examination.

On Monday, 2nd October, the two men were brought before the magistrates at the County Gaol, when several witnesses preferred charges against them. They were remanded till the following Thursday.

5th October, Thursday. The men were remanded till the following Monday.

Early on Sunday, 1st October, a farmhouse and buildings, the property of D. H. Harris, Esq., called Nantyranell, near Llanwrda, was razed to the ground by Rebecca. The tenant who rented it had made himself obnoxious to Rebecca's children, of whom there were about 150 engaged on the destruction of the house.

Monday, 2nd October. A proclamation was agreed to at a Privy Council held by Her Majesty, Queen Victoria, at Windsor Castle. It reads as follows:

By the Queen. Proclamation Victoria R.

Whereas in certain districts of South Wales, more especially in the counties of Pembroke, Cardigan, and Carmarthen, tumultuous assemblages of people, disguised, and armed with guns and other offensive weapons, have taken place by night, and outrages of the most violent description have been committed upon the lives and properties of divers of our subjects; and whereas in contempt of the restraints of law and order, these tumultuous assemblages have pulled down toll-gates, and have violently entered and destroyed toll-houses; and whereas they have also attacked the mansions of individuals, extorting from them sums of money by threats or by violence, and have destroyed by fire the hay, corn, and other property of divers of our subjects; we therefore have thought fit, by, and with the advice of our Privy Council, to issue this our Royal Proclamation; hereby strictly commanding all Justices of the Peace, Sheriffs, Under-Sheriffs, and all other Civil Officers whatsoever, that they do use their utmost endeavours to repress all tumults, riots, outrages, and breaches of the peace, and to discover, apprehend, and bring to justice the persons concerned in the riotous and wicked proceedings aforesaid, and we do strictly enjoin all our Liege Subjects to give prompt and effectual assistance to our Justices of the Peace, Sheriffs, Under-Sheriffs, and all Civil Officers in their endeavours to preserve the public peace; and as a further inducement to discover offenders, we do hereby promise and declare, *That any person or persons who shall discover and apprehend, or cause to be discovered and apprehended, the author's abbettors and perpetrators of any such incendiary fires as aforesaid, or of any such outrage upon the person of any of our subjects by which life shall have been sacrificed*, so that they or any of them shall, be duly convicted thereof, shall be entitled to the sum of **five hundred pounds** for each and every person who shall be so convicted, and shall receive *our most gracious pardon* for the said offence in case the persons making such discovery as aforesaid shall be liable to be prosecuted for the same, except he be the actual perpetrator of such outrage or of such incendiary fire as aforesaid.

And we do also promise and declare that any person or persons who shall discover and apprehend, or cause to be discovered and apprehended, the authors, abettors, and perpetrators of any such outrages, *other than those last above mentioned*, in the said counties, so that they or any of them may be duly convicted thereof, shall be entitled to the sum of **fifty pounds** *for each and every person who shall be so convicted*, and shall receive our most gracious pardon for the said offence in case the person making such discovery as aforesaid shall be liable to be prosecuted for the same.

Given at our Court at Windsor this 2nd day of October in the year of our Lord 1843 and in the seventh year of our reign.

God save the Queen.

Rebecca in London. The first week in October Mr. Hill, porter to the gate of the London University College (which crossed Gower Street, New Road, and which prevented carriages from passing along the front of the Hospital), received a letter signed "Rebecca." She declared it to be the intention of herself and others to remove the "obstruction" called a gate on the following night.

Mr. Hill, believing the matter a joke, took no notice of the incident, but to his surprise the following morning he was awakened by the night porter, who informed him that the gate had disappeared.

On examination it was found that the large padlock by which the gate was fastened had been broken and carried away, the gate itself had been filed off its hinges, taken into the college grounds, and hidden behind some shrubs.

The gate was replaced; but Mr. Hill received another letter, informing him that it was the intention of "Rebecca and her daughters" to effect its entire destruction. It is due to Rebecca to say that suspicion mainly rested on a number of the students themselves, as being the instigators of this proceeding, and the letters signed "Rebecca" were probably forgeries.

The Law in Motion

Rebecca on the Stage

Dolau Hirion Gates near Llandovery, were, for the second time, destroyed on 3rd October by a troop of 'Becca's daughters, who must have lain in ambush in an adjoining plantation during the whole of the night, waiting for the departure of the policeman and constables who guarded the gate. At dawn the policeman went home, leaving two constables near the place; he had scarcely arrived at his lodgings when the constables followed him, breathless with haste, stating that about 150 persons had commenced destroying the gates. The policeman immediately remounted his horse and galloped off into the midst of the gate-levellers, who had by this time completely destroyed the gates, and were unroofing the tollhouse. They, however, did not remain to complete their work, but scampered off as fast as their legs could carry them.

The policeman recognised two of the party, who were subsequently taken into custody.

The turnpike-gate placed by the Main Trust on the road from Llandovery to Trecastle, near the confines of the county, was destroyed the same night. Previous to its being destroyed, the party paid a visit to a farmer residing at Caecrin Mill, whom they threatened in the most awful manner, with 'Becca's extreme vengeance, unless he relinquished some law proceedings against a late tenant.

Cefn Llanddewi turnpike-gate (Breconshire), midway between Builth and Llandovery, was also levelled the same night and completely destroyed.

Public interest in Rebecca's doings had by this time risen to such a pitch that she was even dramatised.

On 4th October, at the Royal Amphitheatre, Liverpool, a new play was produced, entitled "*Rebecca and her Daughters.*" It, moreover, was declared to be a drama of "extraordinary interest!"

The bill was somewhat as follows:—

On Wednesday, ——, 1843, the performance will commence for the first time of an interesting drama entitled *Rebecca and her Daughters, or Paddy the Policeman.*

Sir Watkin Wiseacre (a Welsh Justice of the Peace)	Mr. T. Williams.
Captain Squibb, of the Ponty Puddle Yeomanry	Mr. Abbott.
Cornet Cracker	Mr. Blew.
Sir Henry Honeycomb (nephew to Sir Watkin)	Mr. Coe.
Taffy Tibbs, Head Constable of Ponty Puddle	Mr. Holloway.
Paddy Whack (a policeman of the A division No. 1, consequently first man in the force)	Mr. Fisher.
Lady Winterblossom (sister to Sir Watkin)	Mrs. Fife.
Belinda and Floranthe (her sisters)	Mrs. Coe and Mrs. Johnson.
Jenny Jones (their attendant)	Miss Fife.

PROGRAMME OF SCENERY, ETC.—Vigilance of the civil and military Authorities—£100 Reward for the apprehension of Rebecca, and £10 for each of her daughters—False alarm—Invincible courage of the Yeomanry—Arrival of the London Police in disguise—Paddy Whack undertakes to capture the delinquents—Admonition to the Constabulary—The Inspection—Mysterious appearance of Rebecca and her Daughters in the Glen of Llandilo at midnight—Trial before the Justice of the Peace—Happy Denouement.

On 7th October the outhouses and stables connected with Aberduar, Carmarthenshire (about six miles from Lampeter), the property of the Rev. Thomas Rees, were wantonly set on fire and totally consumed.

Three parts of the premises were almost simultaneously fired.

Mr. Rees had received several notices from "'Becca" because he had given a tenant notice to quit, without sufficient ground, in her ladyship's opinion, for his doing so.

On the same night (7th October) Mr. Thomas Thomas's house, Pantycerrig, near Llanfihangel Rhosycorn, Carmarthen, was attacked. A large quantity of butter and cheese and all the property the rebels could find were destroyed. This was done in revenge. Mr. Thomas had given evidence which led to the committal of David James Evans (his servant). The latter had entered his house and extorted money from him by threats.

On the morning of 9th October John Evans and John Lewis, two Sheriff's officers from Carmarthen, were sent to Tyrypound, in the parish of Llangunnor, to make a distress on the goods and chattels of William Philipp for £7 10s., being half a year's rent, due the previous September. They were attacked by about twenty-five of the 'Beccas, and beaten in a dreadful manner. The latter were all disguised, some with their faces blackened, and others wearing bonnets and gowns.

John Evans was compelled to go on his knees before them, and put the distresses and authority to distrain in the fire. He was then made to take his oath on the Bible, which one of them put in his hands, that he would never again enter the premises to make another distress. He was compelled to make use of the following words: "As the Lord liveth, and my soul liveth, I will never come here to make any distress again." After taking the oath, he was set free, and the two bailiffs returned to town.

After Cefn Llanddewi Gate had been destroyed on the 3rd, two policemen were detached from Brecon to guard the tollhouse and to prevent any further outrage. However, these two Guardians of the Peace, and the Pikes, found their avocation rather dry and insipid, and accordingly on the 9th retired to a house a short distance off, to have a drop of something wet and comfortable. The ever-watchful 'Becca immediately seized the opportunity afforded by their temporary absence to set fire to the house, and the whole building was consumed before the policemen or any others could render assistance towards extinguishing the flames.

Rebecca on the Stage

On 11th October about fifty of the A division of London Police, under Inspector Martin, arrived at Carmarthen, and also several companies of the 76th Regiment.

The same night a Sheriff's officer was in soft repose at a farm called Towy Castle, in the parish of Llandeveilog, where he was lawfully in possession under a Sheriff's warrant for £130. He was suddenly disturbed by the sound of a horse, which he at once guessed to be the signal of the approach of the lawless Rebecca. He hid himself under the bed, rolled up in a counterpane, using every effort in his power to prevent coming in contact with a lady of whom he had heard so much. But Rebecca insisted on an interview, which the poor man ultimately consented to, under the assurance that her ladyship would do him no harm if he but obeyed her injunctions. Staggering and trembling, he ventured to meet her. Rebecca greeted him most graciously, told him he was not to blame, urged him at once to depart and make the best of his way to Carmarthen, or else vengeance would overtake him. The alarmed bailiff immediately consented, and proposed making his way home through the fields, that way being as he stated, much shorter and more convenient. "Your convenience," said 'Becca, "is not to be consulted. You must go on the main road, that my daughters may see you go."

"Any way that will please you," said the officer; "only let me go!" and away he scampered as fast as he could.

The man who personated 'Becca had a horse's mane hanging down his back, and a large feather in his cap. All the members of the party were disguised and well armed, with guns, swords, and other destructive weapons. They saw the bailiff clear off the premises, and fired several shots after him, to make him quicken his pace.

They afterwards returned to Towy Castle, and wished to take away the whole of the property, but Mrs. Phillipps, the landlady, begged of them not to do so, as the whole would be settled in a few days. Rebecca replied that unless the business was settled to her satisfaction, she would pay them another visit.

About this time Rebecca commenced the Radnorshire and Montgomeryshire circuits. She began on the Monday night with Llangurig Gate, which, though actually in the county of Montgomery, is yet on the borders of Radnorshire, and situated about twenty-three miles from Aberystwyth.

On 11th October three other gates were broken down and demolished at Rhayader, in Radnorshire. They were Rhayader Old Gate, the Cwmglyn Gate, and the Cross Lane Gate. The destruction of the Rhayader Gates was attended with all the pomp and paraphernalia of Rebeccaism. Her ladyship, dressed in full costume, was attended by about 200 well-mounted followers, with a due proportion of horn-blowing and firing of guns.

A most wanton act of incendiarism was committed on 12th October on the farm of Penllwynys, near Llanddarog, Carmarthenshire. It was the property of Mr. Pugsley, and occupied by a Mr. Thomas. A large quantity of corn was consumed, and had not the inhabitants of the neighbourhood exerted themselves in extinguishing the fire, the whole of the premises would have been burnt to the ground.

The same night an attack was made on the house of R. P. Beynon, Esq., St. Clears, one of the magistrates of the county. A party of between 200 and 300 persons, with horns and guns, and disguised in various ways, went to the house of a labouring man named James Thomas. This man had some time previous lost an arm by an accident, and had since been chargeable to the parish. Knocking loudly at the door, the Rebeccaites aroused the inmates. The wife, who first answered the summons, exhibited much alarm. They told her there was no cause for apprehension, for they came as friends, and thinking she and her husband had long enough suffered from poverty, they had provided a better dwelling for them, and were come to convey them to it. They then, without paying any regard to remonstrances, packed up the furniture and effects in the house, and placed them in a cart they had brought with them for the purpose. Having made the man and his wife get in also, they carried them to the Pwlltrap Toll-house, which had been unoccupied since the recent destruction of the gate. There they deposited their load and passengers, and formally installed them in possession of the premises, requiring of them only that they should remain there and not take toll of any person. They then left their bewildered tenant to settle himself in his new habitation, and proceeded to the house of the Mr. Beynon. After shouting and making a considerable noise, they fired into his bedroom, and threw several large stones through the windows of the adjoining bedroom. It fortunately happened that Mr. Beynon was not at home, for on his return he found eleven slugs lodged in various parts of his bedroom. They also affixed to his door the following notice:—

> I beg that Rebecca Gav Posesion to James John of the House that was formerly Belong to Pwlltrap Gate, and if any Person will com and Throw him out, Rebecca will and her Children will remember him in future time. The First will come that there shall be drag between 4 horses —Rebecca and her Children.

The following day a similar notice, with the sum of fourpence, was placed under the door of the Crier of Bethlehem Chapel in the neighbourhood, with a note commanding him to publish it in the usual manner on the next Sunday (the 15th). James Thomas and his wife remained in possession of the premises for some time, no clue being found for the detection of those who placed them there.

Twenty-one London Police officers arrived at Carmarthen on Sunday, 15th October. They were divided into sections among the military throughout the entire county.

Some Threatening Letters

Mr. Kynaston, of Blaencorse, received a threatening letter on 15th October, of which the following is a copy:

> To Mr. F. Keniston, Blaencorse, nr. St. Clears, Carmarthenshire.
>
> Sir,
>
> I am known by the name of Rebbecka, I have purpose to visit many places and persons, whenever and with whoever there is injustice; untill we shall the world plain: *Sir* I am well acquainted of all persons in all parts of the Kingdom and I have heard that you, Sir, have not made justice with John and Ann David at your yearly settlement. You do not consider that the times has been so bad and low prises for everything that the poor people could not make up the money which they promise. Now I have consider that Justice is for you to have all that they made of the cows and *no more*.
>
> You should give them the cows this following year. Hoping the times will come better in steed of Driving the poor people out Door with short notice therefore I do hereby give you notice that without you shall give the said persons all their owns The 2 calf pigs and all furniture I shall in few nights come to visit you, and you may depend that the best way for you to take notice of this Because I have got the world in my hand to do Justice Justice Justice. Your beloved friend, Rebbecka.
>
>   Neibourhood and Kingdom, October 13, '43.

This characteristic letter needs a word of explanation. Some time previously Mr. Kynaston leased some cows to a person named in the letter, and upon his becoming indebted in about £20, Mr. Kynaston applied to the surety, who was a relative of Davies, for payment. At the request, however, of the surety, he obtained from Davies some furniture and other things as security for his debt.

Some Threatening Letters

About 11 p.m. on 14th October a lawless mob, consisting of from fifty to sixty persons, assembled at Blackpool Weir (in Pembrokeshire), the property of the Baron and Baroness de Rutzen, which they entirely demolished, but not without considerable difficulty in consequence of its strength. They were occupied from eleven at night until four in the morning, during the time keeping watch over the old man in a cottage adjoining. The latter was ordered with threats not to make his appearance. As usual, no clue was left by which to trace the depredators.

Arrest of one of the Rebecca Leaders in Carmarthenshire. On 16th October four of the Metropolitan Police, led by Jones, a Llandovery Police officer, arrested a leader of the Rebeccaites named John Jones. The latter was a farmer living at Danygarn, near Llangadock. He was taken into custody, under a warrant granted by David John Lewis, and Lewis Lewis, Esqs., for sending a letter to Mr. Thomas Williams, auctioneer. The letter threatened to deprive him of his life if he refused to give up the title-deeds of a small farm which he had purchased from John Jones. Unless Rebecca's request was immediately acceded to, Mr. Williams should be dealt with much worse than she had dealt with the Rev. William Jones of Llansadwrn.

The following day John Jones was committed to take his trial at the next gaol delivery, and was sent in custody of the police, accompanied by an escort of dragoons, to Carmarthen Gaol.

The haggard of Mr. Henry Thomas, of the White Lion public-house, in the village of Llanddarog, about eight miles from Carmarthen, was wantonly set on fire by a party of Rebeccaites, and entirely destroyed on 19th October.

The same night (19th October) the "Crossvaen" turnpike-gate on the road between Llantrissant and Cardiff, was removed, and taken entirely away. The toll-collector stated that the deed was done between 11 p.m. and 5 a.m. She heard no noise during the night. It was supposed that the gate must have been taken some distance, and either thrown into a coal-pit, or burnt in a lime-kiln. A request had previously been made for the removal of the gate, but the authorities of the Trust had declined, though there was reasonable ground for such a demand.

The following was received that week by a toll-collector at Llanddowror:—

Habe omnes

The Days of Vengeance!!!
$$\overline{\wedge}+$$

*By blood and fire Christ strikes the blow,
And London falls like Jericho:
Behold the monsters die around,
Whose grave-diggers may not be found.
    Erin go Bragh
Pour Dieu et mon Droit.
O'Connell shines some people say,
Who admits none, except they pay*

The Piper.

To the Toll-Collector at the Turnpike-Gate, West Side, near Llanddowror, Carmarthen.

The neighbourhood of Brechfa was thrown into a state of alarm in consequence of the farmhouse of Gwarygraig having been found on fire on 21st October. The farm in question was the property of Mrs. Nicholls, and the whole of the outhouses, together with the dwelling-house, which was uninhabited, were entirely consumed. The act was supposed to be one of revenge because Mrs. Nicholls had caused the goods of the late tenant to be distrained for the arrears of rent.

The same night the farm of Tynymynydd, near Penbank, in the neighbourhood of Llandilo, was also discovered to be on fire, and the dwelling-house and outhouses entirely destroyed. A party of the 4th Light Dragoons, stationed at Llandilo, was immediately called out. The soldiers speedily repaired to the scene of the outrage, but no clue had been left as to the origin of the fire, or the supposed author of the mischief. Both fires, however, were supposed to have been the work of an incendiary.

25th October. Queen Victoria issued a commission on the 11th instant, consisting of Thomas Frankland Lewis, Robert Henry Clive, and William Cripps, Esqs., to inquire into the state of the laws which regulated turnpike roads, highways, and bridges in South Wales. On the 25th the first and last named were at Carmarthen, with their Secretary, George Kettilby Richards.

Some Threatening Letters

On the same night the turnpike-gate at Sutton Weeks, near Chewstoke, Somerset, was taken down, carried to a considerable distance, and thrown into a farmer's yard.

The tablet of tolls was also removed from the front of the toll-house, and placed over the door of a shoemaker living some distance away.

The following are a few of Rebecca's letters sent during that week:—

To Mr. George Wood at Whitland.

Sir,

For as much as I have heard your careter in this neighbourhood, I therefore take my pleasure to write you these few lines, hoping that it will have an effect on you, as you are an agent under Mr. Yelverton you thought yourself a monk in Parish, but I mean to reduce your little, hearing that the poor and hungry are calling sometimes at your door, but they are turn off like dogs without having nothing, and therefore you are a hard gentleman to be amongst us Welshmen, for we usually give to the poor when calling for at our doors in a work. It is a pity that such a farm as Whittland a lett in the following manner, having a good tender by trustworthy persons this year to Rent the said farm by a fair Articles, but you are there and your laws are so strict nobody can put up with it and therefore such a large farm are let out to by holders that there a labourer might not have a days work for his good through the whole year. A parcel of idle fellows are living there a agent a keeper, underkeeper that there is no good to the rich man nor poor of them in a word that you are to quit the neighbourhood both of you George Wood, thomas Anthony and Joseph thos within four days after this note at your peril there is about nine hundred years since an imposed have been on Whittland before at the time of Cromwell was set to fire that time and if you disobey the letter it shall be same again. I do not care to call 300 of my children at the same time to level the place in less than an hour time Either by powder or digging or shotting or put the place to fire—fail not at your peril for the sake of your master.

Youngest Rebecca in Correspondent with the old one.

To Miss Yelverton of Whitland I therefore give you notice after read your carrater in the neighbourhood that you doest not good to others nor yourself. You living here and your God in dublin and it therefore cannot be good on you the best plan for you to go along and live with God it will be more comfortable I will take of your land I mean to rent tanybont to some person that are without a place to do him good fail not at your Peril to quit the place within a four days to Ireland take you that with

Rebecca.

To Thos. Wm now living at forge—take Notice Sir in consequence that you quite an high farmer retaining three farms in your hands you have heard the law Sir, towards such a person I may quash a persons that disobey the laws of Rebecca because she want very much to reform things that are out of the way you lately living at Bryngwyllin and holding the fallage the three farms at the same time. Brave fellow that you are and some are without one you are to fall into the laws of Rebecca immediately within four days after this note at your Peril of losing your goods.

Rebecca is here learning you.

The Special Commission for the trial of the Rebecca prisoners was opened at Cardiff on the 26th October, before the Honourable Sir John Gurney, Knight, the Hon. Sir Cresswell Cresswell, Knight, and John Homfray, Esq., Llandaff House, High Sheriff.

John Hughes, for demolishing Pontardulais Toll-house, and destroying the house of William Lewis, was found guilty, but recommended to mercy. Sentence, *Twenty years' transportation.*

David Jones and *John Hugh*, for aiding at Pontardulais, found Guilty—*seven years' transportation.*

William Hughes—The Bill was ignored.

Margaret Morgan (25) 6 months in prison.

Rees Morgan (23), 12 months in prison. *John Morgan*, 12 months in prison. (These would have had hard labour in addition, if they had not been of "good character.")

Morgan Morgan (57) and *Esther Morgan* (63), the father and mother, were discharged on their own recognizances of £50 each, to appear and receive judgment whenever called upon. These were tried for the attack on Captain Napier to prevent the apprehension of Henry Morgan.

Lewis Davies (31), captured by Mr. Chambers at Pontardulais, pleaded guilty, and was discharged on his own recognizances of £50, to appear when called upon.

On 3rd November an incendiary fire took place on a farm occupied by a man named Evans. The farm, called Cefnmystrich, belonged to Lady Hamlyn Williams, and was situated in the parish of Merthyrbach, near Newchurch.

A stack of barley in the centre of the haggard was set on fire. There were about twenty stacks in the haggard, and had it not been for a person fortunately passing at the time, and giving the alarm to the farmer and his family, the whole of the haggard would inevitably have been consumed.

Rebeccaites at Rhayader

Sergeant Shew, of the A division of London Police, who had been sent down to Rhayader, observing a little more stir than usual on 2nd November, and seeing groups of people standing about, was induced to take measures, in case of an outbreak, and the laws being violated. He accordingly called up six special constables who had been sworn in *pro tem*, to act during the night, in case of any violence.

Between two and three o'clock the following morning, when the moon had sunk beneath the horizon, Sergeant Shew received intelligence that a large body of men had attacked, and were levelling the North Gate, and on his running up to the place, he found that the gate had been taken down, hewn to pieces, and the fragments strewn around. Rebecca and her children had disappeared, having proceeded across the fields to the East Gate, for the purpose of avoiding the town, through which they must otherwise have passed on their way thither; thus at least showing their intimate knowledge of the country, which anyone knowing the *locale* will admit is a very difficult one.

The sergeant proceeded to the East Gate with the utmost speed, but arrived too late. It was utterly demolished, and the fragments were lying about as at the North Gate. He, however, obtained some clue as to the direction Rebecca and her progeny had taken, and with the six men under his charge, came up with them at the "Bear" public-house. One of the special constables went close to the Rebeccaites, and was cautioned by one of them in an undertone "to keep off." Another of the constables, named Morris, then went up to them, when a musket was presented to his breast. Morris immediately cried, "For God's sake, don't kill a poor fellow!"

Another of the constables pressed forward in the endeavour to recognise some of them, but he was struck to the ground by one of the Rebeccaites with a musket, and received a violent blow across the shoulders.

After this melee the Rebeccaites marched forward four deep, with a slow and measured pace, keeping step as regularly as any skilled men, and it was observed by some eyewitnesses that every man appeared to submit and be guided by a leader.

Sergeant Shew said to them, "My men, I hope you will not fire." But no answer was returned. They proceeded round the "Lion and Castle" public-house, which was undergoing some repairs; there was accumulated a quantity of stones. The road being rather narrow round the corner, and the party marching four abreast, one might expect some confusion, but they marched in perfect order. Those at the front and rear bore muskets, which were loaded with ball and slugs. The men who marched in the centre fired off as many as ninety blank cartridges. This took place in the North Street.

The sergeant and constables continued to follow the Rebeccaites, imagining that they were about to proceed to the New Gate on the Aberystwyth road, but through not being close enough to them, and owing to the darkness of the night, they lost sight of them soon afterwards. The rebels went to the mill kept by Mr. Jones Harvey, who had rendered himself obnoxious to them, in consequence of his having allowed a gate which belonged to him to be erected in place of one which had been taken down by a party of Rebeccaites. They called him by name, saying that "they would forgive him that time for allowing the gate to be erected at Llangwing," but told him never to do so again, "or they would pull his castle down to the ground." They then fired several times, and soon after disappeared.

Their cunning was evident in the destruction of the Wye Bridge Gate or West Gate. The constables stationed at this place had not been there long before two decently clad women came up and informed Wilding and James that the Rebeccaites were at the New Gate. Unfortunately the ruse succeeded too well, for the constables left the spot, and immediately a party of Rebeccaites came up to the gate, a few of whom were placed along the bridge as a guard, whilst the others demolished the gate and house, throwing the portions of wood into the river which runs near the spot.

The following particulars were gathered from the keepers: *The North Gate.* This gate was kept by John Francis, and was situated on the old road to Llanidloes. The distance from the town was not a quarter of a mile, and the locality was by no means lonesome, there being a number of houses adjacent. The gate-keeper stated that about two o'clock in the morning he and his wife were awakened by hearing persons tapping at his window, and soon after they heard a person speak as through a mouthpiece: "Lie still, or death will be your doom." Afterwards he heard a person say, "Work away, little wenches," and then told Francis if he took toll again, they would not only take the gate down, but also the house. The party, after firing several guns, departed.

The East Gate was on the road from Penybont to Rhayader, and close to the latter place. The tolls were received by an old woman named Sarah Rees, and the toll-house was tenanted by her and her daughter.

They stated that about three in the morning they were awakened by hearing a person say, "Lie still in bed; we don't wish to injure you or the house, but we have come to hew down this old gate." They then heard saws and axes at work, and a person called out, "Work away, my little wenches." Afterwards addressing Rees, the same voice said, "Don't be frightened, we won't injure you; it is only the little wenches hewing chips against the door." In about a quarter of an hour they had completed the act of demolition, when one of them said, "Take notice, if a gate should again be put up in this place, we will take the house down level with the turnpike road!" The tablet of tolls was also taken down from the front of the house, and hewn into small strips. After the gang had discharged several firearms, they departed.

The West Gate was adjoining the Wye Bridge, and situated about the same distance as the other two from the centre of the town. There were several houses near the spot, and therefore it was by no means in a lonely situation. The work of demolition began here about four o'clock. The only débris left was a large heap of stones on the spot where the toll-house formerly stood. The gate-keeper, in consequence of information received, had removed his family from the toll-house, but he had not removed his furniture, although strongly urged to do so by the men who assisted him. The furniture was found underneath the ruins of the house, but considerably injured.

Rebeccaites at Rhayader

The gate-keeper stated his loss to be only a few pounds, as he had not anything of particular value upon the premises. Although the night was dark and foggy, the dress which the Rebeccaites wore was pretty distinct. They all had their faces blackened, and the lower portion was muffled up. They had on mostly dark-coloured bonnets, but a few wore hats; a short cloak was thrown around the shoulders, and petticoats hung from their waists. Each man was well armed, those in front having muskets, and those in the centre carrying gun, sword, or hatchet. The men in the rear were supplied with a gun each.

Sergeant Shew said that in the North Street he placed his men across the road, for the purpose of endeavouring to intimidate the Rebeccaites from proceeding farther, but they turned off to the right, walking in close column. Each man who was stationed in front presented his musket towards the constables ready to discharge it, whilst those in the centre were continually firing blank cartridges over the heads of the constables as they passed them.

It was fortunate, as it turned out, that the special constables were not provided with firearms; had they made any attempt to capture anybody, the rebels were determined to fire those guns, which were loaded, and from their being so well organised there is no doubt that the consequences would have been fatal. There were not less than 200 rioters assembled at the West Gate, three bands of them having apparently met there.

A detachment of the 4th Dragoons, under Captain Arkwright, arrived at Rhayader from Carmarthen on the morning of 4th November.

General Brown, the commanding officer, arrived the following morning, and proceeded to make inquiries. Two men were taken up, but nothing being elicited to warrant their committal, they were held to bail to appear again, if any charge should be preferred against them.

It being ascertained that the foot-soldiers would be more effective than the horse, the dragoons were replaced by a number of the 7th Fusiliers on 5th November. They were stationed in the old Vicarage House. The town and neighbourhood were by that time quiet, but a number of the London Police who had been sent down by the Secretary of State, were out every night, patrolling the town and the surrounding parts.

On Monday night, 6th November, twenty-five men were taken prisoners in the neighbourhood of Aberdaugleddyf, and they were confined in the market-place, under the charge of the military. The leader in the attacks on the toll-gates was there, having been lured through the promise of a prize (gift) by the Queen's Proclamation. He turned traitor, and accused his companions in evil-doing, and gave in the names of thirty-four.

The cavalry rode to Aberdaugleddyf from Cardigan to help the county officers.

The following important address from the men under sentence of transportation was about this time freely distributed through the country:—

To the public generally, and to our neighbours in particular.

We John Hughes, David Jones, and John Hugh who are now confined in Carmarthen, having been found guilty of the attack made on the Toll-gate at Pontardulais, and on the persons appointed to defend it and having been sentenced to penal servitude across the sea desire, and we call seriously on others to take note from us to stop their wild acts before they fall to a similar judgment.

We are guilty and have been sentenced to suffer, when hundreds have escaped. Let them all take heed lest they be led again to spoil possessions Government or personal, and oppose the force of the law, because they are certain to be caught, and they will be brought to destruction.

We are but in prison now—in a week or two we shall have been transported as if felons, to be slaves to strangers in a strange land. We in the flower of our manhood must leave our pleasant homes to live and work with slaves of the worst type, and to be looked upon as thieves.

Friends, neighbours, all—but especially young men, Keep away from night meetings. Beware of doing injustice, and fear the anger of the Judge.

Think what we *must* do, and what you *may have to suffer* before you do what we did.

If you would be peaceful, and live again like honest men, through God's blessing, you can expect success, and we, exiled and miserable creatures may thank you for the mercy of the Crown—for on no other ground but *your* good behaviour will mercy be shown unto us or others who may fall into our almost hopeless situation.

Signed John Hughes.
David Jones.
His mark x John Hugh.
Witness John B. Woods, Governor.

Cardiff Gaol,
Nov. 21st, 1843.

A Table of Grievances

The following is a *Verbatim et Literatim* copy of a Statement of Grievances sent to the Commissioners of inquiry held at Carmarthen on the 7th November, 1843:—[1]

Evan Edwards, David Graville, and John White were called in and examined as follows:

Where do you live?

Evan Edwards. "We all live in the parish of Llandeveilog in this County.

David Granville. "I have brought a statement which I beg to have read." (The same was delivered in, and read as follows):

Statement of Grievances made in a Committee of the Parishioners of the Parish of Llandeveilog county of Carmarthen October 31st 1843, viz. 1st Causes, 2nd Signs, 3rd Treatment.

1st. *Causes.*

Bad Government, before King Henry VIII £10 per cent of the land was consecrated to maintain the poor and religion, but at his time some of it sold and some given to relations and friends; and again a law made to mend the wrong of King Henry VIII in the reign of William IV in part for the same purpose.

Injustice and ungodliness of some of County rulers.

2nd. *Signs.*

1. No hear at Parliament.
2. Public meetings in several places in England Manchester, Birmingham, Bristol etc. and some in Wales, Monmouth and Glamorgan etc.

---

[1] Report of Commissioners, "Rebecca Riots," pp. 110, 111, 112

A Table of Grievances

3. Nocturnal Meetings—some in England, Scotland but multitude in Wales.
4. Pulling down Gates, destroying plantations burnings robberies, loss of lives, and some on the way to transportation.

3rd. *Treatment.* Something like as under:—

1. High Rents, some sensible, some not.
2. Tithe. It is now thrice as much as it was 35 or 40 years ago, and has been very expensive and troublesome. Summer before last, they called a meeting to put it in one parish under the new law; and about thirteen of the higher class of the parishoners meet that morning to hold a committee to consider the same first, and agreed that from £500 to £550 yearly was a great sum for it; but when we appeared at the meeting £700 was the lowest sum and no more; and after conversing a little, we took it for that enormous sum for fear that we should get it worse again, and that was true; said sum increased to £756 before we leave the room; in that state it is since, and it will be better to be as it is than for us to have our corn valued according to London markets. Tithing-man offer it for £500 between 10 and 12 years ago. The above sum is enough to maintain the poor and religion without a church-rate. The vicar receive only £11"13"4 from the tithe.

   1st. If Tithe to maintain Church and poor.

   2nd. And to be reduced £30 per cent.

4th. *Poor Law.*

1. Overseers to gather and pay all.
2. This to be done under directions of Guardians.
3. No separation of husband and wife.
4. Bastardy clauses better under old law.
5. Free liberty on Lord's day etc. for religious purposes.
6. Chaplain not wanted in or near towns.
7. Visiting Workhouse paupers gratis as others.
8. Passing accounts in parish meetings.

5th. County Stock.

1. To separate it from the Poor Rate.
2. Officers for collecting the Rate.
3. As ratepayers had to pay for making the rate.
4. As ratepayers had to pay the rate.
5. As ratepayers had to pay for collecting the rate.
6. Justice to be under the control of the ratepayers.
7. Quarterly accounts of money expended.

6th. *Gates, Bars, and Chains.*

1. Unlawfully to be removed.
2. Letting each separately and annually.
3. Sum collected be expended on roads which it clears.
4. People employed, being parishoners, which road passes.
5. All manure free of toll.
6. Cart, one horse 4d.; horse 1d.; ass ½d.; carriages as before.
7. Toll once a day.
8. Free for religion.
9. Magistrates not to be Trustees of Roads.
10. Quarterly accounts of money collected and expended in each Trust.

7th. *General Highway Act.* Very well make—cannot be better—cruelty before—much afraid that some bad person will offer to alter this good law again; we done our duty now at half expense.

7th. *Corn Law.* Repealed two or three years ago for trial; no sliding scale.

8th. *General Act.* Reformed; no local Act nor bye-laws at all.

9th. *Income Tax.* No income to farmers and county tradesmen in present years; but outgoings all on many, and more than that on some.

10th. *Butter and Cheese.* By 36 Geo. III Cap. 86 S 7 deemed good for farmers etc. to be repealed, and like the following instead—

> And every diaryman, maker, dealer, or seller of butter shall repack in any such vessel or vessels as aforesaid, Provided such vessel or vessels being of the same construction as

aforesaid and likewise such vessel or vessels deemed well and good repacking the same on pain of forfeiting the butter and vessel so repacked.

11th. *Magistrates' Fees.* Few we can get to sign a single assessment etc. under 2s. 6d.; when overseer, surveyor etc. must travel many days in every three months of the year for nothing in the world, for serving the same, and when electing Member to Parliament or some county or parish officer as high constable, guardian, overseer, surveyor, etc. and if some one now and then, that are poor etc. meet some of the magistrates at their petty sessions to have a discharge of a horse, or a dog, or the like, such thing will be for us as a sort of a plague, continued for a long time, and to many families for their whole lives, and can reckon ourselves as already sold to Mr. Gooch, cotton plantation Cashawshire, South Carolina. To remedy this etc. etc. a vote by ballot is so very desirable at this time of our most liberal and gracious Queen Victoria.

12th. *Mortmain Act.* That it will be beneficial for the comonalty to repeal as much of that Act as will enable a Devisor of being capable by his last Will and Testament to give and bequeath out of real property, annually, as much as £1 to £20 or £30 towards education of poor children, or for Bible or Missionary Society, or to be distributed among poor people (without expense as in other causes) of a city town, borough, or village, parish, hamlet or hamlets connected with parish, church, chapel, or meeting house of any denomination. Requested that this be stated before the noble Commissioners of her most Excellent Majesty.

13th. *Rural Police Constables.* We are willing to take oath to preserve peace in our neighbourhood and county to the utmost of our ability and same expense.

14th. *Pensarn Chain on a by-road.*

15th. *Workmen on road, Steward, Agent, Tithe, petition.*

16th. *Barracks.*

Some remarks from Scripture:—

1st. Henry on Nehemiah Chap. 2 Verse 2 and 3 sorrow of heart.

2nd. Henry on Ecclesiastes Chap. 3 Verse 16. Place of righteousness and judgment.

- 3rd. Henry on 1 Kings Chap. 12, Rehoboam refusing Elders' council.
- 4th. Henry on Proverbs Chap. 10, V. 9 Walketh uprightly, God will guard us.
- 5th. Henry on Isaiah Chap. 60. V. 17 and 18, Officers peace, Exactors righteous.
- 6th. Henry on Romans, Chap. 13 V. 1 to 7. Duties to Magistrates and State Officers 8–11 Love fulfilling the Law.

Cwmtoyddur Hill Gate, situated about 7½ miles from Rhayader, was totally destroyed on 7th November, about twelve o'clock, by a party of Rebeccaites, about a hundred in number. They levelled it to the ground, and broke several panes of glass in the toll-house. They then separated, discharging their guns as they passed along the road. They were dressed *à la femme*, wearing petticoats, cloaks, and bonnets.

On 7th November one of the parties concerned in the destruction of the Parcymorfa and Fishguard Gates (11th September) laid information against about thirty of the persons engaged in that affair. Accordingly the London Police officers stationed at Fishguard, and a troop of dragoons effected the capture of the persons accused.

The latter were examined by the magistrates, at Fishguard, when they were committed to the next Assizes.

William Owen (the lady Rebecca on that occasion), James Gwynne, and Thomas Gwynne were allowed bail of £100 each, and two sureties in £50 each, and the remaining twenty-three in £50 each, and two sureties of £25 each.

About 4.30 o'clock on the morning of 14th November the outhouses of a farm called Llwynffynongro, in the parish of Llanegwad, about two miles from Brechfa, were set on fire, and the whole entirely destroyed. Luckily the dwelling-house escaped the fire, in consequence of the wind blowing from the north. The farmhouse was unoccupied, but a new tenant was expected to take possession on the following day. Evidently 'Becca and her daughters thought proper to have recourse to this mode of revenge upon the incoming tenant, because he became the successor of another who had given his landlord notice of quitting, and accordingly left the place on the 29th September previous. The outhouses were set on fire in four different places, and some person in the neighbourhood passing at the time saw a man with a light in his hand on the premises, but passed on, naturally thinking he was the new tenant.

A toll-collector, Thomas Jackson by name, in the employ of Mr. Bullin, was brought before the Neath Petty Sessions about the middle of October.

Lewis Lewis, a farmer, charged him with having, at the West Gate, Aberayon, exacted full toll three times in one day for one horse and cart, contrary to the Act of Parliament.

Mr. Bullin, who was unable to be present owing to a committee meeting of the Bridgend Turnpike Trusts, sent a message to the magistrates, saying he had instructed his collector to take tolls in the manner complained of, because he thought he was legally entitled to them. If, however, the magistrates should rule otherwise, he would willingly submit to their decision, and give directions to his collector not to make similar charges in future.

The clauses of the Act (General Turnpike Laws) which related to the case were the 11th, 12th, and 13th sections of the 1st Wm. IV, which was an Act passed to amend the Act 7th and 8th George IV for the more effectually repairing and otherwise improving the roads in the county of Glamorgan.

Section 11 enacted "That no more than one full toll in any one day (to be computed from 12 o'clock at night till the following midnight) shall be demanded or taken for, or in respect of, the same horse, or horses drawing the same vehicle; or for the same horse, horses, etc., laden or unladen, not drawing, passing and repassing through any of the Gates along the line of the said roads."

Section 12 repealed the provisions of the 7th and 8th George IV respecting stage coaches and other vehicles.

Section 13 enacted that "stage coaches and other vehicles should pay every time of passing, but not more than twice in any one district."

Eventually Mr. Bullin consented to concede the point, provided the magistrates inflicted a nominal penalty only. The magistrates, upon condition of Mr. Bullin's refunding all the expense attending the prosecutors, including the expenses of witnesses, on this occasion inflicted the nominal fine of one shilling.

On 20th November the Mardy Toll-Gate, within five miles of Corwen, on the Holyhead road, in the parish of Llangwm

(Denbigh), and belonging to the Bala Trust, was entirely taken away. The posts were parted with a saw, and a note put under the door informing the toll-keeper that the breach was committed by Sister Rebecca, with a caution against placing another in that neighbourhood.

Early on the morning of 10th December Waunystradfeiris Gate, in the parish of Llangadock, was destroyed, and the windows of the toll-house were smashed in. The act was daring in the extreme, as it was committed within a few hundred yards of Llangadock, where a detachment of the 4th Light Dragoons and the Metropolitan and the Rural Police were stationed at the time. This gate had been destroyed four times, and the old toll-house had been set on fire, and afterwards razed to its foundation; but both had been re-erected at great expense to the local Trust, only to be destroyed again.

6th December, 1843. Examination of Francis McKiernin and George Laing, at Llanelly, by the Commissioners.[2] (The Right Hon. Thomas Frankland Lewis in the chair.)

"What are you?—(Mr. McKiernin) I am a mailcoach proprietor from here to Swansea, and a coach proprietor from Swansea to Carmarthen and back. My great grievance is the tolls upon the road from Llanelly to Swansea and back; a four-horse coach pays 16s. for 11 miles."

"What is your fare?—3s. outside and 5s. inside. I very frequently go with the mail, and I do not take 18d. Mr. Laing is a carrier living near to me; he goes two days a week, but he is obliged to give it up because the tolls are so heavy. If I had not the contract for the mail, I could not keep it on, but that frees me the tolls but I have my mileage to pay the same, 1½d. a mile, and I am allowed £59 a year for conveying the mail to Swansea and back."

"Are the turnpikes free?—Yes, otherwise my gates would amount to £164 12s. 6d. at 8s. per day. The first gate is 1s. and the next 1s. 6d. Then there is the Lougher Bridge, which I should say of all things ought to be made a County Bridge. Then you pass over that Bridge, and you do not go more than

---

[2] Report of Commissioners, "Rebecca Riots," pp. 358, 359.

A Table of Grievances

three or four hundred yards before you get to the other Gate. Things are so bad that unless the tolls are reduced, the other coach I have I must give up."

"Are there any other tolls besides these, which you feel?—I have nothing to say of other tolls, save and except that I have to say that the roads are not kept, in this part of the district, adequate to what they are in other districts. From here to Lougher the Kidwelly line of road, the lower road, is not kept in a state equal to what the roads are in the interior parts of the county."

"Suppose the new road was finished across the Gwendraeth, do you think that the other road might be left to the parishes to repair, and left out of the Turnpike Trusts?—I think it might."

"What do you think of the other road that comes from Carmarthen to Kidwelly by Minke Gate; do you think that could be left to the parishes?—I do not think it could up to Minke, but it might from Minke to here, for nothing is done to it except from Minke to Carmarthen. Mr. Saunders takes good care that one-half the money collected in that district is expended on that part of the road. From the part where his own estate is, there is more material broken and piled by the side of the road in different places than there is in all the rest of the district together; there is nothing done on this side; he appoints his own Surveyor and draws the money, and manages as he thinks proper."

"You know the upper part of the road between Carmarthen and Minke, and Llangadar?—Yes."

"You say that all the roads in that part are much better repaired than they are in the lower part?—Yes, ten to one."

"And less incommodated with turnpikes?—Yes. There is no Gate from Llangadar to Carmarthen, but Mr. Saunders takes care to put Gates there. From here to Pembrey, I am given to understand, by a man who worked for him, that Mr. Saunders put a Bar after the parish of Pembrey and the borough of Llanelly had joined together to make the road. The parish of Pembrey have spent nearly £1100 in making that road. There were three Bars taken away by the lessees of the tolls, by the man who has caused all the row in this country, that is William Lewis."

"Has he been often summoned?—I have had him several times before the magistrates, and I have had him fined, but the magistrates never inflict the penalty, or return me the money that he overcharged."

"How were you overcharged?—Before my neighbour, Mr. Laing, came upon the road, I had a carrier's waggon, and when this waggon used to go into Swansea empty, he used to charge full toll for going empty and returning. I used to take those tickets each way, and I found that the man had extorted money from me which he ought not, in charging me for the empty waggon when I was going in. It was not a regular carrier's waggon. I fetched hay and corn from Swansea for my horses. The magistrates decided that it was illegal, that he had no right to charge. I produced tickets to the amount of £2 8s. 9d., which he was ordered to return to me, but I never had a farthing. Mr. Thomas Atwood, the magistrate's clerk, I applied to, and I never got a farthing back."

"Was William Lewis the renter of gates in Glamorganshire as well as in county?—Yes."

"Was any penalty imposed upon Lewis as well as returning the money?—No, not at that time."

"Had he to pay the cost?—Yes."

"When was it you went before the magistrates?—Four years ago."

"Who were the magistrates? Mr. Hewson, Mr. Thomas Edward Thomas, and, I think, Colonel Jones."

"Have you heard of this man Lewis being summoned lately before the magistrates?—Yes."

"Have you summoned him yourself?—I have not. In fact, I do not speak to him, for I do not have anything to do with him but paying him, through my coachman, his money for the coach every Monday morning. Mr. Lewis himself came once and took three bars away one morning within half a mile of each other."

"What did he take them away for?—They were threatened to be taken down, and he knew they were illegal."

"Did he put them up himself?—Yes."

"Without the authority of the trustees?—I cannot say. I think the magistrates in this hall had given him liberty to put them up, but he took them all away one morning; they were not more than half a mile from each other, all three, they were to catch different roads. It is very hard that a farmer cannot go to his own land without paying a gate. I rent a good

A Table of Grievances

deal of land under Mr. Chambers, and I cannot go to my land without paying tolls for manure, or if I carry lime."

"Do you think the trustees could keep the roads in repair if they took off the toll upon lime?—I do not. We are paying more considerably to the county rate than we paid formerly. This is a place that I think they ought to look more to than any other part, where there is so much shipping, and so many copper works, and there is a large population of persons that are merely labouring persons, who pay considerably more than is paid in the interior of the country; there are farmers who are paying seven times, to all accounts, as much rates as they are in some places in the country, and there has not been a ditch opened in any one place except by Llewellyn Thomas; he is a relieving officer and farmer. On the part of the road, up to where Mr. Saunders, or the trustees, and a magistrate lives, the road is very good. With respect to the bridge, it cost a good deal of money to build, and I never complain of paying the bridge, but the gate on the other side I complain of."

Mr. Laing. "It costs me 6s. 1½d. per day for going to Swansea and back, that is gates and duty."

"What are the gates?—3s. 4½d."

"Have any of these gates been pulled down?"

Mr. McKiernin. "Yes, we are both out on bail, charged with having pulled the gates down."

Mr. Laing. "And that a gate we never wanted to come through."

Mr. McKiernin. "I never was out of my house that night, but a drunken fellow informed against me, and I was admitted to bail."

(The witnesses withdrew.)

Becca Before the Bar

On 19th December about forty Rebeccaites assembled in the peaceful village of Llanddausant (Anglesea), having been summoned by sound of horn, and firing of guns. They proceeded in good order, armed with bludgeons and branches of trees, to the house of a certain D—— W——, a shopkeeper. Two bailiffs were there in possession of the goods and chattels under execution from the North and South Wales Bank of Holyhead.

Having entered the house by bursting open the door, Rebecca ran upstairs, followed by some of her daughters. She ordered the bailiffs, who were in bed at the time, to be up and going in five minutes, or to prepare for a good drubbing. The bailiffs promptly obeyed, but were driven forth by a bodyguard of the rioters, who escorted them some distance, pushing and driving the poor men in front of them. At last they were allowed to depart to their homes on a sincere promise of not returning.

On Monday night, 25th December, the gate in the village of Glasbury, on the Radnorshire side of the River Wye, was removed. The posts were sawn off about half a yard above the ground, and the gate, after being sawn in two and otherwise mutilated, was thrown into the River Wye.

The old woman who collected the tolls saw only three men employed, and they told her to keep quiet, as they would not injure her. About fifty persons were secreted near the place, to be of assistance if necessary.

Having finished their dastardly work, the whole party gave three cheers, and marched through the village in the direction of the Woodlands. Shouts of "'Becca for ever!" and the noise of firearms brought some of the inhabitants out, but they were peremptorily ordered back to their homes.

The road on which the gate was placed was repaired by the parish of Glasbury, and some time previous the inhabitants of Glasbury and the adjoining parishes had signed a petition to remove the said gate, but the Radnorshire Turnpike Trust took no notice of the petition. There were two gates adjoining the toll-house viz. the one on the road leading to the village, which was destroyed, and the other on the road leading to Rhydspence, which was not touched.

A reward of £50 was offered by the magistrates acting in the hundred of Paincastle for information which would lead to the conviction of the parties by whom the act was committed.

The Carmarthen Winter Assizes opened on 22nd December, 1843. Sir Cresswell Cresswell, one of Her Majesty's justices, arrived on the 25th. Sir Frederick Pollock, the Attorney-General, also arrived on the same afternoon.

The court began on Tuesday, 26th December, owing to Christmas Day intervening.

John Jones (Shoni Scuborfawr) was indicted for unlawfully and maliciously shooting at Walter Rees at Pontyberem on 25th August, for shooting at Miss Slocombe, for destroying a house at Spudder's Bridge, for destroying a house in Porthyrhyd, and for destroying a house in Tyrynys. He was found *Guilty*. Sentence—Transportation for life.

David Davies (Dai'r Cantwr) was tried for riot in Coalbrook Works and Spudder's Bridge. Transported for twenty years.

A *nolle prosequi* was entered against *William Walters*, who was charged with demolishing the house of Thomas Walters at Spudder's Bridge, Pembrey Parish, on the previous 8th April.

Thomas Morris pleaded guilty. He was charged with the same offence. He entered into his own recognisance of £50 to appear and receive judgment when called upon.

John Jones and *David Davies* pleaded guilty to a charge of demolishing the same house on the previous 17th September. Sentence—*vide* above.

Lewis Henry. For stealing in "The White Gate," Abergwili, was sentenced to transportation for ten years.

David Jones was charged with sending a threatening letter[1] to Thomas Williams, auctioneer of Llanwrda, Carmarthenshire. Found *Guilty*. Sentence, eight months' imprisonment.

Evan Williams, Joseph Williams, David Williams, William Williams, were charged with having destroyed Pentrebach Gate on 4th October. The Attorney-General entered a *nolle prosequi* against David Williams, he being only thirteen years old. The other three retracted their plea of not guilty, and pleaded guilty. The Attorney-General did not press for judgment against Evan and Joseph Williams. Evan, being of age, entered into his own recognizance of £100 to appear and receive judgment when required. Josiah Williams bailed Joseph Williams to the same effect. William Williams had six months' imprisonment with hard labour.

Bridget Williams was charged with having sent a threatening letter in the name of Rebecca to Benjamin Evans,[2] of Penyrherber, in Cenarth. Verdict *Guilty*. Sentence, three months' imprisonment.

John Jones was charged with sending a letter to Thomas Williams, of Llanwrda threatening to murder him on 9th October. Verdict, *Not Guilty*.

Daniel Mainwaring, Isaac Mainwaring, Thomas Mainwaring, and *John Powell*, were indicted for destroying the house of Mary Rees, in the parish of Llandebie. Verdict, *Not Guilty*.

David Evans (20), farmer, and *James Evans* (25) were charged with having on 30th September last, with divers others, assembled at Pantycerrig, and assaulted one Thomas Thomas, and with force demanding the sum of 40s. from him, with intent to steal the same. (Thomas was drowned a week previous to the Assizes.) Verdict, *Guilty*. Sentence, twelve months' imprisonment.

John Jones (21), *William Jones* (17), *Thomas Jones* (14), *Seth Morgan* (21), *Henry Thomas* (21), and *Thomas Harris* (a young lad) pleaded guilty to having (with others) destroyed the toll-house at Porthyrhyd on 7th August last. They were discharged on their own recognizances to appear when called upon to receive judgment.

George Daniel pleaded guilty to having committed a riot on 10th November at Blaennantymabuchaf, Llanegwad. Discharged as above.

---

[1] See page 175.

[2] Benjamin Evans was an ancestor of the Rev. Herbert Evans.

John Jones Smith pleaded guilty to having committed a riot and an assault at Llandilo Rwnnws Bridge on 7th July. Discharged as above. The Government would not proceed against *Francis McKiernin* and *George Laing*[3] who were charged with the demolition of a turnpike-gate at Llanelly.

William Davies (farmer), *Benjamin Richards* (farmer), *W. Evans* (labourer), *Arthur Arthur* (labourer), charged with various Rebecca outrages, were discharged by proclamation. (Dai Joshua the toll-keeper of Glangwili, informed.)

Thomas Morgan (28) and *Thomas Lewis* (24), (labourers), were charged with having, on 3rd October, demolished Dolau hirion Toll-gate in Llanegwad. The case was removed by *Certiorari* into the Court of Queen's Bench. In the course of a few minutes, perceiving their companions in tribulation set at liberty, they wished to withdraw their plea of not guilty, and to substitute guilty, but the judge told them they were too late.

Philip Philip and *William Philip*, father and son, received twelve months' imprisonment for having committed a riot and beaten the bailiff, etc., at Pound.

David Morgan (34), *James Morgan* (30), *George Thomas* (17), *John Lewis* (20), were charged with a burglary and riot at Llanarthney on 5th September. *David Morgan* pleaded not guilty, and was discharged, the evidence being inconclusive.

The others pleaded guilty. Sentence, two months' imprisonment.

David Jones was charged with attempting to suborn and instigate Daniel Lloyd, a mason of Priory Street, to commit perjury, or to withhold his evidence. Found *Guilty*. Sentence, one year's imprisonment.

. . . .

About the end of January, 1844, a certain Evan Rees, carrier from Shrewsbury to Aberystwyth, was proceeding with a waggon-load of timber from Aberystwyth to Llanidloes. On arriving at Pantmawr Turnpike-gate, the toll-collector demanded the usual toll. Rees offered him half, which the toll-keeper refused.

---

3 See evidence, page 189

The waggoner then ordered his servant to hook the team of horses to the gate posts. This frightened the collector so much that he immediately opened the gates for the sturdy Rebeccaite to pass through.

Shortly after Rees was visited at the Black Horse Inn, Aberystwyth (of which he was landlord), by a bailiff. The latter requested him to meet the magistrates of the hundred of Llanidloes at Llandinam on a certain day. Rees, who dared not refuse, turned up at the time appointed.

The magistrates, after going into the case, informed him that they would deal leniently with him on that occasion. If, however, he made his appearance before them again, the utmost penalty of the law would be inflicted. On this occasion they would only impose upon him the sum of £5 and costs. This was immediately paid.

Rebecca and about 200 of her daughters assembled at Llangerrig, near Rhayader, on 7th February. They soon demolished the turnpike-gate. This was one of four within a distance of twelve miles on the road from Rhayader to Aberystwyth. At two of the gates travellers had to pay 8d. for a horse and gig. All four gates had been previously taken down by Rebecca, as it was considered that two were ample within such a short distance.

On 21st February, 1844, about forty men, disguised in various ways, levelled Plasbach Gate, situated near Llanyhyther, on the Carmarthen and Lampeter road.

The Pembrokeshire Spring Assizes for 1844 opened before his Honour Judge Sir W. H. Maule on the 12th March at Haverfordwest.

William Walters and *David Vaughan*, for a riot and unlawful assembly at Prendergast Gate on the 25th August, previous, were found guilty of "unlawful assembly."

They were sentenced to twelve months' imprisonment each.

On Wednesday, 13th March, Mr. Vaughan Williams moved that the recognizances of the prisoners from No. 2 to No. 27 on the calendar be discharged. In these cases the prisoners were held to bail for having been concerned in the riotous proceedings at Fishguard in the previous September, the Crown proceeding no further with them. The motion was granted.

March 19th, *John Lewis, John Charles, Job Evans, John Harris*, of Talog, *David Williams*, and *David Thomas* were tried for unlawfully assembling at the Union Workhouse, Carmarthen, on 19th June, 1843. They were found *Guilty*. John Harris had twelve calendar months' hard labour, and the three others eight months each.

John Jones, Jonathan Jones, Howell Lewis, Jonathan Lewis, David Davies, and *David Lewis* were tried for having committed a riot and assault at Talog, in the parish of Abernant on the previous 12th June. John Jones was acquitted, the others were found guilty, and sentenced to eight months' imprisonment with hard labour.

Thomas Lewis and *Thomas Morgan* were indicted on the charge of having destroyed the turnpike-gate and toll-house at Dolau hirion, near Llandovery. Verdict, *Guilty* of being present, but not of breaking the gate. His lordship observed that was equivalent to a verdict of *Not Guilty*, and directed a verdict to that effect to be entered.

John Jones, Thomas Hughes, and *Benjamin Jones* were tried for having destroyed Pontarllechan Gate and Toll-house on the night of 1st August previous. Verdict, To come up for judgment when called upon.

Thomas Powell, John James, John Thomas, Thomas Thomas, John Thomas, Evan Davies, and *David Evans*, were tried for having, with others, entered the house of Daniel Harris of Pantyfen and stolen a sovereign, and *David Thomas* was charged as having been accessory to the fact. All found *Guilty*. David Thomas was sentenced to twenty years' transportation, and all the others to ten years' transportation each.

James Thomas and *Thomas Thomas* were acquitted of having aided and abetted "Shoni Scuborfawr" in firing a gun at one Margaret Thomas, with intent to murder her, or do her some bodily harm. They were also acquitted with having on the previous 5th Stepember caused, with others, a riot, etc., at Porthyrhyd.

The Assizes terminated on 21st March, 1844.

. . . .

On 27th March about a dozen of "Rebecca's Best" visited Pensarne Gate, Cardigan, and totally demolished and removed it. When the police visited the place at an early hour in the morning, all was right; and then all was done in about ten minutes or a quarter of an hour at furthest. It was a daring act to be attempted in a town where there were stationed about forty marines and several policemen.

On 17th April the side-gate for foot passengers attached to the turnpike-gate of Brynlloi, three miles from Llandebie, was entirely destroyed by Rebecca and her daughters.

A party of men, numbering from forty to fifty, suddenly assembled on 21st April at Plasbach Gate, about four miles from Llanybyther, on the Lampeter Road; they destroyed both toll-house and gate.

At the Carmarthenshire Quarter Sessions for April, 1844, William Lewis, Collector of Tolls on the Three Commotts Trust, was indicted for having illegally erected a toll-bar across a high road between Porthyrhyd and Voelgastell Gates.

He pleaded guilty. The Chairman addressed the defendant thus: "You have pleaded guilty to an indictment charging you with having illegally erected a turnpike-gate on a public road. Many of the magistrates think that this is a fit case for the imposition of imprisonment, but the majority on the Bench are of the opinion that the justice of the case will be met by the infliction of a fine. You, and men like you, by your iniquity and corruption, have first of all exasperated and provoked the people to outrage and violence, and you are therefore far worse, far more culpable, far more wicked than they. Who shall say, that of those misguided men who unfortunately have lately been banished beyond the seas, or otherwise punished for offences against the law, some were not provoked to raise their hands against that law by your injustice, misconduct, and oppression? The sentence of the court is that you pay a fine of £50 to the Queen, and that you be imprisoned until such fine is paid."

The defendant immediately paid the fine and left the court.

21st May. The detachment of the 4th Light Dragoons left Carmarthen.

22nd May. A detachment of the 13th Light Dragoons arrived at Carmarthen under Captain Dickson and Lieutenant Derem.

18th June. The 76th Regiment left Carmarthen.

20th June. Two Companies of the 41st Foot arrived.

25th June. The 7th Company of the 41st arrived under Captain Vaughan.

13th July. The Summer Assizes opened before Sir Robert Monsy Rolfe. On Tuesday, the 16th, *David Evans* was tried for being concerned in pulling down and destroying Llanfihangel-ar-arth Gate, and found "Guilty of being in the company, but not guilty of demolishing." On Wednesday (17th) he was again tried for destroying Gwarallt Gate. The jury having been locked up all night, and not agreeing, the judge ordered the prisoner to be discharged, but told him that he might be called again at the next, or any other Assizes to be tried for the same offence before another jury.

3rd September, 1844. *Henry Evans* was committed to the county gaol at Carmarthen, for being engaged in some of the disturbances. He was tried in March, 1845, and sentenced to eighteen months' imprisonment. His term ended in October, 1846, and he was thereupon discharged.

He was the last of those unfortunate men who were committed for various terms of imprisonment on account of their Rebeccaite dealings.

When Evans entered the gaol he was not able to speak a word of English, nor did he know his alphabet, but when he was discharged he could speak English fluently, and was able to read the Bible. On leaving prison he repeated the third chapter of Matthew, which he had learnt, to his chaplain, who expressed great satisfaction at his rapid progress.

Appendix A

Anno Septimo and Octavo Victoriæ Reginæ, Cap. XCI

An Act to consolidate and amend the Laws relating to Turnpike Trusts in South Wales. [9th August, 1844.]

A Summary:—

It first refers to the Commission appointed on the 7th day of October, 1843, "to make a full and diligent Inquiry into the State of the Laws as administered in *South Wales* which regulate the Maintenance and Repair of Turnpike Roads, Highways, and Bridges."

The report was made to Her Majesty bearing the date 6th day of March, 1844. In it the Commissioners recommended, among other things, that the Debts then chargeable upon the several Turnpike Trusts, in *South Wales*, should be ascertained and redeemed; also that the several Trusts in each of the respective counties then existing should be consolidated and placed under uniform Management and Control; and that the Laws and Regulations relating to the Collection and Application of Tolls should be revised and amended.

The Act commends:—

1. The appointment of not more than three Commissioners by the Lord High Treasurer, or the Commissioners of Her Majesty's Treasury for the time being, or any Three or more of them by any writing under their hands, to be Commissioners to carry this Act into execution.

2. The Powers given under the Act to such Commissioners to absolutely cease and determine on September 29th, 1845.

3. The said Commissioners to be styled "The Commissioners for consolidating and adjusting the Turnpike Trusts in

Appendix A

South Wales"; to have Powers and Authorities comprising the six counties following: Glamorgan, Brecknock, Radnor, Carmarthen, Pembroke, and Cardigan.

4. The orders of the Commissioners to be binding, and not to be removed by *Certiorari*.

5. A secretary to be appointed, whose work, and the Salaries and Allowances to Commissioners and their officers to be regulated by the Lord High Treasurer or the said Commissioners of Her Majesty's Treasury.

6. Commissioners to proceed through South Wales.

7. Notice to be given by Advertisement.

8. Inquiry to be made by Commissioners into circumstances of all the Trusts, their Debts, etc.

9. Commissioners to summon Witnesses and call for Papers.

10. Penalty for giving false Evidence to be deemed guilty of a misdemeanour.

11. Commissioners to record their Proceedings.

12. Commissioners to ascertain and estimate all Debts, and to award the Sums, and name the Persons to whom due. Sums due to Infants and Lunatics may be awarded to Guardians and Committees, etc. Persons dissatisfied with the Award could appeal.

13. Commissioners to appoint Time and Place for Arbitration.

14. The Selection of Arbitrators, their Power, Awards, and Expenses of the Arbitration how borne.

15. Awards, Advertisements, and other Instruments to be free of Stamp Duty.

16. Provisions made in case of Creditors not applying within Time limit; Creditors after twelve months barred.

17. Commissioners to report Result of Awards to Secretary of State.

18. Sums awarded to be paid by Public Works Loan Commissioners.

19. Sum not exceeding £225,000 to be charged upon the Consolidated Fund.

20. Commissioners for the Reduction of National Debt to be Trustees of South Wales Turnpike Trust Fund, and to cause separate Account to be opened at Bank of England for the purpose.

21. When powers of Commissioners have ceased, the Charge to be executed by the Secretary of State.

22. All Local Acts to be repealed from a Day to be declared by the Commissioners.

23. Justices in Quarter Sessions to elect members of County Roa4 Boards.

24. Certain Persons in each County to be ex-officio Members of the County Roads Boards.

25. The above Boards to have the Superintendence, Control, and Management of all Turnpike Roads, and part of the Turnpike Roads situated in any of the said counties respectively.

26. Existing Officers of Trusts to give Account of all moneys, etc., taken.

27. Provisions made as to existing Leases of Tolls.

28. Debts due to Trust to be vested in the County Roads Boards.

29. Materials to be the Property of the County to which they shall be adjudged by Commissioners to belong.

30. Mortgagees not to take possession of the Tolls.

31. Mortgagees in possession to deliver up Possession and to account to County Roads Boards.

32. Lands or Persons liable to Repair of any Roads to continue liable.

33. County Roads Boards may continue existing Toll Gates.

34. County Roads Boards may remove Toll Gates if desirable.

35. Rates of Tolls to be taken under this Act (see second schedule).

36. Equal Tolls to be taken at all Gates in same county.

37. Distinction as to Breadth of Wheels to be abolished.

38. Toll once paid, to clear seven miles in same, or two in adjacent county.

39. Where any Toll payable within the specified Distance is a higher one, the Difference only is to be paid.

40. Provision as to Stage Coaches and Stage Waggons.

41. Post Horses to be charged on every fresh Hiring.

42. Exemption from Toll.

No Toll "for any Horse or other animal carrying, drawing, or conveying any Agricultural Produce which shall have grown or arisen on Land or Ground in the occupation of, or

Appendix A

cultivated, used, or enjoyed by the Owner of any such Agricultural Produce, and which shall not have been bought, sold, or otherwise profitably exchanged or disposed of, nor be going to be bought, sold, or otherwise profitably exchanged or disposed of, or for any sheep going to be washed, or returning therefrom, or for any Horse or other Animal drawing, or not drawing, which shall not pass more than Three Hundred Yards along, or upon such Turnpike Road, whether the whole or any Part of such Three hundred Yards shall have been traversed before passing through any Gate or Bar, or shall be traversed after passing through the same."

43. Exceptions not to be defeated on account of Regulations as to Breadth of Wheels or as to Weight.

44. Lime to be charged Half Toll.

45. Toll not to be taken within Limits of Towns.

46. Toll Tables to be fixed at the Gates.

47. Penalty for Want of Toll Tables 40s. per diem for every Day during which Collector shall continue to collect Tolls without such Table being affixed.

48. County Roads Boards empowered to reduce Tolls in schedule.

49. Meetings of County Roads Boards not less than four times in a year, "and may adjourn themselves to meet at any other Place or Places."

50. Three to be Quorum when Tolls are to be let.

51. Tolls may be let at any Meeting without putting them up at the sum before realized.

52. After mentioning Repeal of Part of 3 Geo. 4th c. 126 and part of 3 and 4 Wm. 4th c. 80. The Annual General Meeting of County Roads Boards for the purpose of auditing and examining the Accounts.

53. General Superintendent of County Roads to be appointed to Office and Duties.

    (1) To overlook Management of Roads.
    (2) To attend Meetings of County and District Boards.
    (3) To examine Accounts at Annual Meetings.
    (4) To prepare Statements and Estimates.
    (5) To transmit Statements and Estimates to Commissioners.
    (6) To report from Time to Time.

54. Books to be kept and to be open to Inspection.

55. Plan of County Roads to be made by the Authority of the Commissioners.

56. Roads rejected by the Commissioners to become Highways.

57. County Roads Boards to make special Reports in certain cases.

58. Local Boards to be appointed, called "District Roads Boards."

59. If the Commissioners deemed it expedient they could appoint additional members.

60. Members of the County and District Boards could act as justices.

61. The Tolls collected (to be called "County Roads Funds") to be applied as follows:—
> (a) To the Payment of such Annuity as should be charged upon such County Roads Funds.
> (b) Subject to No. 1 should be applicable to the Repair, Maintenance, Management, and Improvement of the several Turnpike roads.
> (c) To the Salaries of the officers.

62. If the County Roads Fund proved insufficient for the Purposes required, County Roads Boards should certify the Amount required to the Quarter Sessions.

63. Justices in Quarter Sessions to make a rate to supply the Amount required.

64. Occupiers paying Road Rate could deduct it from the Rent paid to their Landlord.

65. Llandilo Rhwnws Bridge, and Towey Suspension Bridge to become County Bridges, Wych Tree Bridge to become a County Bridge, Loughor Bridge to be maintained as a County Bridge between the Counties of Glamorgan and Carmarthen jointly.

66. Part of the Debt of Rumney Bridge Trust to be borne by the Newport Turnpike Trust, Rumney Bridge to be maintained as a County Bridge between the Counties of Glamorgan and Monmouth jointly.

67. The Act not to apply to Hay Bridge nor to the Haverfordwest or Boughrood Bridges.

First Schedule

7° AND 8° VICTORIÆ, CAP. XCI

Appendix A

Schedules to which the foregoing Act refers:—
1. Act in George IV, 3rd year.
2. Act in George IV, 4th year.
3. Act in George IV, 7th and 8th years.
4. Act in George IV, 9th year.
5. Act in William IV, 1st and 2nd years.
6. Act in William IV, 2nd and 3rd years.
7. Act in William IV, 3rd and 4th years.
8. Act in William IV, 4th and 5th years.

SECOND SCHEDULE

Rate of Toll to be taken in the Counties to which this Act refers:—

For every Horse or other Beast drawing any Coach, Chariot, Berlin, Landau, Landaulet, Barouche, Chaise, Phaeton, Vis-a-Vis, Calash, Curricle, Car, Chair, Gig, Hearse, Caravan, Litter, or any such like Carriage	0 0 6
For every Horse or other Beast except Asses, drawing any Waggon, Wain, Cart, or other such like Carriage	0 0 4
For every Ass drawing any Cart, Carriage, or other Vehicle	0 0 2
For every Horse, or Mule, laden or unladen, and not drawing	0 0 1½
For every Ass laden or unladen and not drawing	0 0 0½
For every Drove of Oxen, Cows, or Neat Cattle, the sum of Ten-pence per Score, and so in proportion for any greater or less number	
For every drove of Calves, Hogs, Sheep, or Lambs, the sum of Five-pence per Score, and so in proportion for any greater or less number.	
For every Carriage drawn or impelled by Steam or other Power other than Animal Power, having Two Wheels	0 1 0
And for every such last-mentioned Carriage having more than Two Wheels	0 2 0

Appendix B

The following account, taken from *Yr Haul* August, 1843, shows that the various expenses incurred by Rebecca's Raids, fell, in the long run, on the people themselves:

The Welsh Goblins

Let not Rebecca and her Daughters think it is all honey for them. As likely as not, some of them will have to scratch their heads when making up the losses caused by their late depredations. The expense is falling sweetly on the County this quarter again. On looking over the "Carmarthen Journal," last issue, in the accounts of this County, amongst other things, we see the following respectable items:

Paid George Martin and other Police Officers for their attendance at St. Clears to protect Gates, etc.	185 19 0
Paid David Jones Nantyclawdd Gate for injury done to Nantyclawdd Toll House	22 8 10
Paid David Jones Bwlchyclawdd Gate for injury done to Bwlchyclawdd Gate	24 1 0
Paid William Davies, John's Town, for watching Royal Oak Gate	2 2 0
Paid David Edwards, John's Town, Carmarthen, for watching Royal Oak Gate	2 2 0
Paid David Rees and others appointed in the Hundred of Commott, etc.	3 15 0
Paid David Rees and others for watching Llanfihangel Turnpike Gate	22 9 0
Paid Thomas Thomas for watching Troedrhiwglyn Gate	5 2 0
Paid for protecting Glangwili Gate	6 6 6

Appendix B

Paid John Evans and others for protecting
    Glangwili Gate   7 0 3
                                                        £281 5 7

During last month a large number of gates have been broken and destroyed in the county of Carmarthen, in the Three Hundreds, Llangadock, Pumpsaint, and the middle region near Llandovery; the whole cost will fall on each Hundred where the destruction took place, according to the 7th and 8th George IV. They do not make a penny cost to the Trusts.

Appendix C

Can newydd sef ychydig o hanes Bywyd Rebecca a'i Merched

Fel y maent yn tori'r Tollbyrth mewn amrywiol fanau.
I'w chanu ar y Mesur—"Pray, what will old England come to?"

          Cyneswch yn awr Gymry mwynion,
          Ymdyrwch yn dirion ym mlaen;
          Rhowch osteg ar unwaith yn ddiddig,
          Ac yna gwnaf gynnyg rhoi Cân;
          Nid ydwyf yn awr yn enllibio,
          Na beio nid oes arnaf chwant;
          Rhof 'chydig o hanes fel medraf,
          O fywyd Rebecca a'r plant.
Byrdwn.   Nid amal y bu ffasiwn beth!

          Rhyw ddynes go ryfedd yw Becca,
          Am blanta mi goeliaf yn siwr;
          Mae ganddi rai cannoedd o ferched,
          Er hyny 'does ganddi'r un gwr;
          Mae hyn yn beth achos rhyfeddu,
          I bawb yn gyffredin trwy'r wlad,
          Pa ffordd y mae Becca yn medru,
          Rheoli'r holl blant heb un tad
                 Nid amal, etc.

          Mae hanes fod Becca a'i merched
          Yn myned ar gerdded y nos,
          I dori yn ddarnau'r holl Durnpikes,
          Rhag talu am dramwy ffyrdd croes,
          Mae rhai yn ei chanmol am hyny,
          A'r lleill am ei chospi yn llym,

Appendix C

A llawer dyn call gellwch gredu,
Yn tewi a pheidio dweyd dim
    Nid amal, etc.

Aeth Becca a'i merched calonog,
Ryw noswaith yn arfog a hy,
Torasant y tollborth yn hollol
Yn ymyl pen Heol Llwyn-du;
Rhoed hwnw yn gryfach i fyny,
A physt haiarn bwrw'n ddi ball,
Drachefn daeth Rebecca a'i merched
I'w falu mor llwyred a'r llall
    Nid amal, etc.

Bu yno gwnstebli a *Soldiers*
A'r *Cavalry* hefyd yn hir
Roedd pawb ar eu goreu yn gwylied,
Rhag Becca a'i merched mae'n wir;
Er cymaint oedd yno yn bugeilia,
Aeth Becca'n llawn ffwdan a ffrwst,
At gate y Drefechan a'i merched,
Fe'i torwyd mor faned a dwst.
    Nid amal, etc.

Argraffwyd ar bapur fod gwobr,
O gan' punt am roi eglurhad,
A chael y gwirionedd yn berffaith,
Am Becca neu ryw rai o'r had:
Daeth hen Borthmon moch, ac achwynodd,
Pan glywodd fod arian i'w cael,
A rhoed dau ddyn parchus yn ngharchar,
O achos ei gelwydd di sail.
    Nid amal, etc.

Ca'dd rhei'ny eu cadw dan gloion,
Waith dichell echryslon a thwyll;
Ond gwelwyd y camwedd anmherffaith,
'Nol chwilio y gyfraith mewn pwyll;
Hwy gawsant eu rhyddid oddiyno
'Roedd llawer yn bloeddio wrth chwant,
'Roedd digon o dystion nad oeddynt

Can newydd sef ychydig o hanes Bywyd Rebecca a'i Merched

Yn perthyn i Becca na'i phlant.
　　Nid amal, etc.

Er cymaint yn awr sy'n bugeilia,
Mae Becca yn uchel ei phen,
Gate Pwll-y-trap gadd ei thori,
Ryw noswaith, a Gate Efelwen,
Mae'n anhawdd i'r bobl fugeilia,
Plant Becca sy'n gymaint o rif,
Bu rhywun wrth weitio'r hen lodes,
Mi glwais dan ddanedd y llif!
　　Nid amal, etc.

'Rwyf finnau yn crynu ar droion,
Rhag ofn cwrdd Becca a'i phlant bach;
Ond gartref arosaf yn ddiddig,
'Does angen am feddyg i'r iach;
Mae'n well i mi lechu yn rhyw gornel,
Heb Dobaco na Snisin na The,
Na chwrdd a Rebecca a'i merched,
Wrth dori hen lidiard rhyw le.
　　Nid amal, etc.

Aeth Becca a rhai o'i chenedlaeth,
I Arberth, mi glywais y sôn,
Dinystriwyd y Gwaliau a'r Llidiardau,
A thorwyd y pyst yn y bôn;
Hwy aethant a'r cwbl i'w canlyn,
'Doedd yno na ysglodyn na phren;
'Roedd llawer yn barod pryd hyny
I waeddi mai Becca oedd ben.
　　Nid amal, etc.

Fe dorwyd rhai clwydi yn Llandyssul,
A rhai wrth Llansawel yn syn,
A Gate Bwlch y Clawdd a ganfyddais,
Wrth ddarllen yr hanes fel hyn;
A Gates wrth Lanbedr-Pont-Stephan,
Llanon Aberaeron, mewn gwir,
A Gate Abergwaun yn bur hynod,
Lle tiriodd y Ffrancod i'n tir.
　　Nid amal, etc.

Appendix C

> Mi glywais fod Becca a'r werin,
> Gerllaw i Gaerfyrddin yn siwr,
> Ryw noswaith yn gweithio'n ddinystriol,
> Yn ymyl pen Heol-y Dwr,
> Gate arall nid pell o Dremadog,[1]
> A ddrylliwyd yn llidiog i'r llawr;
> Gall llawer i feddwl wrth hyna;
> Mai Becca yw Trust y ffordd fawr.
>   Nid amal, etc.
>
> Y Gate oedd gerllaw i Dregaron,
> A daflwyd i'r afon yn lân;
> Ac hefyd, tri thollborth yn Mrechfa.
> A dorwyd yn ddarnau pur fân;
> Fe ddrylliwyd y gate yn Mhenllwynan,
> A gates y Felindre fel earth;
> Heblaw Castellnewydd-yn-Emlyn,
> Pencader, Llanfihangel-ar-Arth.
>   Nid amal, etc.
>
> Rhyw 'chydig o hanes fel yma
> Sydd genyf am Becca a'i phlant,—
> Mae'n ddrwg genyf wel'd aflonyddwch,
> Gwir heddwch sydd arnaf fi chwant;
> Gobeithio y chwilir y llwybyr
> Sydd gy wir, drwy synwyr heb sen;
> A chariad gan bawb at ein gilydd
> A fyddo byth beunydd yn ben.
> *Byrdwn.* Wei felly dymunwn ei bod.
>
>   D. D. J., Ll-n-b-th-r a'i cant.

---

1 Near Portmadoc, North Wales.

Appendix D

Excerpts from the letters of Col. Trevor

13 August 1843

I have just heard that on Thursday last there was a meeting held in the village of Pontyberem, attended by 2 or 300 persons, most of whom, it is said, were armed and disguised, and that there were several hundred more who appeared to be lookers on. These men, it is said, made the inn-keeper swear not to entertain Lewis, the Toll Collector, and also made some special constables promise not to serve, and took away their staves.

13 September 1843

About 2 o'clock, on 9 September, a party of men disguised in white dresses, went to Hendy Gate, about half a mile from Pontarddulais. They carried out the furniture from the toll-house, and told the old woman, whose name was Sarah Williams, to go away and not return. She went to the house of John Thomas, a labourer, and called him to assist in extinguishing the fire at the toll-house, which had been ignited by the Rebeccaites. The old woman then re-entered the toll-house. The report of a gun or pistol was soon afterwards heard. The old woman ran back to John Thomas's house, fell down at the threshold, and expired within two minutes. She had received several cautions to collect no more tolls. On 11 September an inquest was held before William Bonville, Coroner. Two surgeons, Ben Thomas, Llanelli, and John Kirkhouse Cooke, Llanelli, gave evidence that on the body were marks of shot, some penetrating the nipple of left breast, on

Appendix D

in the armpit of the same side, and several shot marks on both arms. Two shots were found in the left lung. In spite of all this evidence the jury found "that the deceased died from effution of blood into the chest occasioned, suffocation, but from what cause is to this jury unknown." ...

...[T]he Secretary of State will authorise the offer by you of Her Majesty's most gracious pardon to any person concerened in the murder of the woman at Ponthendy gate, who shall give information and evidence so as to convict the offenders, excepting such persons as actually fired the shot which deprived her of life. And also that he will recommend of the payment of a further reward of £200 in addition to that sum offered by Mr. Chambers for the detection of the persons who set her property on fire, excepting always anyone who actually set fire to the premises and stacks, and so that no principal offender shall receive any part of the award in question. He will advise in this case the grant of Her Majesty's most gracious pardon to an accomplice under the same restriction, namely, that it is not to be extended to any one who actually set fire to any of the property consumed.

Appendix E

The Riots of Rebecca and Her Daughters[1]
by George Thomas, of Ely.

In the early part of his paper Mr. Thomas pointed out that the phrase "Rebecca and her Daughters," by which the turnpike rioters of South Wales were known, had probably a Biblical origin, being assumed in irreverent allusion to the blessing pronounced on Rebekah, Isaac's wife,—"Be thou the mother of thousands of millions, and let thy seed possess the gate of those which hate them." (Genesis xxiv. 60.) The name "Becca" was not confined to one individual, but was given to the leader for the occasion. Similar disturbances had occurred in Gloucestershire and Herefordshire as far back as 1730, accounts of which appear in the public prints of the time.

The "Becca" riots in South Wales took place in 1843. They originated in the circumstances of the turnpike roads being held under separate trusts, the trustees of which found it necessary, in order to protect the interest of the tally-holders, to place their gates near the confines of their districts, so as to prevent persons from other districts travelling over their roads free of charge. It thus happened that, while persons living and travelling within any given district were usually charged with only one toll for the use of a considerable length of road, those living on the borders and having occasion to travel out of the district had frequently to pay at two gates within a comparatively short distance. This was not unnaturally felt to be a grievance, and Becca's action was at first directed to its removal, though not by legitimate means. "She"

---

[1] Read before the Cardiff Naturalists Society

Appendix E

was at first disguised in woman's clothes, and when attacking a gate called on her "children" to pull it down. Persons more ill-disposed than the original malcontents were soon mixed up in the disturbances, which speedily assumed a serious aspect, and culminated in threatening letters, theft, arson, and murder. Several country gentlemen in the County of Carmarthen appealed through the Press to the better feelings of the people. Amongst others were Mr. Johnes, of Dolau Cothi, who issued an address to the inhabitants of Conwil Gaio: Col. Trevor (afterwards Lord Dynevor), who issued a proclamation as Deputy Lord-Lieutenant; Mr. Fitzwilliams and Mr. William Chambers, junior. The bard "Tegid" (once Hebrew Professor at Oxford) made a fervent appeal to the people of Nevern parish; and "Brutus," the talented editor of the Haul, firmly supported the unpopular side of law and order. The chief incidents in connection with Becca's proceedings began in the neighbourhood of St. Clears and Whitland on January 16th, 1843. Trefechan Gate was destroyed, Pentre and "Maeswholan" soon followed. February 5th, Mynydd-y-Garreg Gate destroyed; 13th, Tavernspite and Lampeter Gates destroyed; 21st, Bwlch-y-Clawdd Tollhouse demolished; April 7th, Bwlchtrap Gate destroyed; 22nd Trefechan Toll-house demolished; May 3rd, Pont Twelly and Troed-y-Rhiw Gribyn Toll-gates destroyed; 26th, Water Street Gate, Carmarthen, destroyed. After Water Street Gate was destroyed, some persons from Talog passed through before it was replaced, and refused to pay toll. For this they were fined by the Magistrates at Carmarthen Petty Sessions, and constables were sent from Carmarthen to levy the fines. The constables were, however, forced to return without executing the distress warrants. About 30 pensioners were then sworn in to assist in executing the warrants, and having seized the goods of one Harries, of Talog, they were on their way to Carmarthen, surrounded by about 400 of the Beccas (about one hundred of whom carried guns) and obliged to fire their pistols in the air and to give them up. They were then forced to march to Trawsmawr, the residence of Captain D. Davies, who had signed the warrants, and to return emptyhanded to Carmarthen. The walls round Trawsmawr were demolished, and it was reported that the pensioners were compelled to assist in their destruction. Further damage was done to the walls and plantations at Trawsmawr by the rioters on the night of Saturday, the 10th of June. Two days later, Penllwynau Gate and House destroyed. On the 13th, riots took place at Talog, and on the following day meetings were held in the evening at Trelech, Talog, Blaen-y-Coed, and Conwil, at which it was resolved that 'Becca and her children should visit Carmarthen on the ensuing Monday. Rich and poor were required to be present at the Plough and Harrow Public-house, Bwlch Newydd, at eleven o'clock, on pain of having their houses and barns burnt. On the 15th, Melindre Siencyn Toll house was demolished, and next day Bwlch-y-Clawdd Toll-house shared the same fate. On the 19th, 'Becca was discomfitted at Carmarthen Workhouse by the 4th Dragoons (Queen's Own) under Major Parlby. On this occasion, the late John Lloyd Davies, of Blaen-dyffryn, with his friend, John Lloyd, of Alltyr-Odyn, met a large body of men on their march to Carmarthen, with the view of "showing their strength," and tried to dissuade them from their unwise purpose, promising to exert himself to get their grievances inquired into. His patriotic counsel was given in vain. The procession reached from the gaol through Spilman Street, Church Street, St. Peter Street, to the King Street end of Conduit Lane, and numbered from 2,000 to 2,500 persons. A man disguised with long hair rode in front on rather a low horse. It is believed that at first there was no intention to commit excesses, and that the country people were led to the workhouse by some town roughs. Others maintain that the attack on the workhouse was deliberately resolved on at the meetings held the previous Wednesday at Talog and other places. Be that as it may, to the workhouse they went. The dragoons were expected earlier than they arrived, having, it is said, been misdirected by a countryman whom they met between Pont-ar-Ddulais and Carmarthen. They came just in time to save the workhouse, and possibly the neighbouring brewery, the contents of which might have given further impulse to the fury of the rioters. They were met by Mr. T. C. Morris, Mayor, who rode on with their officer. Sweeping through Red Street and Barn Row, they charged, at gallop, up the hill, their armour glistening in the sun. Just at this instant, the work of destruction had begun, the beds being thrown out through the windows. It was amusing to witness the consternation the arrival of the soldiers occasioned. The country people fled in every direction, like ants when an ant-hill is disturbed, fleeing they

Appendix E

knew not whither, none seeming to look back. A goodly number were taken within the workhouse walls, many of them being merely curious spectators of what was going on. June 27th, Penygarn Toll-house destroyed. July 7th, Llandilorhwnws Toll-house destroyed. July 15th, riot at Talog. August 1st, Pont-ar-Lechau Toll-house destroyed; August 7th, Porth-y-Rhyd Toll-house demolished; August 22nd, the house of D. Harries, Pant-y-Fen, invaded; murderous attack on Mr. Edwards, Gelli Gwernen, near Llanon. August 25th, Glangwili Tollhouse demolished. Riot at Pont-y-Berem 29th, £500 offered for discovery of the ringleader. September 5th, Llanddarog Toll-house attacked. September 9th, Sarah Williams, aged 75, toll-collector of Hendy Gate, Llanedy, was shot at the gate-house; hitherto the riots had been free from bloodshed. The first life taken was that of the old woman; she had ignored repeated summonses served upon her by Rebeccaites to quit the place, and in the small hours of a Sabbath morn woke to find her thatched cottage in flames. Rushing out, she raised piercing cries, and hurrying to the house of a neighbour piteously appealed for assistance—er mwyn Duw—to put out the fire. He, grasping the situation, and fearful of the consequences, refused to move. She returned, and was making frenzied efforts to save her "household goods" from the flames, when the report of a rifle was heard, and staggering forward, the woman fell dead, the bullet having pierced her breast. Some consolation for this cowardly deed may be obtained from the fact supplied by a subsequent confession that it was the thoughtless act of a youth, and that there had been no intention whatever to injure the poor, offenceless creature. This tragic incident filled the party with consternation, and they quickly returned from whence they came. Actions such as these caused a revulsion in public feeling, and as disintegrating influences were actively at work within the ranks of the rioters, the task of the authorities, especially as their arrangements gained completeness, became easier. After this about a dozen toll-houses and gales were destroyed, and the house of Mr. Rees, Llandebie, demolished.

Much was expected by the reverse suffered by the rioters at Carmarthen, but subsequent events showed that those had been oversanguine who, in the first flush of victory, had been tempted to believe the campaign over. Far from being

The Riots of Rebecca and Her Daughters

the end, it was merely the beginning. Carmarthen was the scene of the first open defiance of the law.

In July the police and the 'Beccas came into collision at Pontardulais. Acting upon the statement of an "informer," Captain Napier, the superintendent, and eight armed police, lay in ambush near a threatened gate. "Mid-night gave the signal sound of strife." A body of mounted men galloped down the road, dismounted and wrecked a smithy, and then the adjacent gate. They had well nigh completed their self-imposed task when the police "broke cover." Volleys were exchanged with disastrous results, for the rioters, in the lurid glare of the torches they carried, afforded excellent targets for practice for the police. A battle ensued, and the rioters, demoralised by the surprise, fled, leaving six prisoners in the hands of the law. Once clear of the melee, they rallied and attempted a rescue, but the police, having meanwhile being reinforced by some soldiers, easily beat off their assailants. One of the prisoners, who had been severely wounded, was a young farmer of Llannon, John Hughes by name, subsequently transported for twenty years. He was a few years back a wealthy landowner in Tasmania. The increased vigilance of the authorities; the reaction in public sentiment; and the growing heinousness of the acts committed in the name of Rebecca were factors in promoting the rapid decline of the movement. On the 25th of October, the Royal Commissioners formally entered upon their duties; I knew two of them personally,—the Hon. Robert Henry Give, Lord Windsor's grandfather, and Major Bowen, father of the late Mr. Bowen, Q.C. They made full and diligent enquiry into the state of the laws administered in South Wales regulating the maintenance of turnpike roads, highways, and bridges; and also into the circumstances which led to acts of violence in certain districts. The suppression of the riots was followed by this inquiry into their cause, and the result was the passing of the South Wales Turnpike Act, which remedied the evils that led to them. The disturbances may be said to have terminated with the capture of "Shoni 'Scybor Fawr," whose violence and daring made him the terror not less of the police than the country folk with whom he professed to be in sympathy. A noted pugilist of magnificent physique, Shoni had used his giant's strength like a giant. I knew Shoni, and recollect him fighting at a Llandaff fair, and I can recall when he engaged to fight

Appendix E

Harry Jones, of Cardiff, on the Great Heath. In this they were disturbed by county magistrates acting in the Hundred of Kibbor, when two justices, the late T. W. Booker Blakemore, of Velindre, and the late Rev. R. Prichard, came on the scene. Shoni and Harry, with hundreds ot their backers, fled, and having crossed the river Rhymney by a wooden bridge near Coedygoras, they fought on the other side of the river in the county of Monmouth, and out of the jurisdiction of the Glamorgan Justices. Shoni was a native of Yscubor Fawr, Penderyn, near Merthyr Tydfil, and a brassfitter by trade. He was taken by a band of constables of A Division of the London Police, at the Five Roads Tavern, Pontyberem, who pounced upon him unawares, and before he could grasp his gun had his wrists in the embrace of the "darbies." It was with a sense of relief the people received the intelligence of his capture. About twenty of those captured at Carmarthen on the fateful day of the demonstration, were tried before Baron Gurney and Mr. Justice Cresswell, were found guilty, and ten of them sentenced to be transported. Amongst the prisoners found guilty before Judge Cresswell, were two of more notoriety than the rest: "Shoni 'Scybor Fawr," and "Dai y Cantwr." Shoni, an ignorant ruffianly fellow, convicted of the more heinious offences committed during the period, was sent to transportation for life. "Dai," whose sentence was for twenty years, was a man of a different stamp, and deserved the pity generally extended to him. He was a native of Treguff, in the parish of Llancarfan. While imprisoned, awaiting his removal, "Dai y Cantwr," who was a poet of considerable merit, composed a lament, which, if your good patience will allow, I will read to you.

Lament of DAVID DAVIES (Dai'r Cantwr) when in Carmarthen Gaol for the Becca Riot.

(Translation by Evan Watkin, Jun., Pentyrch, from the Welsh).

Alas! what a sight to the world I shall be,
I have lost all the fame I could win were I free,
Unworthy is the brand and heavy the blow,
And sad is the way I was brought to my woe.
While yet but a youth I've misfortune and pain,
My freedom I lose and my bondage I gain;
Commencing life's journey, an exile am I,
Sent forth from my country, it may be to die.

The Riots of Rebecca and Her Daughters

My father I'm leaving—his kindness and care,
In a land among; negroes my home they'll prepare.
O'er seas I'll be carried far from this loved shore,
How sad the misfortune—I'll see no more.
I am going as an exile, I am going in my tears,
I am borne into bondage for twenty long years,
Ah! long will it be ere I'll see you again,
For sore are the means and the sorrow'll remain.

The song that I sing is a farewell song
To the dear native land I have loved so long,
For the good I have got, in the days that are past,
On the banks of her rivers so famed and so fast.
Farewell unto Cambria—to leave thee I am bound,
Farewell every meadow and bush-covered mound;
If in the whole world there's a garden to see,
Oh! beautiful Britain 'tis thee, it is thee.
Farewell, sons of Gomer, for soon I shall be
Sent forth to a land that's a Babel to me;
My journey is long, o'er the ocean's wild wave,
May God be my guardian—He's mighty to save.
Farewell, lovely maidens, so fresh and so fair,
The beauty of none with your own will compare;
As nature has power by pain to atone,
This David must leave you to suffer alone.

Treguff with its palace will soon be forgot,
For anguish and sorrow is David's sad lot,
The thought of journey is melting my heart,
As far over the billows I soon must depart.
Saint Athan rich parish must read in my rhyme,
And Cadoxton, too, where I dwelt for a time,
And often and long I'll remember Bridgend,
May God be with all to protect and defend.
Oh! noble Glamorgan, I bid thee good cheer,
Thy bells will be tolled never more on my ear,
To tell of thy meadows and dales I will dare,
The Garden of Eden was never more fair.
Farewell unto Monmouth so dear to my heart,
And Troed-y-Rhiw'r Clawdd which is strong on my part;
And as for the people who dwell at Tredegar,
To do me a kindness they ever were eager.

It may be that someone will ask with delight,
The name of the bard who has striven to write;
And seeing that now he is going away,
I'm certain you'll grant him permission to say.
In the land of Glamorgan this gladsome youth dwelt,
And now in his fetters his heart would fain melt,

Appendix E

> In a Carmarthenshire prison he's safe in his cell,
> By anguish more torn than he ever can tell.
> Llancarfan's the parish that had my life's morn,
> Treguir, in that parish, is where I was born.
> And now, as I am going to quit your bright shore,
> I'll give you my name, for I'll see you no more;
> My name's David Davies, I bid adieu;
> May God give long life and protection to you.

In conclusion, I may say I am greatly indebted to Mr. Spurrell's "Caermarthen and its neighbourhood," and to Mr. David Davies, for his account of "Rebecca and her daughters" in the Red Dragon, vol. XI.

Chronological Index

to the attacks on the various toll-houses, toll-gates, and toll-bars

1839.

> June: Efailwen.
> " 15 St. Clears Gate and House.
> July 17 Efailwen (chain).
> Dec. 12 Llanfihangel, and Tawe Bridge Gates.

1843.

> Jan. 16. Trefechan (Trevaughan) Gate.
> " 16. Pentre.
> " 16. Maeswholan.
> Feb. 5. Mynydd y Garreg Gate.
> " 13. Tavernspite and Lampeter Gates.
> " 14. Trefechan two Gates and House.
> " 17. Llanddarog Toll-bar.
> March 6. Robeston Wathen, and Canasten Bridge Gates.
> " 13. Kidwelly Toll House.
> " 17. Penclawdd Gate and House.
> " 29 Narberth Gate.
> " 29. Plaindealings Gate.
> " 29. Cott's Lane Gate.
> April 6. Prendergast Gate.
> " 7. Bwlchtrap Gate.

Chronological Index

" 18. Bwlchclawdd Gate and House.
" 22. Trefechan Gate and House.
" 29. Llanfihangel Gate.
May 5. Pontweli and Troedyrhiw-Gribyn Gates.
" 12. Fishguard Gate.
" 26. Water St. Gate (Carmarthen).
June 12. Penllwynan.
" 16. Bwlchyclawdd Toll-house.
" 19. Carmarthen Workhouse (attack on).
" 21. Adpar Gate.
" 21. Henafod Gate.
" 21. Kerry Gate.
" 23. Pensarne (Rhos) and Rhydyfuwch Gates, Cardigan.
" 27. Penygarn Toll-house.
" 27. Scleddy Gate.
" 29. Gurreyfach Gate.
" 30. Llanddarog Gate.
July 6. Goppa Fach Bar and House.
" 6. Pumpsaint Gate.
" 7. Bolgoed Bar and House.
" 7. Llandilo Rhwnws Toll-house.
" 8. Bronvelin Gate.
" 10. Gwarallt Gate.
" 14. Porthyrhyd Toll-house.
" 14. Minke Toll-house.
" 15. Pontyberem Gate.
" 15. Pompren Gate.
" 15. Pumfry Gate.
" 20. Ystradfeiris Gate.
" 22. Cenarth Gate.
" 23. Brynefal Gate.
" 24. Abergwili Bar.

to the attacks on the various toll-houses, toll-gates, and toll-bars

      " 25. Tyllwyd Gate and Toll-house.
      " 26. Croeslwyd Gate.
Aug. 1. Alltfawr Gate and House.
      " 1. Pontarllechan Bar.
      " 1. Llannon Gate and House.
      " 3. Red Lion Gate.
      " 3. Sandy Lime-kiln Gate and House.
      " 3. Aberayron—two Gates.
      " 3. Burton Gate.
      " 3. Tycoch Bar.
      " 4. New Inn Gate.
      " 5. Porthyrhyd Gate and House.
      " 7. Llandilo Walk Gate and House.
      " 9. Penygarn Gate.
      " 16. Bwlchclawdd (Chain, etc.).
      " 19. Porthyrhyd (third time).
      " 23. Croeslwyd (Chain, etc.).
      " 23. Llandebie Common (enclosures).
      " 23. Gellygwernen Private House.
      " 25. Glangwili Toll-house.
      " 25. Little Newcastle.
Sept. 1. Greencastle Toll-house.
      " 5.? Pontardulais Gate.
      " 8. Sanders Bridge Gate.
      " 9. Hendy Gate (Sarah Williams shot).
      " 12. Parcymorfa Gate and House.
      " 12. Fishguard Gate and House.
      " 13. Llechryd Weir.
      " 14. Mansant Farm.
      " 14. Carregsawdde Gate and Toll-house.
      " 14. Pontarllechan Gate and Toll-house.
      " 14. Mountain Gate and Toll-house
      " 14. Waunystradfeiris Gate and Toll-house.

Chronological Index

    " 14. Pontardulais Gate.
    " 17. Pontardulais Bar.
    " 18. Porthyrhyd Gate.
    " 21. Dwelling-house and Buildings at Gwynfe.
    " 29. Cwmdwr Gate and House.
Oct. 1. Nantyranell Farm.
    " 3. Dolau hirion Gate and House.
    " 3. Cefn Llanddewi Gate.
    " 7. Aberduar (stables).
    " ? Llangurig Gate.
    " 11. Rhayader Old Gate.
    " 11. Cwmglyn Gate.
    " 11. Cross Lane Gate.
    " 12. Penllwynys Farm.
    " 14. Blackpool Weir.
    " 19. Cross vaen Gate.
    " 21. Gwarygraig Farm.
    " 21. Tynymynydd Farm.
    " 25. Sutton Weeks Gate.
Nov. 3. North, East, and West Gates, Rhayader.
    " 7. Cwmtoyddur Hill Gate.
    " 14. Llwynffynongro Farm.
    " 20. Mardy Gate.
Dec. 10. Waunystradfeiris Gate.
    " 19. Llanddausant.
    " 25. Glasbury Gate

1844.

Feb. 7. Llangerrig Gate
    " 21. Plasbach Gate.
March 27. Pensarne Gate.
April 17. Brynlloi Side-gate.
    " 21. Plasbach Gate and House.

General Index

(Note: uses English alphabetization for Welsh names)

"Assizes", 7, 18, 26, 36, 57, 73, 75–76, 86, 88, 99, 117, 143, 145–146, 152, 187, 194–195, 197–198, 200
Aylesbury, 20

A

Aberaeron, 62, 211
Aberayon, 188
Aberayron, 98, 225
Aberceri, 14
Aberdare, 146
Aberdaugleddyf, 181
Aberduar, 166, 226
Abergorlech, 98
Abergwili, 69, 78, 89, 137–138, 147, 194, 224
Abernant, 44, 128, 198
Aberystwyth, 67, 98, 168, 178, 196–197
"Act", 2, 4, 21, 34, 39, 79, 116, 129, 146–147, 185–186, 188, 201–206
"Address", 20, 30, 55, 63–64, 68–69, 71–72, 101–104, 119–123, 141, 181–182
Adpar, 48, 68, 224
Albion Inn, 65
Alltcynadda, 148
Alltfawr, 97, 225
Allt-yr-Odyn, 217
Amersham, 20
Anglesea, 193

B

Bala, 189
Bancllynllech Owen, 155
"Bear", 177
Bettws, 12
"Black Horse", 197
Black Mountain, 158
Blackpool Weir, 172, 226
Blaencoed, 48
Blaencorse, 171
Blaen-dyffryn, 217
Blaenffrwd, 145
Blaen-gilfach, 131
Blaennant Lane, 63
Blaennantymabuchaf, 195
Blaen-y-Coed, 217
"Blue Boar", 30–31, 37
Bolgoed, 78, 93, 96, 224
Bolton, 20
Boughrood, 205
Brechfa, 17, 159, 173, 187
Brecknock, 202
Brecon, 75–76, 167
Breconshire, 22, 165
Bridgend, 77, 188
Bristol, 88, 183
Bronfelin, 16

227

General Index

Bronvelin, 76, 224
Bronwydd, 68
Bronyfelin, 82
Bryn Dyleth, 161
Brynchwith, 44
Brynefal, 89, 224
Bryngwyllin, 175
Brynlloi, 199, 226
Builth, 16, 159, 165
Burton, 99, 225
Bwlch Newydd, 217
Bwlchclawdd, 37, 129, 224–225
Bwlchnewydd, 43–44, 51
Bwlchtrap, 36, 216, 223
Bwlch-y-Clawdd, 216–217
Bwlchyclawdd, 46, 207, 224
Bwlchydomen, 37, 74

C

Cadoxton, 85
Caecrin Mill, 165
Canasten Bridge, 35, 223
Cardiff, 172, 175, 182
Cardigan, 13–15, 17, 48, 67, 70, 85, 88, 111, 115, 143, 157, 162, 181, 198, 202, 224
Cardiganshire, iii, 17, 46, 61, 68, 71, 85, 101
Carmarthen, 4, 7–8, 13, 15, 17, 25, 27, 29–30, 41–42, 45–46, 48, 51–52, 56, 63, 68–78, 81–82, 86, 88, 90–91, 101, 115–116, 119, 125, 127, 130–131, 136–138, 144, 146, 154–156, 159–162, 167–168, 170, 172–173, 180–181, 183, 189–190, 194, 197–200, 202, 205, 207–208, 216–220, 224
Carmarthenshire, 3, 6, 14, 17–18, 25, 31–32, 62, 68, 76, 82, 89, 91, 101, 104, 109, 115, 128, 131, 133, 146, 150, 155, 166, 169, 171–172, 194, 199
Carnfig, 155

Carregsawdde, 157, 225
Castell Maelgwyn, 17
Castellrhingyll, 65, 77
Cefn Llanddewi, 165, 167, 226
Cefnbralam, 5
Cefnmystrich, 175
Cenarth, 88, 195, 224
"Chartist", 2–3, 6–7, 146
Cheddar, 19
Cilgerran, 157–158
Cilmaenllwyd, 30
Cleddau, 10, 13
Coalbrook, 16, 194
"Coburg", 113
Coedmore, 157
Colby Scott, 143
"Commission", 20, 173, 175, 201
"Committee", 68, 73–74, 87, 183–184, 188
Commons, 97
Commott, 207
Conwil, 36–37, 44, 48, 89, 119, 128, 145, 216–217
Corn Law, 3, 128, 148, 185
Corwen, 188
Cothy Bridge, 130
Cott's Lane, 36, 223
Cresselly, 145
Croes Ifan, 12
Croeslwyd, 90, 131, 225
Cross Hands, 155
Cross Inn, 81
Cross Lane, 169, 226
Crossvaen, 172, 226
Crugebolion, 131–132
Crymych, 9
Cwm Cille, 97
Cwm Cillefach, 94
Cwmblewog, 131
Cwmduad, 43
Cwmdwr, 159, 226
Cwmfelinboeth, 5
Cwmglyn, 169, 226
Cwmgwili, 81
Cwmifor, 86, 89, 104
Cwmmawr, 89, 91

Cwmtoyddur, 187, 226

D

Danygarn, 172
Darlington, 131, 136
Denbigh, 189
Derllys, 39
Dinas, 38
Dolau Cothi, 123, 216
Dolau hirion, 16, 158, 165, 196, 198, 226
Dolhaidd, 158
"Dragoons", 55–56, 58–59, 69–70, 73, 75–76, 78, 82, 88, 90–91, 110, 114–115, 125–127, 137, 144, 150, 155–156, 158, 172–173, 180, 187, 189, 199, 217
Duffryn, 158
Dyffryn, 68
Dynevor, 114

E

East Gate, 177, 179
Efailwen, 5–8, 13–15, 25–26, 211, 223
Eglwyscummin, 30
Elephant, 20
Elfed, 38, 44, 48, 51, 63–64 (Elvet)
Emlyn Cottage, 68–69

F

Factory Bill, 102
Fairwood Common, 127
Felingigfran, 156–157
Felinwen, 154
Ferryside, 7
Ffosgrech, 159
Ffynondeilo, 130
Ffynonwen, 131
Fishguard, 36, 38–39, 70, 151, 153, 187, 197, 224–225
Five Roads, 161, 220
Forest, 77
forge, 175
Fountain Hall, 42, 53
Francis Well, 73
Friends, Society of, 131, 136
Furnace Lodge, 98

G

Ganneg, 29
Gelli, 147
Gelli Gwernen, 218
Gellyglynog, 156
Gellygwernen, 133–135, 225
Glamorgan, 183, 188, 202, 205
Glamorganshire, 3, 85, 150, 152, 191
Glangwili, 42, 69, 137–138, 144, 146, 196, 207–208, 218, 225
Glanrhydw, 77
Glasbury, 193–194, 226
Golden Grove, 78
Goppa Fach, 76, 224
Gower, 85, 127, 163
Green Castle, 146, 225
Green Hall, 42, 46
"Grievances", 1–3, 5, 17, 20–23, 49, 52, 54–55, 63–64, 69, 71–72, 86, 101–104, 106–108, 120–121, 128, 130, 138, 147–148, 155, 183–187
Griffiths, Lewis, 33
Guildhall Square, 54, 68
Gurrey fach, 72, 224
Gwarallt, 81, 200, 224
Gwarygraig, 173, 226
Gwendraeth, 83, 160, 190
Gwernant, 81
Gwynfe, 158, 226

H

Haverfordwest, 29, 33, 35–36,

General Index

141–143, 197, 205
Hay Bridge, 205
Henafod, 14, 48, 224
Hendy, 152, 213, 218, 225
Henhafod
 see Henafod
Highbridge, 19
Holyhead, 188, 193
Howells, 35

I

Inclosure Acts, 22
"Infantry", 73, 88, 96, 116, 125, 155, 180
Ivy Bush, 55

K

Kencoed, 145
Kerry, 48, 224
Kibbor, 220
Kidwelly, 29, 35, 77, 97, 151, 153, 190, 223
Kilgwynuchaf, 75
Kilmaenllwyd, 30
King's Lodge, 145

L

Lampeter, 16, 32, 39, 76, 81, 88, 98, 115, 158, 166, 197, 199, 216, 223
"Land League", 1
Laugharne, 30
"Lion and Castle", 178
Little Newcastle, 225
Liverpool, 20, 165
Llanarthney, 82, 131, 145, 196
Llanboidy, 26, 30
Llanddarog, 75, 82, 169, 172, 218, 223–224
Llanddausant, 193, 226
Llanddewi, 30
Llanddowror, 173

Llandebie, 16, 97, 131, 195, 199, 218, 225
Llandeveilog, 147, 168, 183
Llandilo, 72, 76, 78, 83–84, 86, 89, 104, 110, 114–115, 145, 154–155, 159, 166, 173
Llandilo Walk, 98, 114, 225
Llandilo-rhwnws, 218
Llandilo-rwnws, 77, 196, 205, 224
Llandilo-Talybont, 93
Llandinam, 197
Llandovery, 16, 75–76, 82, 84, 115, 119, 158, 165, 172, 198, 208
Llandyssilio, 5, 9, 25, 30
Llandyssul, 38, 46–48, 211
Llanedy, 128, 218
Llanegwad, 70, 143, 145, 187, 195–196
Llanelly, 77, 98, 109, 116–117, 125, 133, 136, 138, 149–150, 152, 161, 189–190, 196
Llanfallteg, 5, 30
Llanfihangel, 27, 30–31, 78, 207, 223–224
Llanfihangel-Abercowin, 30
Llanfihangel-ar-arth, 200, 212
Llanfihangel-rhos-y-corn, 17, 167
Llanfihangel-Yeroth, 48
Llanfynydd, 159
Llanfyrnach, 30
Llanfyrnwyd, 98
Llangadar, 190
Llangadock, 83, 88, 97, 104, 157–158, 172, 189, 208
Llangain, 30, 32
Llangefelach, 93
Llangeler, 128
Llangendeirne, 97, 125
Llangennech, 77
Llangerrig, 197, 226
Llanginning, 30
Llangludwen, 30
Llangoedmore, 14, 67

Llangranog, 61, 70, 111
Llangunnor, 154, 167
Llangurig, 168, 226
Llangwing, 178
Llangwm, 188
Llanidloes, 179, 196–197
Llanllawddog, 138, 145
Llannewydd, 75
Llannon, 97–98, 127, 133, 136, 149–150, 219, 225
Llanon, 218
Llanpumpsaint, 74
Llansadwrn, 109, 160, 172
Llansamlet, 99
Llanstephan, 65
Llantrissant, 172
Llanvihangel, 38
Llanvihangel-Yeroth, 48
Llanwrda, 159, 162, 194–195
Llanwrtyd, 76
Llanybyther, 81, 199
Llanyhyther, 197
Llechryd, 17, 85, 156–157, 225
Lletty, 93
Llwyndryssi, 32, 35
Llwynffynongro, 187, 226
Llynydd Styfle, 138
Llysnewydd, 68
London, 4, 17, 37, 91, 136, 163, 166, 168, 170, 173, 177, 180, 184, 187
"London Peace Society", 141
Lougher, 149
Lougher Bridge, 189
Loughor Bridge, 205

M

Machynlleth, 7
Maesgwenllian, 153
Maesgwynne, 5
Maeswholan, 29, 216, 223
Mansant, 156, 225
"Mansel's Arms", 78
Mardy, 188, 226

Marines, Royal, 70, 85, 156–157, 199
Mark, 19
Melindre Siencyn, 217
Merlin's Hill, 78
Merthyr Bach, 176
Merthyr Tydfil, 220
Middleton Hall, 82, 113, 154–155
Milford, 4
Minke, 77, 83, 190, 224
Missenden, 20
Moelycwan, 43
Monmouth, 183, 205
Monmouthshire, 3
Montgomery, 168
Montgomeryshire, 168
Morlais, 133
Mount Pleasant, 90
Mountain Gate, 225
Mydrim, 62
Mynachlogddu, 7, 10
Mynydd Selen, 134, 138, 148
Mynydd y Garreg, 223
Mynydd-y-Garreg, 216

N

Nantgaredig, 77
Nantgwyn, 16
Nantyclawdd, 74, 207
Nantyranell, 162, 226
Narberth, 9, 25, 27, 35–36, 72, 223
Neath, 99, 131, 136, 149, 188
"Nelson, The", 112
New Bridge, 77
New Gate, 34, 178
New Inn, 14, 81, 225
Newcastle Emlyn, 14–15, 36–38, 48, 61, 64, 68–70, 73–74, 81, 88, 115–116, 128, 146
Newcastle Trust, 48
Newchurch, 48, 128, 176
Newport (Mon.), 26

Rebecca and Her Daughters 231

General Index

Newport (Pem.), 38
Newport Turnpike Trust, 205
North Gate, 177, 179
Norton's Brewery, 56

P

Paincastle, 194
Pantmawr, 196
Pantycaws, 5
Pantycendy, 44, 51, 68
Pantycerrig, 16–17, 167, 195
Pant-y-Fen, 218
Pantyfen, 116, 198
Pantyfenwas, 15
Pantylleifion, 67
Parcymorfa, 151, 153, 187, 225
Pembrey, 46, 190, 194
Pembroke, 4, 7, 25, 29, 31–32, 70, 99, 162, 202
Pembrokeshire, 32, 51, 172, 197
Penbryn, 46
Penclawdd, 36, 223
Pencoed, 38
Penderyn, 220
Penlan, 56, 104, 138, 145
Penllwynan, 46, 224
Penllwynau, 217
Penllwynys, 169, 226
Pensarne, 13, 15, 67, 198, 224, 226
(Rhos)
Pentre, 29, 216, 223
Pentrebach, 16, 195
Pentregalar, 9
Penty-park, 33
Penwalk, 70
Penybank, 145
Penybont, 179
Penygarn, 70, 115–116, 218, 224–225
Penyrherber, 46–47, 195
Penyrhoel, 145–146
"Petition", 5, 7, 52, 55, 71, 98, 102–103, 128, 153, 155–156, 194
Plaindealings, 36, 223
Plas Llangledwen, 15
Plasbach, 197, 199, 226
"Plough and Harrow", 48, 51, 217
"Police", 17, 22, 29–30, 37–39, 43, 46, 52, 58, 90–91, 93, 96, 98–99, 104, 108–109, 115, 120, 127, 130, 142, 144, 149–151, 160, 165–168, 170, 172, 177, 180, 186–187, 189, 199, 207
Pompren, 83, 224
Pont Twelly, 216
Pont-ar-Ddulais, 217
Pontarddulais, 213
Pontardulais, 76–78, 93, 96–97, 133, 149, 151–152, 157, 175, 181, 219, 225–226
Pont-ar-Lechau, 218
Pontarllechan, 15, 98, 157, 198, 225
Pontarselly, 74
Pontbrengwyddon, 74
Pontnewydd, 65
Pontprenaneth, 157
Pontweli, 38, 47, 224
Pontwelly, 73–74
Pont-y-Berem, 218
Pontyberem, 16, 65, 77, 83, 89, 160–161, 194, 213, 220, 224
Pontycleivion, 67
Pontyeates, 77
Poor Law, 4, 87, 116, 127–129, 147, 154–155, 184
Porth-y-Rhyd, 218
Porthyrhyd, 82, 112–114, 126, 157–158, 194–195, 198–199, 224–226
Portmadoc, 212
Potato Famine, 3
Pound, 16, 39, 196
Prendergast, 36, 142–143, 197, 223
Prescelly, 10

232 *Rebecca and Her Daughters*

"Proclamation", 136, 162–163, 181, 196
Pumfry, 224
Pumpsaint, 16, 76, 208, 224
Pwlltrap, 30, 169–170

R

Radnor, 202
Radnorshire, 22, 159, 168–169, 193–194
Raymond's Lodge, 147
Rebecca and her Daughters, 20, 165–166
"Red Lion", 98, 149, 225
Redstone, 35
Rhayader, 159, 169, 177, 179–180, 187, 197, 226
Rhos
  see Pensarne
Rhydspence, 194
Rhydyfuwch, 14, 67, 85, 224
Riot Act, 55, 58
Robeston Wathen, 35, 223
Round House Yard, 144
Royal Oak, 207
Rumney, 205

S

"Salutation Inn", 68
Sanders Bridge, 151, 225
Sandy Lime Kiln, 98, 136, 225
Sandy Turnpike, 117
"The Scamber Inn", 9
Scleddy, 70, 224
"Sessions", 18, 29, 69, 71, 90, 107, 115, 186, 188, 199, 203, 205
Shrewsbury, 196
Somerset, 174
Spudder's Bridge, 194
St. Clears, 7, 25–26, 29–32, 36, 39, 62–63, 70, 88, 90, 169, 171, 207, 216, 223

"Stag and Pheasant", 161
Steam Mill, 76
Sutton Weeks, 174, 226
Swansea, 85, 88, 90–91, 93–95, 98–99, 127, 149–151, 155, 189, 191–192

T

Talog, 15, 44–45, 48, 57, 75, 86, 198, 217–218
Tavernspite, 32, 216, 223
Tawe Bridge, 27, 223
Teify, 39, 73, 85, 89
Three Commotts, 17, 77, 98, 199
"The Three-Cornered Piece", 142
Three Crosses, 85
"The Times", 86, 97, 104, 128
Tivyside, 17
Towey, 205
Towy, 77–78
Towy Castle, 168
Trawsmawr, 44, 46, 216
Trecastle, 165
Trefechan, 13, 29, 32–33, 38, 216, 223–224
Treguff, 220
Trelech, 12, 30, 48, 128, 131, 217
Tremadoc, 89
Tretoisaf, 131
Treto-uchaf, 131
Trevaughan
  see Trefechan
Trevor, George Rice, 213–214
Trimsaran, 161
Troedrhiw-gribyn, 38
Troedyraur, 79
Troedyrhiw (Card.), 47
Troedyrhiw (Carm.), 75
Troed-y-Rhiw Gribyn, 216
Troedyrhiwgribin, 47, 224
Tumble, 161
Tycoch, 99, 225
Tyllwyd, 82, 90, 225

General Index

Tymawr, 93
Tynymynydd, 173, 226
Tynywern, 156
Tyrynys, 194
Tyrypound, 167

U

Union, Farmers', 106

V

Velindre, 37, 74, 94, 220
"Victoria Arms", 13
Voelgastell, 199

W

Water Street, 41–44, 48, 53–54, 131, 216, 224
Waunystradfeiris, 157, 189, 225–226
Wedmore, 19
Wells, 19
Welshpool, 7
Wernfach, 128
West Gate, 178–180, 188
"The Wheaten Sheaf", 62
White Gate, 194
"White Lion", 172
Whitland, 5–7, 13, 17, 27, 32–33, 35, 174, 216
Williams, Sarah, 225
Windsor, 162–163
Woodlands, 193
Woolwich, 88
Wych Tree, 205
Wye, 21, 179, 193
Wye Bridge Gate
see West Gate

Y

Yeomanry, 29, 31, 70, 72, 88, 115, 166

Ystrad, 77
Ystradfeiris, 88, 224

Index of Persons

(Note: uses English alphabetization for Welsh names)

Brown, Miss, 61
"Brutus", 216
Bryant, Capt., 29
Buchan, Dóroma, 31
Bullin, Mr., 31, 188

A

Adams, Ed., 113, 154–155
Allen, Seymour, 145
Arkwright, Captain, 180
Arthur, Arthur, 138, 145, 196
Attwood, Thomas, 96, 191
Attwood,Thomas, 149

B

Barrett, William, 135
 (William Bassett)
Beauport, (Duke of), 22
Bennett, Sergeant, 96
Bevan, John, 158
Beynon, John, 68
Beynon, R.P., 169
Bird, Dr., 95–96, 151
Blakemore, T.W. Booker, 220
Bonville, William, 152, 213
Bowen, Dr., 125
Bowen, Maj., 219
Bowen, Michael, 42
Bowen, Samuel, 44
Bowling, Maj., 72
Bowring, Dr., 20
Brown, General, 180

C

Cameron, V.P., 150
Cameron, William, 150
Cantwr, Dai'r
 see Davies, David
Carnabwth, Twm
 see Rees, Thomas
Cawdor, Earl, 78
Chambers, Mr., 109, 156, 175, 192, 214
Chambers, William, 138, 149, 151, 216
Charles, John, 198
"Charlotte", 41, 159–160
Clive, Robert Henry, 173
Coedygoras, 220
Collins, Henry, 153
Cook, Mr., 113
Cooke, John Kirkhouse, 152, 213
Cracker, Cornet, 166
Cresswell, Cresswell, 18, 175, 194, 220
Cripps, William, 173
"Miss Cromwell", 87

235

Index of Persons

D

Daniel, George, 195
David, Ann, 171
David, John, 171
Davies, Captain, 44, 46, 216
Davies, Charles, 145
Davies, David, 18–19, 61, 83, 161, 194, 198, 220–222 (Dai'r Cantwr)
Davies, Evan, 198
Davies, Gabriel, 8–10
Davies, Henry, 93
Davies, Howell, 89, 145
Davies, John, 15, 68
Davies, John Lloyd, 52, 217
Davies, Lewis, 152, 175
Davies, Morris, 14
Davies, Mr., 113, 143, 160, 171
Davies, Mrs., 145
Davies, Rebecca, 8
Davies, Samuel, 96
Davies, Thomas, 7–8
Davies, William, 116, 196, 207
Derem, Lieut., 199
Dickson, Capt., 199
Dillwyn, E.A., iv
Dillwyn, Lewis, 149
Dynevor, Lord
  see Trevor, George Rice

E

Eaton, William, 85
Edwards, David, 207
Edwards, Evan, 183
Edwards, Miss, 134–135
Edwards, Mr., 128, 133–134, 147, 218
Edwards, Mrs., 134
"Eliza", 48
Evans, Allen Raine, 70
Evans, Benjamin, 70–71, 195
Evans, Captain, 51–52, 68
Evans, David, 45, 195, 198, 200
Evans, David James, 167
Evans, Eleazer, 111
Evans, Frances, 75
Evans, Gwladys Tobit, iii, 23
Evans, Henry, 200
Evans, Herbert, 195
Evans, James, 195
Evans, Job, 198
Evans, John, 130–131, 167, 208 (Skippo)
Evans, Mr., 77–78, 175
Evans, Mrs., 54–55
Evans, Mrs. John, 130 (Shan Ionath)
Evans, O. Beynon, 15
Evans, Thomas, 46
Evans, W., 196

F

Fitz-Williams, Mr.
  see Hall, Mr.
Francis, John, 179
Frost, John, 26

G

Genteel, Jeremy, 159
Give, Robert Henry, 219
Glamorgan, 220
Gower, Abel Lewes, 17, 157
Graham, James, 43
Graville, David, 183
Grove, Mr., 127
Gurney, John, 26, 175, 220
Gwehydd, Ianto'r
  see Thomas, Evan
Gwynne, James, 187
Gwynne, Thomas, 187

H

Halket, Capt., 76, 82
Hall, Lloyd, 49, 63–64, 68–69
Hall, Mr., 14, 91, 104, 128, 216

(Mr. Fitz-Williams)
Harries, David, 15, 218
Harries, Mr., 216
Harris, D.H., 162
Harris, Daniel, 198
Harris, John, 44–45, 57, 86, 198
Harris, Thomas, 195
Harvey, Jones, 178
Henry, Lewis, 194
Hewson, Mr., 191
Hill, Mr., 163
Homfray, John, 175
Honeycomb, Henry, 166
Howell, David, 32
Howells, David, 35–36
Howells, Thomas, 32, 35–36
Hugh, Jenkin, 136
Hugh, John, 152, 175, 181–182
Hughes, John, 150–152, 175, 181–182, 219
Hughes, Rev. John, 46–47
Hughes, Mr., 57
Hughes, Thomas, 198
Hughes, William, 152, 175

I

Ionath, Shan
see Evans, Mrs. John

J

Jackson, Thomas, 188
James, John, 198
James, Mr., 178
Jenkins, D.M., 146
Jenkins, William, 93, 95
John, James, 170
Johnes, John, 119–123, 216
Jones, Benjamin, 198
Jones, Col., 191
Jones, Daniel, 151
Jones, David, 93, 151–152, 175, 181–182, 194, 196, 207
Jones, Harry, 220
Jones, Jane, 154
Jones, Jenny, 166
Jones, Job, 86
Jones, John, 18, 77, 93, 161, 172, 194–195, 198, 219–220
(Shoni Scuborfawr)
Jones, Jonathan, 198
Jones, Josiah Thomas, 146
Jones, Rev. J., 160
Jones, Mr., 26, 172
Jones, Thomas, 195
Jones, William, 12, 138, 145, 172, 195
Joshua, D.W., 138
Joshua, David, 42, 137, 144, 146, 196

K

Kearns, Mr., 73
Kirkman, Lieut., 88
Kynaston, F., 171

L

Laing, George, 117, 189, 191–192, 196
Leach, Henry, 29, 70
Leach, Lieut., 29
Lewis, Benjamin, 68
Lewis, David, 96, 198
Lewis, David John, 172
Lewis, Henry, 95
Lewis, Howell, 198
Lewis, John, 76, 167, 196, 198
(John Pengelly)
Lewis, Jonathan, 198
Lewis, Lewis, 172, 188
Lewis, Mr., 78, 97
Lewis, Thomas, 196, 198
Lewis, Thomas Frankland, 173, 189
Lewis, William, 175, 190–191, 199
Llewellyn, Dillwyn, 149

Rebecca and Her Daughters

Index of Persons

Lloyd, Daniel, 196
Lloyd, John, 217
Lloyd, Mr., 65, 77
Lloyd, Thomas, 68, 157
Llwynpatria, Will, 83
Love, Col., 70, 73, 75

M

M'Kennel, John, 153
M'Kiernin, Francis, 117
Mainwaring, Daniel, 195
Mainwaring, Isaac, 195
Mainwaring, Thomas, 195
Mami, John, 83
Mansel, Capt., 70
Mansel, John, 98
Martin, George, 207
Martin, Inspector, 168
Maule, W.H., 18, 36, 197
McKiernin, Francis, 189, 192, 196
Moggridge, Matthew, 149
Monmouth, 220
Morgan, David, 196
Morgan, Esther, 175
Morgan, Henry, 93–94, 175
Morgan, J., 156
Morgan, James, 196
Morgan, John, 94–95, 175
Morgan, Margaret, 175
Morgan, Mathew, 93
Morgan, Morgan, 93, 175
Morgan, Rees, 175
Morgan, Seth, 195
Morgan, Thomas, 196, 198
Morgan, William, 93
Morganwg, Dick, 112–114, 126
Morris, Charles, 56–57
Morris, David, 154
Morris, Lewis, 68
Morris, Mr., 90, 177
Morris, Thomas, 194
Morris, Thomas Charles, 55, 217
Morris, W., 44

Morse, James, 55
Mortimer, Mr., 153
Moses, David, 130

N

Napier, Capt., 93–97, 149, 151, 175, 219
"Nelly", 8, 68
Neville, Mr., 109
Newman, Mr., 161
Nicholas, Mr., 77
Nicholls, Mrs., 173
Nott, Mr., 144

O

Owen, Hugh, 71
Owen, William, 187

P

Paget, Lord, 158
Parlby, Maj., 56, 217
Peak, Supt., 96
Pengelly, John
  see Lewis, John
Philip, Philip, 196
Philip, William, 196
Philipp, William, 167
Phillipps, Mrs., 168
Phillips, J.W., 98
Phillips, Mr., 36
Pollock, Frederick, 18, 194
Popkin, Mr., 145
Porthyrhyd Lion, The
  see Thomas, Evan
Powell, John, 195
Powell, Mother, 112–113
Powell, Mr., 5, 97
Powell, Thomas, 198
Powell, Timothy, 38
Powell, W.E., 71
Price, J. Lloyd, 69
Price, Mr., 131, 136

Price, R.D. Green, 22
Price, R.D.Green, 21
Prichard, R., 220
Pugh, David, 107
Pugh, Mr., 107
Pugsley, Mr., 169

R

Rees, David, 46, 116, 207
Rees, Evan, 196–197
Rees, Mary, 195
Rees, Mr., 16, 65, 93–95, 97
Rees, Rev., 127
Rees, Richard, 42–43
Rees, Sarah, 179
Rees, Thomas, 7–10
   (Twm Carnabwth)
Rees, Rev. Thomas, 166–167
Rees, Walter, 194
Rees, William, 119
Rhymney, 220
Richards, Benjamin, 138, 145, 196
Richards, George Kettilby, 173
Richards, Mr., 158
Roger, Henry, 152
Rogers, Dr., 95
Rolfe, Robert Monsy, 200
de Rutzen, Baron & Baroness, 172

S

Saunders, J.E., 77
Saunders, Mr., 190, 192
Scott, Richard Andrew, 115
Scuborfawr, Shoni
   see Jones, John
Shew, Sgt., 177–178, 180
"Skippo"
   see Evans, John, 130
Slocombe, Miss, 194
Slocombe, Mr., 161
Smith, C.H., 150
Smith, John Jones, 196
Squibb, Capt., 166
Stacey, Edmund Hills, 44, 56

T

Taylor, Capt., 88
"Tegid", 216
Thomas, A. Goring, 74
Thomas, Ben, 152, 213
Thomas, David, 138, 145, 198
Thomas, Evan, 82, 112–114, 126
   (Ianto'r Gwehydd)
   (The Porthyrhyd Lion)
Thomas, George, 196, 215
Thomas, Henry, 172, 195
Thomas, Jacob, 112
Thomas, James, 159, 169–170, 198
Thomas, John, 91, 152, 198, 213
Thomas, Llewellyn, 192
Thomas, Margaret, 198
Thomas, Mr., 63, 143, 169
Thomas, Rees Goring, 68, 98, 133
Thomas, Thomas, 17, 44–45, 167, 195, 198, 207
Thomas, Thomas Edward, 191
Thomas, Titus, 71
Tibbs, Taffy, 166
Tierney, Mr., 160–161
Trevor, George Rice, 68, 71–72, 75, 90, 98, 115, 145, 216
   (Lord Dynevor)

V

Vaughan, Capt., 200
Vaughan, David, 197
Vaughan, Griffith, 96–97, 149
Victoria, 162–163, 173

W

Walters, Thomas, 194

Index of Persons

Walters, William, 194, 197
Watkin, Evan, 220
Whack, Paddy, 166
White, John, 183
Whylock, Maj., 70
Wil, 47
Wilding, Mr., 178
Williams, Bridget, 195
Williams, David, 195, 198
Williams, Edward Lloyd, 79–81
Williams, Evan, 195
Williams, H., 131
Williams, Hamlyn, 176
Williams, Hugh, 7, 128, 139
Williams, Joseph, 195
Williams, Josiah, 195
Williams, Mr., 90, 98, 142–143
Williams, Sarah, 152, 213, 218
Williams, T., 166
Williams, Thomas, 152, 172, 194–195
Williams, Vaughan, 197
Williams, William, 195
Williams, Zephaniah, 26
Lady Winterblossom, 166
Wiseacre, Watkin, 166
Wood, George, 174
Woods, John B., 182

Y

Yelverton, Miss, 174
Yelverton, Mr., 174
Yscubor Fawr, 220

My Thoughts are Murder to the State:
Thoreau's Essays on Political Philosophy

Thoreau's *Civil Disobedience* continues to inspire and shape lives today. If you have not yet sought out his other writings on political philosophy, this collection will show you Thoreau's insights applied to nonviolence & violent insurrection, technological utopianism & environmentalism, conscience & the State, abolitionism, and heroism.

This collection includes:

- *Resistance to Civil Government* (*Civil Disobedience*)
- *Slavery in Massachusetts*
- *A Plea for Captain John Brown*
- *Remarks After the Hanging of John Brown*
- *The Last Days of John Brown*
- *Sir Walter Raleigh*
- *Reform and the Reformers*
- *Paradise (to be) Regained*
- *Herald of Freedom*
- *Wendell Phillips Before the Concord Lyceum*
- *The Service*
- *Life Without Principle*

http://www.createspace.com/3330261

The Price of Freedom: Political Philosophy from Thoreau's Journals

"Classic Thoreau presented in a thorough, illuminating volume."

— *Kirkus Discoveries*

"extremely clear and thorough... excellent notes and references... Thoreau is among the best political thinkers—and certainly among the best writers—in our language."

— Crispin Sartwell

Henry David Thoreau's private thoughts on law, government, man in society, war, economics, duty, and conscience.

Thoreau had to be cautious when speaking or publishing, but in his journal he felt free to entertain thoughts that have been described as "blasphemous, revolutionary, or, at best, politically incautious" and were never published during his lifetime

These show Thoreau as uncompromising in his disgust with the government, with church authority, with the news media, and with slavery and those who would accommodate it. They also show Thoreau defending wilderness against "improvement," as curious about economics as he was about trees and turtles, wrestling with arguments for animal rights, and moving from thinking of soldiers as almost mythological heroes to thinking of them as "powder monkeys" who had mortgaged their consciences to no good end.

Thoreau sided with freedom. The passages in this volume are part of what he considered "the price of freedom"—his attempts to mine the richest vein of observations about human and political life, and to preserve what he found free from all censorship.

http://www.createspace.com/3330815

We Won't Pay: A Tax Resistance Reader

"…magnificent …an amazing resource for historical information on conscience, dissent, government, militarism, nonviolence, patriotism, peacemaking, religious freedom, responsibility, revenue refusal, tax redirection, truth, violence, and war."

—Don Kaufman

"well worth the considerable reading time… captures in one indexed volume many individual acts and campaigns of conscientious objection to war and of revenue refusal to tyrannical governments… sincere voices and challenging arguments."

— Clare Hanrahan

Tax resisters have been violent revolutionaries like John Adams, and pacifist nonresistants like John Woolman; communists like Karl Marx, and capitalists like Vivien Kellems; solitary consciences like Ammon Hennacy, and leaders of resistance movements like Mahatma Gandhi.

Some refused to pay a tax because they would not support with their money what their consciences condemned. Others refused to pay taxes that were being unfairly or illegally assessed. Others resisted as part of a campaign to overthrow the government.

This book tells their stories, in their words, and will provide inspiration and education for generations of tax resisters to come.

Includes writings by Mahatma Gandhi, John Woolman, John Adams, Paul Cuffe, Larry Rosenwald, William Lloyd Garrison, Henry David Thoreau, Leo Tolstoy, Benjamin Ricketson Tucker, Lucy Stone, Elizabeth Cady Stanton, Ammon Hennacy, Karl Marx, Karl Hess, Juanita Nelson, Allen Ginsberg, Milton Mayer, Bernard Offen, Peace Pilgrim, Julia "Butterfly" Hill, Gene Sharp, and many more!

http://www.createspace.com/33396598

American Quaker War Tax Resistance

"...a marvelous historical compilation of 167 intelligent and intense writings on the challenging question of whether people of conscience should pay for war.... People struggling with this moral issue today will be guided by the writings in this book and may find some wonderful language to use in their own statements of conscience... a straightforward and compelling book."

— Elizabeth Boardman, *Western Friend*

"What difference is there, in principle, between killing a fellow man in war and paying another man to kill him?"

This book illuminates the evolution of Quaker war tax resistance in America, as told by those who resisted and those who debated the limits of the Quaker peace testimony where it applied to taxpaying.

Among the writers found in this volume are Isaac Sharpless, Thomas Story, William Penn, James Logan, Benjamin Franklin, John Woolman, John Churchman, James Pemberton, Joshua Evans, Anthony Benezet, Job Scott, Warner Mifflin, Timothy Davis, James Mott, Isaac Grey, Samuel Allinson, Moses Brown, Stephen B. Weeks, Rufus Hall, Gouverneur Morris, Elias Hicks, Joshua Maule, and Cyrus G. Pringle.

http://www.createspace.com/3347562

Against War and War Taxes

Classic Quaker arguments why Christians should neither fight in wars nor pay others to fight in their place by paying taxes that sustain the military.

Among the writers in this volume are Thomas Story, Philalethes, John Woolman, John Pemberton, Samuel Allinson, Joshua Brown, Benjamin Mason, William Swayne, Joshua Pusey, Richard Barnard, Isaac Coates, Amos Davis, Samuel Cope, William Lamborn, Samuel Parsons, Pacificus, Thomas P. Cope, Thomas Howland, Joseph Snowdon, Joshua Maule, Joseph Scattergood, Richard Moore, John Sellers, Jos. C. Turnpenny, Henry W. Moore, William Dorsey, and Caleb Clothier.

http://www.createspace.com/3396846

Printed in Great Britain
by Amazon